Healthy Food, Farms & Families

Hunger 2007

17th Annual Report on the
State of World Hunger

 Bread for the World
Institute

50 F Street NW, Suite 500
Washington, DC 20001
USA

Bread for the World Institute

President
David Beckmann

President Emeritus
Arthur Simon

Vice President of Policy and Programs
James L. McDonald

Director
Marco Grimaldo

Senior Editor
Todd Post

Policy Analyst
Eric Muñoz

Contributing Writer
Michele Learner

Project Assistants
Margaret Munroe
Gihani Perera

Design
Hilary Kay Doran

© 2006 by Bread for the World Institute
50 F Street NW, Suite 500
Washington, DC 20001
Telephone (202) 639-9400
Fax (202) 639-9401
E-mail: institute@bread.org
www.bread.org

Printer: HBP, Hagerstown, MD

Cover photo: © Richard Lord

Manufactured in the United States of America
First Edition Published in January 2007
ISBN 1-884361-16-1

Table of Contents

Acknowledgments

This report was completed thanks to the support of many people.

For their insights on farming, rural development, trade and nutrition, we are grateful to George Alford, Molly Anderson, Brother Dave Andrews, Audrey Arner, Bruce Babcock, Amy Bacigalupo, Jon Bailey, Geoffrey Becker, Eric Bell, David Bieging, John Boyd, Julie Brewer, Delia Brand, Traci Bruckner, Randy Capps, Sheila Christopher, John Cook, Delaine Cooper, Willie Datcher, Shelley Davis, Stacey Dean, Reid Doster, Anne Effland, Scott Faber, Frances Ford, Keira Franz, Stephanie Gambrell, Barbara Grant, Bob Gronski, Robert Guenther, Joe Guinan, Ilan Gutherz, Allan Hance, Sissy Hembree, Everett Henderson, Kari Herman, Ray Higgins, Walter Hillman, Cassi Johnson, Jean Jones, Tim Kautzma, Fred Kirschenmann, Jerry Kobs, Kathy Link, Joseph Llobrera, Stephanie Lundberg, Tammy Maul, Derrick Miller, Josh Miner, Kevin Miskell, Joe Moton, George Naylor, Tony Nertoli, Mark Nord, Ben Newell, Dennis Nuxoll, Christine Olson, David Orden, Eugene Paul, Daryl Perkins, Lorette Picciano, Miles Petrie, David Pope, Carolyn Powell, Barbara Prather, Rev. Cedell Raggs, Flo Raitano, Charles Ray, John Clyde Riggs, Susan Roberts, Beatrice Rogers, Lauren Rosapep, Joyce Rothermel, Susan Sechler, Debra Shoopman, Joe Shultz, Carol Smith, Ben Steinberg, Keith Stern, Robert Thompson, Ann Tutwiler, Terry VanDerPol, Ellen Vollinger, Nancy Weed, Parke Wilde, and Carla Wynn.

In the summer of 2006, the following people participated in an expert consultation and reviewed draft chapters: Bev Abma, Marv Baldwin, Mari Castellanos, Amy Chevalier, Edward Cooney, Jimmy Daukus, Trevor Dean, Kimberly Elliot, Sarah Ford, Raquel Gomes, Alan Hunt, Julie Justus, Joseph D. Keesecker, Jeremy Lewis, Jennifer Ng'andu, Carolyn Race, Sandhya Rao, Kim Stietz, Rick Swartz, Patty Kupfer, Mary Minette, Karen Vagley, Janet White. Some of the same people cited in the paragraph above also participated in the consultation and/or reviewed draft chapters.

We are especially grateful to Antoine Bouët and Marcelle Thomas for their study on the effects of economic growth in developing countries.

Finally, we would like to acknowledge the collective contribution of our colleagues at Bread for the World, Bread for the World Institute, and the Alliance to End Hunger for their dedication in working to end the scourge of hunger. It is a pleasure to work with all of you.

Foreword

Rick Reinhard

My mother grew up on a farm in Nebraska. She had to leave home when she was 16, because her family could no longer afford to feed her. Times were tough for farmers, and her father was ill. She got a job in Lincoln as a live-in helper and sent part of her earnings home to help her family. Mom never got to go to college.

My father came from a nearby small town. He and my mother worked hard together to advance his education and career, and then to give me and my three sisters a strong start in life. I still have lots of family ties to rural Nebraska.

Most people in the United States now live in cities, but many urban people, like me, have rural roots. We know from our own family's experience about both the strong values and economic struggles of rural America. Poverty and food insecurity are more widespread in rural than in urban areas.

Healthy Food, Farms and Families focuses on how we can address the hunger and poverty in rural America. Farm and rural people in our country are hardworking, resourceful and communityminded. But our current farm policies do little to encourage their entrepreneurial spirit or give a boost to the rural people who most need help.

The current farm bill provides large payments to some farmers, but does little to help small-scale farmers and other rural families of modest means.

The current U.S. farm bill also has a negative impact on rural communities in developing countries. Three-quarters of the world's hungry people live in rural areas of developing countries, and some of them could increase their earnings if they did not have to compete with subsidized crops from the United States and other industrialized countries. More could work their way out of poverty if the industrialized countries fully opened their markets to agricultural exports from developing countries.

Trade is important to progress against hunger and poverty in the developing world. When I recently visited Uganda, most of the farm families I visited were producing crops for export as well as crops for their own consumption. The U.S. Agency for International Development has helped Uganda expand its production and export of vanilla. As I visited farm families who were growing vanilla beans, I saw well-fed children and other clear signs of economic progress—a new cow in the yard, for example.

African leaders know that their countries need effective development assistance, but most African leaders are even more interested in trade justice— an opportunity to sell their countries' products, mainly agricultural, freely and fairly in world markets.

Progress for poor people will benefit the whole world. This report includes new data from the International Food Policy Research Institute. They demonstrate that economic growth in Africa and poor Asian countries will benefit U.S. farmers.

Bread for the World is planning a major campaign in 2007 to push for food and farm policies that are better for rural America and better for hungry and poor people in our country and around the world. The campaign will be called *Seeds of Change: Help Farmers. End Hunger.* You can find out more about it and how you can get involved at www. bread.org.

David Beckmann

Rev. David Beckmann
President, Bread for the World and Bread for the World Institute

Healthy Food, Farms & Families

Introduction

In 2007, anti-hunger groups will be gearing up for the U.S. farm bill. Few other pieces of legislation give federal policymakers such an opportunity to significantly reduce hunger in the United States and around the globe. The farm bill is about much more than farming— it's an omnibus bill that shapes farm subsidies, nutrition programs, conservation, energy, trade, research and rural development.

The current farm bill was signed into law in 2002 and is set to expire in 2007. The reauthorization date is somewhat flexible, and farm groups and some legislators have suggested a delay until international trade negotiations are concluded. But a delay will not lessen the need for reforms.

Traditionally, it has been the commodity crops—primarily corn, wheat, soybeans, cotton and rice—that drive the reauthorization agenda. Of the $51.7 billion in new funding included in the 2002 farm bill, more than two-thirds went to the commodity programs.[1] The next farm bill will be reauthorized under much different circumstances. The 2002 bill was negotiated in 2001, before the escalating federal budget deficit and the war on terror reshaped spending priorities. Though the policy environment may be different, what has not changed is Bread for the World's contention that securing farm bill reform is vitally important.

A change in U.S. agricultural policy is long overdue, and it begins with commodities. Commodity programs force farmers to depend on government subsidies, divert scarce resources needed for rural development, distort agricultural markets at the expense of farmers in the developing world, and contribute to rising obesity rates in the United States. Reforming the farm bill to address these problems is the subject of the 2007 Hunger Report: *Healthy Food, Farms and Families.*

Farm Subsidies Do Not Benefit Most Rural Americans

Rural America has higher rates of hunger and poverty than urban areas. Unemployment and underemployment are higher too, and rural America has higher concentrations of substandard housing. Minority residents of rural areas are worse off than those in metropolitan areas. These conditions may not be caused directly by government payments to commodity producers, but the fact that most people consider farm subsidies a form of rural development explains why so little is left for the development strategies and programs that would improve the lives of most rural Americans.

It is a myth that government payments to farmers support rural America. Areas of the country that receive the greatest share of subsidies, like the Great Plains or the Delta, have some of the highest rates of hunger and poverty, and these communities have been losing people for decades as farms have consolidated, making it increasingly difficult for small farmers to compete. "When I was growing up, our town had all kinds of stores. Now there is nothing," said Ken Gallaway, a small cotton farmer in Olton, Texas. "A lot of this is because there are fewer farmers and they can't support the local commerce."[2] The impact of the commodity programs ripples through rural communities around the nation.

By design, commodity payments benefit the biggest producers. That is how they have encouraged consolidation. U.S. farm subsidy programs do little to help small to medium-sized family farmers, most of whom receive no subsidies and earn most of their household income by working off-farm. Nor do farm programs provide much help to growers of the so-called specialty crops, better known as fruits and vegetables, which are ineligible for subsidies. The notion that U.S. agriculture could not be competitive without the high commodity subsidies is another myth—for one thing, specialty crops remain competitive without subsidies.

Direct government support for farmers started during the Great Depression, when most U.S. farm households were extremely poor. A policy designed to be a temporary solution to address a national crisis has prevailed for three-quarters of a century. Today, average farm household income exceeds the average income of the rest of the country.

The landscape of rural America is also vastly different than during the Great Depression. Less than one percent of the population in the United States is engaged in farming, compared to 25 percent in the 1930s. Roughly the same amount of farmland is being used, but the farms themselves have grown larger and more specialized, due to improvements in technology and the government programs that have encouraged consolidation.

Federal farm policy has not kept pace with changes in the farm sector or with changes in rural America.

Some legislators worry because U.S. agricultural imports are increasing faster than exports. But agricultural imports are serving the widespread U.S. consumer demand for products grown in other parts of the world. Look around Iowa, for example. For many people, the word Iowa signifies farming—yet almost all of the foods Iowans eat come from out of state. Iowa farmers grow lots of corn and soy beans, but very little else. It is not because the soil cannot produce foods other than corn and soybeans. It is because it would be a disastrous business decision for farmers to rethink their planting decisions. Under the current farm program structure, they have become dependent on subsidies that give them little scope to diversify.

Federal farm policy should offer farmers tools for managing financial risk, assistance during times of catastrophic crop failure, and support for practicing good environmental stewardship. But most importantly, federal policy needs to support creativity and an entrepreneurial spirit in farming by encouraging farmers to plant the crops they choose. All farmers should be eligible for this support, not just a small handful of commodity producers.

U.S. farm programs should also provide more help to beginning farmers and ranchers. Under current farm policy, the cost of land has risen dramatically because the value of program crop subsidies is factored into the value of land. Given the high cost of purchasing or renting land, it has become almost impossible for a new generation of farmers to raise enough capital to get started in farming. There are twice as many farmers over 65 as there are under 35.[3]

The significant financial savings from restructuring U.S. farm policy as discussed above should be redirected primarily to boosting rural development and reducing hunger. Rural economic development policy should place a heavy emphasis on small business creation and support for local entrepreneurs, especially in the non-farm sector, because few people in rural America work on farms. Investments in infrastructure such as better transportation systems, broadband and Internet access, education and health care, water and sewage treatment are an essential foundation for economic development. The potential for business development in rural America is great, but without improvements to rural infrastructure, it will not reach that potential.

Commodities and World Hunger

U.S. farm programs favor a few thousand large corporate farming interests, much to the detriment of smaller family farmers like Ken Galloway. But their impact on smallholder farmers in the developing world is even more devastating. Subsidizing commodities encourages U.S. farmers to overproduce them. Selling these excess commodities in world markets at artificially low prices distorts trade and makes it extremely difficult for farmers in developing nations to sell their products. In spite of their much lower production costs, cotton farmers in countries like Senegal, Burkina Faso, Chad and Mali cannot compete against highly subsidized U.S. cotton. For these African nations, where 15 million people earning roughly $1 to $2 per day depend directly on cotton,[4] U.S. farm programs shatter hopes of reducing hunger and poverty.

There are nearly 3 billion people in the world living on less than $2 per day. Raising the income of the poorest people, even by a small amount, could be a great opportunity for U.S. farmers to expand their export markets. One of the first things very poor people do with additional income is to buy more food. The demand for animal protein in particular will quickly outstrip developing countries' own productive capacity. Midwestern producers of feed grains stand to gain from poverty reduction in the developing world.

Thus, strong economic growth in developing countries should be a preeminent concern for U.S. farmers, but so far, farm groups have not used their powerful influence on Capitol Hill to press policymakers to understand the relationship between global poverty reduction and emerging markets for U.S. agriculture, and to take action. In the developing world, reducing poverty depends largely on improvements in agricultural productivity. Three-fourths of the poorest people in the developing world make their living from agriculture. It may be counterintuitive that U.S. farmers should be rooting for farmers in other countries, but without large-scale growth in the agricultural sector of poor countries, broad-based economic development will not occur and the substantial new markets for U.S. agricultural products will not materialize.

For farmers in developing countries to compete in local, regional, and even global markets, they need protection from U.S. commodities that flood the market at prices which are artificially low because they are highly subsidized. They also need access to open markets in developed countries. The Doha Development Round of the World Trade Organization (WTO) is an opportunity to address the inequities that keep billions of people mired in poverty. The United States should

Richard Lord

New Study Shows How U.S. Farm Sector Benefits from Global Development

– Bread for the World Institute

A new study by Marcelle Thomas and Antoine Bouët at the International Food Policy Research Institute (IFPRI) finds that U.S. agricultural exports to Africa and Asia could rise substantially if low- and middle-income countries in these regions were to achieve broad-based economic growth. The study, commissioned by Bread for the World Institute, presents some of the most compelling evidence to date to show how much the U.S. farm sector stands to gain.

IFPRI simulated annual growth rates of 7 percent in Gross Domestic Product (GDP) for three groups of developing countries in Africa and Asia (see Table 1). This level of GDP growth is a sharp increase from recent growth rates in most countries in these regions, but it is clearly within the range achieved by such fast-growth economies as China and India.

"The argument that income growth abroad in low-income countries can benefit U.S. agriculture has a long tradition," IFPRI notes. This is the view championed by renowned agricultural economist Dr. Robert Thompson, whose arguments are discussed in Chapter Three of *Healthy Food, Farms and Families*. Thompson and others who share this position rely on what Thomas and Bouet call a common-sense argument of what happens when hundreds of millions of people living on $1-$2 per day see their incomes rise to $5-$10 per day. As history shows, consumption quantities and diet quality improve as demand for food sharply increases. This is precisely what happened in Japan, South Korea and Taiwan, for example, as they emerged from relative poverty in the 1950s-1960s to become booming economies in the 1980s-1990s. Thompson observes that these countries "became the best markets for Midwestern corn and soybean producers as people

there gained the purchasing power to include more animal protein in their diets."

Building new export markets is a continuous concern for U.S. agricultural producers. While the largest share of U.S. trade is with other industrialized nations, developing countries represent new markets with vast potential. Presently, African and Asian countries (excluding India and China) account for a small share of overall U.S. agricultural exports (see Table 2). As people's livelihoods in these countries improve, U.S. export volumes are bound to increase as they have for Japan, South Korea and Taiwan. "Driven by rising incomes," IFPRI writes, "U.S. agricultural exports have increased to these countries simultaneously with substantial increases in their own domestic agricultural production and despite significant trade barriers."

> Between 2006 and 2020, U.S. agriculture exports would grow by $25.8 billion, according to the study.

Agriculture is the key to development in low-income countries, and that is why it has been at the center of the Doha Development Round of the World Trade Organization. Achieving higher levels of economic growth in the developing world requires support from developed countries. The United States has good reason to be supportive of policies that promote economic development in low-income countries. It is in the best interest of U.S. farmers, and it is in the best interest of poor people around the world.

The full study, Effects of Economic Growth in Developing Countries on U.S. Agriculture: Preliminary Evidence from a Global CGE Model, *is included in Appendix A, starting on page 118.*

Table 1. Regional increase in U.S. exports with 7 percent GDP growth

	Low income Africa	Importers Middle income Africa	Low income Asia
	(in percent)		
U.S. agriculture exports			
Rice	26.43	35.43	3.17
Wheat	32.08	17.73	15.73
Other cereals	31.27	40.70	24.00
Fruits and vegetables	25.65	33.45	19.27
Oilseeds	20.92	33.62	22.43
Sugar	14.01	23.94	13.74
Plant based fibers	20.72	21.02	12.18
Other agriculture	5.62	20.86	16.41
Meat and meat products	9.67	19.34	7.69
Milk	24.61	24.28	9.68
Food products	22.65	31.21	13.89

Table 2. Regional share of total U.S. exports with 7 percent GDP growth

	Low income Africa	Importers Middle income Africa	Low income Asia
	(in percent)		
U.S. agriculture exports			
Rice	7.94	2.55	0.75
Wheat	2.19	18.04	0.70
Other cereals	0.45	11.86	0.09
Fruits and vegetables	0.33	0.61	0.08
Oilseeds	0.05	1.14	0.00
Sugar	0.34	0.76	0.02
Plant based fibers	0.00	0.13	3.44
Other agriculture	0.55	1.14	0.17
Meat and meat products	0.53	1.34	0.09
Milk	0.42	1.30	0.15
Food products	0.69	1.65	0.10

be leading other industrialized countries in reforming agricultural payment and tariff policies that distort trade.

But whether the Doha round is successfully concluded or not, the United States must reform its farm programs. In one of the first cases of its kind, Brazil challenged the legality of U.S. cotton subsidies under WTO rules of trade and won its case. The WTO ruled that U.S. subsidies distorted world cotton markets and harmed the economic interests of cotton-exporting countries like Brazil.[5] As a result, the United States is obligated to reform and restrict its current cotton subsidy programs. Also, the outcome of the cotton case increases the likelihood that subsidies for other U.S. commodities will face similar WTO challenges and be forced to reform. It makes little sense to let the litigation set the pace of reform—it is costly to defend these programs, and it leaves U.S. farmers in a state of uncertainty as to whether the programs they rely on will be available months or years down the road.

Nutrition Programs Protect Families from Hunger

Federal nutrition programs represent an investment in the health and well-being of families by ensuring that low-income Americans have access to food. The Food Stamp Program, the largest federal nutrition program, will be reauthorized in the next farm bill, and so will several other programs that are smaller but still important.

The United States continues to need effective nutrition programs to combat hunger. In 2005, the Food Stamp Program served an average of 25 million people per month. There is much to praise in the Food Stamp Program. "Waste, fraud and abuse" is at an almost negligible level, such that policymakers might hold up the Food Stamp Program as an example of what other federal programs should try to achieve.

But for all the good the Food Stamp Program does for low-income families, it does not ensure them access to adequate amounts of healthy food. The government meal plan that the program is based on, known as the Thrifty Food Plan, does not meet current nutritional guidelines. Improving the Food Stamp Program could benefit families in several key ways. First, it could improve the health of families by making it possible for them to afford healthy foods for the entire monthly benefit cycle. Second, it could help to increase participation; today only 60 percent of eligible people participate in the program. Finally, it could help the United States meet its pledge of cutting food insecurity in half by 2010.

Far too many people in the United States remain food insecure —more than 35 million according to recent government statistics —and yet in these households, as in others, obesity is all too common. According to the latest government data, 66 percent of Americans are considered overweight and nearly half of those are obese. Overweight and obesity affect all income groups but are most prevalent in low-income communities. Calories are cheap and abundant in the United States—it's the nutrients that are expensive. Poverty limits access

to healthy foods. Too poor to afford nutritious meals, many low-income households stock their cupboards with cheap but filling foods, high in fats and sweeteners.

Some public health experts contend that U.S. farm policy, by heavily subsidizing corn and soybean production, is contributing to the obesity problem. High fructose corn syrup and hydrogenated vegetable oil, byproducts of subsidized corn and soybeans, are ingredients used in almost all processed foods.

Especially alarming are the rising rates of obesity among children and adolescents. Obesity is now the most prevalent nutritional disease of children and adolescents in the United States.[6] The percentage of children between the ages of 6 and 19 who are overweight has reached 16 percent.[7] This is a fourfold increase since 1974 for children between the ages of 6 and 11, and a threefold increase for adolescents 12 to 19.[8]

In the next farm bill, policymakers should counter the effects of heavily subsidized foods by promoting healthful relationships between nutrition programs and farm policy. Nutrition programs that provide fresh fruits and vegetables in the schools should receive stronger support, since overweight children have a high probability of growing up to be obese adults. The Food Stamp Program should include incentives to encourage participants to purchase healthy foods. Incentive programs and farm-to-school programs also benefit farmers. In short, the goals of federal farm policy and nutrition policy need to be in accord with public health goals.

Hunger and Farm Bill Reform

Hunger is the lens through which this report looks at the farm

bill. No legislator wants to increase hunger, but sometimes policies do so inadvertently because of conflicting priorities. If it turns out that policies are contributing to hunger, the moral imperative should be to reform them. That does not mean eliminating support for farmers. Rather, policymakers must develop solutions that help struggling U.S. farmers, strengthen rural communities, provide an adequate, nutritious diet for hungry people in this country, and support the efforts of small farmers in developing countries to get their products to market and feed their families.

Mainline Recommendations in this report:

■ The United States should phase out the current system of farm subsidies, which links higher payments with higher production levels.

■ Federal farm policy should offer farmers tools for managing financial risk, disaster assistance during times of catastrophic crop failure, and support for practicing good environmental stewardship.

■ The United States should lead the way in pushing for a swift and successful conclusion to the Doha Round of the World Trade Organization (WTO) negotiations.

■ Savings from limits on trade-distorting farm programs should be redirected to accelerating rural development and ending hunger.

■ Nutrition programs should ensure that participants have access to healthy foods.

Milestones in U.S. Agricultural Policy

1933

Agricultural Adjustment Act: First "farm bill" established the New Deal mix of commodity-specific price and income support programs.

1936

 Soil Conservation and Domestic Allotment Act: First direct links created between soil conservation and commodity programs.

1949

Agricultural Act: Established policy of high, fixed-price supports and acreage allotments as permanent farm policy. Programs revert to the 1949 provisions should a new farm bill fail to pass.

1954

Agricultural Act: Introduced flexible price supports to commodity programs.

1956

Agricultural Act: Established Soil Bank, which introduced use of conservation reserve in addition to acreage control for supply management. The program ended after only 2 years.

1965

Food and Agricultural Act: Introduced new income support payments in combination with reduced price supports and continued supply controls.

1970

Agriculture Act: First inclusion of title for Rural Development in a farm bill.

1973

Agriculture and Consumer Protection Act: Introduced target prices and deficiency payments to replace price supports, coupled with low commodity loan rates, to increase producer reliance on markets and allow for free movement of commodities at world prices.

1977

Food and Agriculture Act: First inclusion of title for Food Stamps and other commodity distribution programs in a farm bill.

1985

Food Security Act: Introduced marketing loan provisions to commodity loan programs to reduce forfeitures by allowing repayment of loans at lower rate when market prices fell, with the intention of aiding in reducing Government-held surplus grain. Re-established a conservation reserve.

1996

Federal Agriculture Improvement and Reform Act: Replaced price support and supply control program with program of direct payments based on historical production. Introduced nearly complete planting flexibility.

2002

Farm Security and Rural Investment Act: Introduced counter-cyclical payments program triggered when current prices fall below a target level, but paid based on historical production. Introduced working-lands conservation payments through the Conservation Security Program. Continued planting flexibility and program of direct payments based on historical production, allowing updating of historical base acres and adding historical soybean acres.

Source: Compiled by Economic Research Service, USDA. The complete texts of U.S. farm bills from 1933 to 2002 are available on the website of the National Agricultural Law Center (http://www.nationalaglawcenter.org/farmbills/).

A Primer on Farm Subsidies:
How Income-Support Payments Work

Farmers can receive three types of income-support payments for the production and sale of wheat, corn, grain sorghum, barley, oats, cotton, rice, soybeans, or other oilseeds. These payments are:

Direct Payments, calculated based on 85 percent of the farmer's historical yield,[1] base acreage,[2] and payment rate.[3]

Counter-Cyclical Payments, calculated based on 85 percent of the farmer's historical yield, base acreage, and a payment per unit[4] that varies depending on market prices. The amount of the payment per unit is determined by the difference between a target price[5] previously determined and the actual market price.

Loan Deficiency Payments, provided when market prices drop below a specified loan rate.[6] These payments are determined by the difference between the loan rate and the market price. Payments are made on 100 percent of production.

Footnotes

[1] Historical yield refers to yields based on calculations for 1998-2001.

[2] Base acreage refers to the number of acres of a particular commodity in production.

[3] Payment rate is set in law and is defined in terms of $ per bushel/ton/pound/hundredweight.

[4] Unit is measured in terms of a bushel/ton/pound/hundredweight per acre.

[5] Target price is set in law and is defined in terms of $ per bushel/ton/pound/hundredweight.

[6] Loan rate is set in law and is defined in terms of $ per bushel/ton/pound/hundredweight.

Terry Smith farms 100 acres in Dawes County, Nebraska.* Her historical base is 100 acres of corn and her historical yield is 136 bushels per acre. This year, she decides to plant 50 acres of corn and 40 acres of soybeans, leaving 10 acres fallow. Her land yields 143 bushels per acre of corn and 41 bushels per acre of soybeans.

Based on her base acreage and historical yield, Terry is eligible to receive a direct payment and a countercyclical payment. As legislated in the 2002 farm bill, the payment rate for corn is $.28 per bushel. Each year, Terry receives a direct payment of $3,237 [(.85 x 100 base acres) x (136 bushels per acre x $.28 per bushel)].

For the same year, the target price for the counter-cyclical payment is $2.63 per bushel. To determine the size of Terry's countercyclical payment, first it is necessary to get the "effective price" for corn, which is the direct payment rate plus either the national loan rate or the national season-average market price, whichever is higher.

If the season-average market price was $2.20 per bushel (higher than the national loan rate of $1.95), the effective price would be $2.48 ($.28 + $2.20). Therefore, the payment rate for countercyclical payments is $.15. Terry would therefore receive a coun-

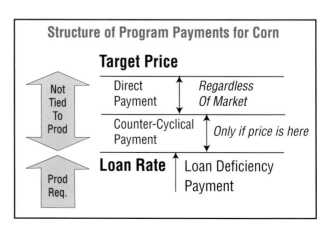

Structure of Program Payments for Corn

Target Price

| Not Tied To Prod | Direct Payment | Regardless Of Market |
| Counter-Cyclical Payment | Only if price is here |

Loan Rate | Loan Deficiency Payment

Prod Req.

Cheryl A. Meyer

Commodity program payments to corn producers are estimated to average $5.4 billion per year and account for 46 percent of total crop payments from 2002-2006.

tercyclical payment of $1,734 [(.85 x 100 base acres) x (136 bushels per acre x $.15 per bushel)].

The third type of payment—loan deficiency—makes up the difference between the market price and the loan rate. Terry decides to exercise her option to collect a loan deficiency payment for both crops on January 20. That day's local price for corn (the Posted County Price) is $1.71 per bushel and the loan rate for Dawes County is $1.90. Terry's loan deficiency payment is $680 [50 acres planted x (143 bushels per acre x $.19 per bushel)]. Since the market price for soybeans on that day exceeds the local loan rate ($4.87 and $4.61, respectively), she receives a loan deficiency payment for soybeans. She keeps her crop and sells it when she chooses.

$3,237	– direct payment
$1,734	– countercyclical payment
$1,358	– loan deficiency payment
$6,329	– total payments

* The example illustrates how the three income support programs fit together for a producer (under policies in effect from fiscal years 2004 to 2007).

	Corn	Soybeans	Fallow
Base acres	100	-	-
Acres actually planted	50	40	10
Historical yield per acre	136 bu/acre	-	-
Actual yield per acre	143 bu/acre	41 bu/acre	-
National loan rate	$1.95	$5.00	-
Local loan rate (Dawes County, NE)	$1.90	$4.61	-
Posted County Price (PCP) on Jan. 20, 2006, when farmer chooses to collect LDP	$1.71	$4.87	-
LDP rate (local loan rate-PCP)	$ .19/bu.	$0	-
National season-average market price	$2.20/bu.		-
Effective price	$2.48/bu.		-
Direct payment rate	$ .28/bu.	$ .44/bu.	-
Direct payment	$3,237	-	-
Counter-cyclical payment	$1,734	-	-
Loan deficiency payment	$1,358	$0	-
Total government payment	$6,329		

Commodities:
Reform Starts Here

Chapter 1

In the most recent farm bill, the Farm Security and Rural Investment Act of 2002, federal policymakers agreed to spend approximately $120 billion over six years on payments to farmers. Nearly $100 billion was intended to subsidize farm revenues and offset the low prices of some crops. Under the farm bill's Commodities Title, these so-called "program crops" were treated generously, with subsidies directed to farmers growing select commodities—wheat, corn, soybeans, rice, cotton and dairy products.[1]

This type of direct government support for farmers started during the Great Depression, when farm household income was only half that of non-farm households. The fact that federal farm programs have been in effect for the intervening 70 years suggests that farms have continued to face the dire economic conditions of the 1930s—but on the contrary, farm household income has closely tracked or surpassed the median income for all U.S. households since the 1970s. In 2004, for example, the average net income of a farm household was $81,000, while the average for non-farm households was $61,000.[2] Currently the poverty rate among farmers is the lowest in U.S. history.[3] It is clear that today's farm programs do not confront the degree of poverty among farmers that they did in the 1930s.

"It is not easy to pin down what farm programs are supposed to accomplish," said agricultural economist Bruce Babcock of the Center for Agricultural Research and Development (CARD) at Iowa State University.[4] One thing is clear: a small group of farmers and landowners benefit from federal programs, and a far greater number of people who live in rural America —including most farmers—do not. This chapter looks at how this has happened and identifies a package of reforms that will enable farm payment programs to better serve both farmers and everyone in rural America.

U.S. farm policies affect all Americans—from rural economic development to environmental impacts to which food products are available on grocery store shelves —so the public has a vested interest in reshaping them. These concerns are central to the reform agenda.

70 Years of Farm Policy

A cursory look at the history of farming and U.S. farm programs reveals that federal support for farmers was born out of necessity. Although the government sought in several ways to support farmers prior to the early 1930s, the first major piece of farm legislation was passed in 1933 in response to the widespread economic devastation of the Great Depression. Between 1929 and 1933, farm gate prices for agricultural commodities fell by more than 50 percent and net farm revenues declined even more precipitously—nearly 70 percent in just four years. The result was a dramatic increase in the number of farm failures.[5]

After the election of Franklin D. Roosevelt, Congress enacted the Agricultural Adjustment Act (AAA) of 1933. The AAA was an unprecedented government intervention into the farm sector. Between 1929 and 1935, the budget of the U.S. Department of Agriculture grew sixfold, from $200 million to $1.2 billion.[6] Under the new legislation, farmers who produced any of several widely-grown commodities were required to participate in a farm program aimed at stabilizing prices and farmer livelihoods. In the language of the law, the AAA would "reestablish prices to farmers at a level that will give agricultural commodities a purchasing power with respect to articles that farmers buy."

Created to "relieve the existing national economic emergency" of the Great Depression, the AAA was supposed to be terminated "whenever the President finds and proclaims that the national economic emergency in relation to agriculture has been ended."[7] The proclamation never came. Since the AAA, 14 separate pieces of major legislation (farm bills) have been enacted to continue and expand farm programs. Several commodities first supported in 1933—corn, wheat, cotton, rice, and dairy products—continue to receive a large share of the funding for federal farm programs.

The government response to the plight of farmers in the 1930s served a second purpose: addressing rural poverty. At the onset of the Great Depression, there were more than six million farms in the United States and farming employed 25 percent of working Americans. Agriculture accounted for nearly 7 percent of the nation's gross domestic product (GDP). Farming was clearly a driving force in the economy. Since that time, however, the number of farms has decreased, as has the number of people employed on farms and the percentage of the nation's total income derived from the agriculture sector. In 2000, only two million farms remained and agriculture contributed less than 1 percent of the nation's GDP. Only about 1 percent of the population is now employed in on-farm activities.[8]

These figures show that since the early 1930s, agriculture has declined quite significantly as a share of the U.S. economy. Over the same period of time, the amount of subsidies paid to farmers has increased quite substantially. And yet rural poverty persists. By the latest estimates, 14.2 percent of the population in

In the U.S., five crops account for 21 percent of our cash receipts in agriculture. Those five crops receive 93 percent of our subsidy payments."

*– Mike Johanns,
Secretary of Agriculture*

rural America lives in poverty. This is about 2 percent higher than the poverty rate for urban areas of the country.[9] As one development expert observed, "Farm payments are not providing a strong boost to the rural economy in those counties that most depend on them. Job gains are weak and population growth is actually negative in most of the counties where farm payments are the biggest share of income."[10] Similarly, a recent U.S. Department of Agriculture (USDA) study found, "Many areas that have consistently garnered high payments from farm programs have lost population decade after decade, even during periods when most other rural areas

were gaining population."[11]

During Congress' negotiation of the 2002 farm bill, most legislators showed little enthusiasm for altering the traditional set of farm subsidies. One notable exception came from a group of senators and representatives who proposed an alternative farm bill that would have lowered the amount of commodity payments transferred to the largest recipients of current farm subsidies. In total, the amendment would have reduced commodity payments by about $19 billion, and these savings would have been directed to conservation programs that could "help small farmers who have been virtually ignored by traditional subsidy programs."[12] Although the proposal enjoyed wide support, it was narrowly defeated. Instead, Congress passed legislation adding an estimated $38 billion to commodity program spending.[13]

Who Wins and Who Loses in the Current Farm System

For the majority of farmers, income from farming constitutes only a small portion of their total household income. Most of their income is derived from off-farm work.[14] By design, commodity subsidies benefit the biggest producers. The bigger they are, the more they are entitled to receive.

Here is how payment amounts for program crops are determined. Compare two farms both growing rice, one with 1,000 acres and another with 10,000 acres. If the farmers are enrolled in the commodity programs, they will both receive direct payments from the government, even if they leave their fields fallow. If they choose to plant and the price of rice falls below a predefined target, the government

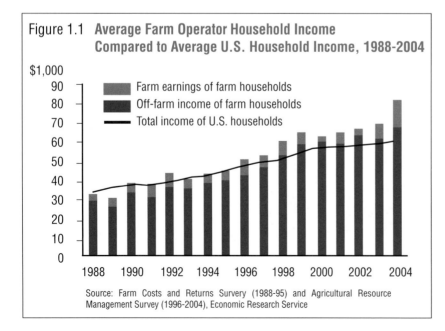

Figure 1.1   **Average Farm Operator Household Income Compared to Average U.S. Household Income, 1988-2004**

- Farm earnings of farm households
- Off-farm income of farm households
- Total income of U.S. households

Source: Farm Costs and Returns Survey (1988-95) and Agricultural Resource Management Survey (1996-2004), Economic Research Service

will provide further compensation to offset the difference between the market and target prices. The amount of compensation is determined by market prices but also by the amount of land in production. The farmer with 10,000 base acres dedicated to rice will receive a larger government payment than the farmer with only 1,000 base acres dedicated to that crop.

"Get big or get out," the often-quoted advice of former Secretary of Agriculture Earl Butz to American farmers in the 1970s, has been the prevailing model for success in U.S. agriculture for the past 70 years, and it holds true today. While the total amount of farmland in production has remained fairly stable since the advent of commodity programs in the 1930s, the average farm is much larger than it was 70 years ago.

Technology and the advantages of realizing economies of scale have played leading roles in the consolidation of farms, but federal farm subsidies are also an important factor. Federal farm payments tend to drive up land values. For example, without federal farm supports, estimates are that the value of farmland would have been about 25 percent lower for the years 1998-2001.[15] Increasing land values make it more difficult for medium-sized farms to expand operations and also more difficult for new farmers to enter farming. Farm consolidation has had the strongest impact on farms of between 50 and 499 acres. The number of farms of this size is declining, while the number of large farms (more than 500 acres) is steadily increasing.[16]

Increasing farm size is encouraged and rewarded by the current system of farm subsidies. In 2004, more than half of the $9.9 billion in commodity payments went to large farms with annual sales of more

Figure 1.2   Operating Profit Margin by Size of Farm, 2003

Farm Sales Class (2003$)

Percent	Less than $10,000	$10,000 - $99,000	$100,000 - $249,000	$250,000 - $499,999	$500,000 or more	Nonfamily
	-98.0	-24.8	-1.8	10.6	16.4	15.3

Source: USDA, 2003 Agricultural Resource Managment Survey

Richard Lord

Why Are Land Values Such An Important Issue?

– Miles Patrie, Bread for the World Institute

Why is the value of farmland such an important issue? Roughly 75 percent of total farm household assets are tied to real estate. Because the land represents such a large portion of a farm household's wealth, renting or selling farmland serves as a retirement plan for many U.S. farmers. Currently, there are more farmers over age 65 than there are under 35, so a change in land values would have an immediate impact on older farmers and their prospects for retirement.

Agricultural economist Willard Cochrane describes the situation as it relates to commodity subsidies: "Every farmland owner, rural banker, farm machinery dealer, fertilizer salesman and Congressman from a farming district from Western Ohio to the Rocky Mountains and from the Canadian border to the Rio Grande knows that the major hunk of wealth, in the form of land values, in that broad sweep of land would simply evaporate if major price and income subsidies to commercial farmers were shut down."

Many people hold this adamant view of the necessity of commodity subsidies, but fortunately for advocates of farm bill reform, it is not shared by everyone. The research of agricultural economist Saleem Shaik shows that efforts to reduce commodity program payments would no longer have the serious effect on land prices that they might have had 30 years ago. Shaik found that in the period 1965-1972, the impact of commodity program payments on land values was nearly three times as great as it was during 1995-2002.

Farmland value is based on the expected income from the land, so there's no doubt that commodity payments increase the value of the land being subsidized. The commodity payment is added to the value of the crops expected from the land to determine the total value of the land. But exactly how much of the value is attributable to subsidies depends on several factors, including which commodities are being produced.

Government payments are not the only factor determining farmland values. The boom and bust cycle that exists within agriculture has also played an important role. Booming exports of grain to Russia in the 1970s and high crop prices led to an extremely rapid increase in farmland prices. During the 1970s, farmland values in Iowa increased by 400 percent. But then, from 1981 to 1986, export levels fell dramatically, interest rates went up, and farmland values fell by 60 percent.

Urban pressures and population growth also exert a strong influence on land values. A 1 percent increase in local population growth adds $64 per acre to the value of farmland. Recently, low interest rates have been a driving force of the strong farmland market, but interest rates are now once again on the rise, and it is unclear what effect this will have on farmland values.

Another factor driving farmland values in many parts of the country is the use of land for recreational purposes. As more land is used for recreation, competition for the remaining farmland increases, driving up prices. In a recent survey by the Federal Reserve Bank of Kansas City, nearly half of all respondents listed hunting, fishing, and other recreation as a major factor in recent farmland price increases.

The value of land in the Northern Plains and Cornbelt regions would be most affected by reductions in commodity payments, due to the large number of acres planted in program crops in these areas. Southern regions that produce a lot of cotton and rice would also be affected, as well as the dairy states around the Great Lakes region and in the Northeast. Non-farming families in nearby rural communities could also be indirectly affected. Property taxes are a critical source of revenue for many communities, representing one-fourth of all public school funding nationwide. If farmland values were to fall significantly, revenue from property taxes would decrease and local governments would have to find new sources of revenue. This could be a serious problem in sparsely populated areas.

Because so many factors affect the value of farmland, the extent to which farmland values would decrease as payments are decreased is difficult to

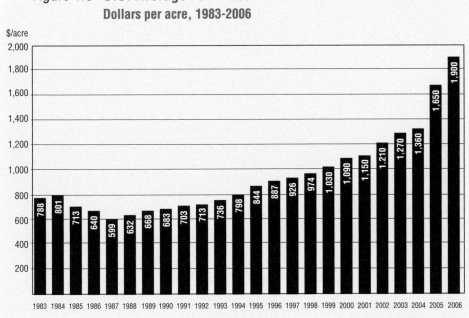

Figure 1.3 U.S. Average Farm Real Estate Value
Dollars per acre, 1983-2006

$/acre

Year	$/acre
1983	788
1984	801
1985	713
1986	640
1987	599
1988	632
1989	668
1990	683
1991	703
1992	713
1993	736
1994	798
1995	844
1996	887
1997	926
1998	974
1999	1,030
2000	1,090
2001	1,150
2002	1,210
2003	1,270
2004	1,360
2005	1,650
2006	1,900

Source: USDA-NASS; August 2006

predict. But perhaps we can learn from other countries' experiences. In 1984, New Zealand decided to swiftly and drastically cut farm subsidies. By 1985, land prices began to decrease, as did farmers' incomes. But by the early 1990s, farmers in New Zealand had adjusted by growing different crops and finding new marketing opportunities. Land values began to rise in 1992 and have continued to do so since then.

In the United States, gradual reform of farm policy could allow farmers time to make these adjustments and thus lessen the effect on land prices. Gradual decreases in farmland values could actually benefit many U.S. farmers in the long run. Reducing farmland prices could improve the ability of U.S. farmers to compete in global markets. Since farmland prices are included in the cost of production, higher land prices mean higher production costs. Some experts have argued that inflated farmland values make U.S. farmers less competitive than farmers elsewhere. South American farmers, for example, are able to produce soybeans for substantially less than U.S. farmers, largely due to lower land values.

The next generation of farmers would also benefit from a phased-in transition to lower land values. Becoming a farmer has never been more difficult than it is right now, because the start-up costs for machinery and land are incredibly high. A significant decrease in farmland prices would make it much easier for new farmers to rent or purchase land. But even these farmers will not benefit from lower land values unless they receive adequate prices for their crops. Gradual reform that maintains a safety net during transition would allow young farmers to adjust to new policies. As the average age of U.S. farmers continues to rise, supporting new and aspiring farmers will be crucial to the well-being of farming and farm-dependent communities across the United States.

Miles Patrie was a Bill Emerson National Hunger Fellow from August 2005 to August 2006. Part of his fellowship included working on national policy at Bread for the World Institute.

Figure 1.4   Eight States Collect Over Half of All Farm Spending

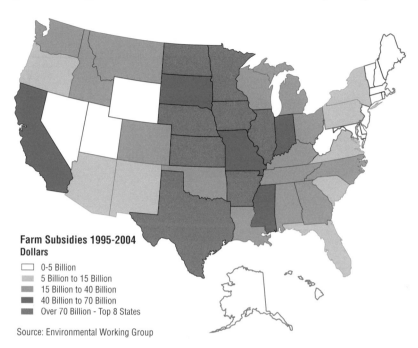

Farm Subsidies 1995-2004 Dollars

- ☐ 0-5 Billion
- ☐ 5 Billion to 15 Billion
- ☐ 15 Billion to 40 Billion
- ☐ 40 Billion to 70 Billion
- ☐ Over 70 Billion - Top 8 States

Source: Environmental Working Group

than $250,000. Operations of this size represent only 7 percent of U.S. farms, although they account for the majority of crop production.[17] In 2004, 37 farming entities (farms and cooperatives) received more than $1 million apiece in commodity payments. That year, Riceland Foods, Inc., a large Arkansas rice cooperative, received by far the largest set of payments: $14.6 million.[18]

The money allocated to commodity programs is not equally distributed among farmers or among regions of the country. Midwestern states such as Kansas, Nebraska, Iowa, Illinois, Indiana, Minnesota and North Dakota, along with California and Texas, receive the highest concentration of payments.[19] Approximately two-thirds of the nation's farmers receive no government payments whatsoever. "For the most part they don't qualify because they grow the 'wrong' thing," observed the Environmental Working Group. "If you want to see what the wrong things are, stroll

through the produce aisle or meat department of your local supermarket."[20] Specialty crops, otherwise known as fruits and vegetables, receive no subsidies.

The question of who receives federal farm payments is important because it is often assumed that when a farmer in rural America receives a farm payment, that money is spent in the community where the farm is located. Although federal farm payments are targeted to the farm operator, in practice it has not been difficult for absentee landowners to capture the value of government payments (either directly or through charging higher rent). If a landowner is not the primary farm operator and does not live in a rural community, then the potential multiplier effects of federal farm dollars into rural economies are greatly reduced.

Huge government outlays for a shrinking farming sector, the concentration of federal farm support payments among a relatively small number of farmers, the inflation of land values by federal farm supports, the promotion of larger farms at the expense of mid-size operations and stagnating rural economies: there is no shortage of problems linked to current farm policy.

Despite a yawning chasm between the amount of money the government spends to support a small proportion of American farmers and the actual impact of farming on the U.S. economy, government farm programs continue to enjoy a great deal of support in Congress. Though many provisions of the farm bill are set to expire in 2007, several policymakers have called for extending existing farm programs for a year or more. The commitment of members of Congress to helping farmers is not

> Commodity program payments shifted to higher income households between 1983-2003."
>
> – USDA

in question. They, like everyone else, realize that a successful agricultural sector is in everyone's best interest. But a significant number of farmers, especially small and medium-sized farmers, are critical of the current farm policy. A good many are frankly convinced that current U.S. farm policy has not been designed to serve their best interests.

What Do "Family Farmers" Think?

It is not easy to define a "family farmer." Many gargantuan farms are family-owned, but when most Americans think of a struggling family farmer, they tend to envision a small or medium-sized operation. USDA defines small and medium-sized farms as those with less than $250,000 in net sales. Farms with sales of less than $250,000 generally have negative profit margins.[21] It is clear that these farmers are indeed struggling. (See figure 1.2).

According to nearly any definition, Kevin Miskell is a family farmer. A fifth generation farmer, Miskell raises corn and soybeans on 700 acres in Stanhope, Iowa. According to his own definition, he is a family farmer because he works the land, makes all the decisions on how it is used and is involved in the farm's operation most days of the year. Miskell benefits from government subsidies—although benefits may not be a word he would use. Does he like subsidies? He abhors them. "I don't know one honest farmer that wouldn't want a farm program structured so that we got our money out of the market, not out of the government," he said, but adds that without the subsidies he would be out of business. Under the current system there is no viable alternative to subsidies for a corn and soy farmer like him.

The problem with farm policy, according to Miskell, is how family farmers like himself have been marginalized to serve the interests of large corporations. He points to the concentration of the livestock industry as an example of this. "Twenty years ago, I wouldn't have cared about the price of corn—it went into hogs. I used to raise corn to feed my livestock to sell as meat—value added. Now you have

a handful of companies controlling the majority of the livestock business in this country. They want cheap inputs, and so what you have is a depressed grain market, which is all that is left for farmers like me. We're dependent on farm payments to make up the difference in what we lose by supplying Cargill, Tysons, and Smithfield (among others) with cheap feed."

If all there is for farmers is to provide cheap grain rather than add value to livestock and sell the meat themselves, then the only way for a farm the size of Miskell's to remain viable is to expand. Once again, we return to "Get big or get out." But not everyone can expand. They must raise the purchase price of additional land, and land is costly, partly because government payments have raised land values. It's not surprising that Miskell feels trapped. But he also worries that reform engineered too hastily will add more to his burdens than it solves. The devil he knows is preferable to the one he does not.

Some entrapment is a matter of perspective. Tim Nissen, who farms 500 acres in his hometown of Hartington, Nebraska, feels that he

has also been marginalized, but he is in a much different place psychologically if not financially. Ten years ago, he was strictly a corn and soy farmer like Miskell. Now he has diversified his operation to include choke cherries and plums. He is getting ready for his first grape harvest in another year. Eventually he wants to open up a winery.

His neighbors think he is either nuts or really on to something. Those who think he's stumbled across a good idea agree with him about the economics of farming but haven't yet figured out what to do about it. Nissen started coming to terms with the hard truth in 2000, following a freak hailstorm that wiped out his entire corn crop for the year. It felt just as if one of the hailstones had hit him in the head, he says. Crop insurance covered the loss of his corn but he had nothing else growing. That's when the possibility of running a different sort of farm occurred to him.

"Until you get off the treadmill it's hard to see there are alternatives," Nissen says. The system does little to encourage farmers to diversify. In fact, Nissen has a neighbor who

Family-operated farms continue to account for most U.S. agricultural production.

was farming 160 acres of corn and decided to experiment by taking one acre out of corn production to grow grapes. Because of that one acre of grapes, the neighbor lost his government payments for the whole farm: according to government regulations, land that is registered for growing commodity crops cannot be used to plant fruits or vegetables. "Rules like that would discourage anyone from doing things differently," said Nissen.

Currently Nissen works part-time in town and will continue to do so for another year until his grape vines start producing. Although he still farms some program crops, he is looking forward to the day when he will be done with them entirely. It's not that he's philosophically opposed to getting help from the government; he applied for and received a Value-added Producer Grant (VAPG) from USDA to start his vineyard and write a business plan for it. The VAPG is part of a rural development program added to the 2002 farm bill to help farmers like Nissen diversify their operations.

"It was painful realizing there is no money in what you thought there was," he says, reflecting on the quandary he faced. "I have friends who raised hogs and were really low-cost producers, but they're out of business now because they didn't have the volume to compete with the big producers. It's not a level playing field. The low-cost producer doesn't win like they say he should in the textbooks."

Tim Nissen and Kevin Miskell agree that current U.S. farm policy needs reform, but they have very different ideas of what should happen. Miskell wants policymakers to address the concentration in the livestock industry, proposing that they do this by enforcing tighter regulations and even turning to anti-trust legislation if necessary. Nissen wants to see more focus on encouraging farmers to diversify and get out of the commodity game if they wish. For the average small- to medium-sized family farmer, either direction may be preferable to where they are today. Probably all would agree that they wish they had a stronger say in the policies that affect their livelihoods.

Clearing Up Myths about Farm Programs

The current system of farm subsidies is outdated and no longer meets the needs of most farmers. Nor is it contributing to rural economic prosperity. The evidence for this is overwhelming and readily available, so one has to wonder why federal policy continues to accord farming a privileged position in the ongoing conversation about how best to support rural America. The likely answer is in the power of several myths about the value of farm programs. These myths are often the basis for arguments against reform, sometimes by people who benefit from the status quo. Each is examined and rebutted here.

Myth One: Subsidies ensure American consumers a low-cost food supply.

It's commonly argued that the flow of federal dollars to certain U.S. farmers helps ensure an abundant and cheap food supply. The low prices that farmers are paid for raw commodities translate into

Figure 1.5   Labor Takes the Biggest Chunk of the Food Dollar

Source: USDA, 2004

Labor — Packaging — Transportation — Energy — Profits — Advertising — Depreciation — Rent — Interest — Repairs — Business Taxes — Other costs

| 19.0¢ | 38.5¢ | 8.0¢ | 4.0¢ | 3.5¢ | 4.5¢ | 4.0¢ | 3.5¢ | 4.5¢ | 2.5¢ | 1.5¢ | 3.5¢ | 3.0¢ |

Farm Value — Marketing Bill

lower food prices for consumers. Two of the most heavily subsidized commodities, soybeans and corn, are widely used as animal feed. In exchange for billions of dollars in farm subsidies, U.S. consumers benefit from a plentiful supply of inexpensive meat. At least this is the logic behind the claims of the National Beef Association and other groups.[22]

But would the cost of meat and other final products rise significantly if farm subsidies were eliminated? Experts answer, probably not. In their raw, unprocessed form, subsidized commodities make up only a modest portion of the value of finished food products. Consider, for example, the retail cost of pork at a local grocery store. The cost of feed corn is only a small share, approximately 11 percent, of the in-store cost of pork. So even if the price of corn were to increase by 5 percent as a result of the elimination of farm subsidies (in itself a questionable assumption), the price of pork would increase by less than one percent. Pork chops that cost $3.00 per pound with farm subsidies would cost about $3.02 without them, says Iowa State economist Bruce Babcock.[23]

The evidence shows that farm subsidies cannot be credited for low food prices at the grocery store. Contrary to the claims of industry insiders, U.S. consumers will not suffer significantly higher food prices even if farm subsidies were eliminated altogether.

Myth Two: Subsidies ensure that the United States does not become dependent on imported food.

"Importing oil may have made economic sense in the short term, but over the long term it has proved

problematic and very costly. Why would we want our food policy to follow the same historic path as our energy policy?"[24]

Sentiments like this, voiced by an executive of the National Association of Wheat Growers and quoted in *The Wall Street Journal*, are part of a highly dubious argument for maintaining current farm policy: the idea that without subsidies the United States might stop producing enough food to feed itself. In the first place, comparing oil to food is a far-fetched analogy. Because oil must first be present in the earth before it can be extracted, the United States is able to produce just a fraction of its overall petroleum needs. But U.S. food production is not similarly handicapped.

A rapidly shrinking trade surplus in agricultural products is playing on public fears of dependency on "foreign food." And in fact, U.S. consumer preference for agricultural imports has been rising faster than new markets have been opening for exports. The untold part of this story, though, is that Americans are choosing to buy the imported foods. "The declining U.S. trade surplus does not signal reduced competitiveness of the U.S. farm sector," USDA acknowledges, "but rather Americans' preference for a wider variety of foods and beverages."[25] Products in high demand include tropical fruits and vegetables, nuts, cut flowers, coffee, cocoa, cheeses and wines. U.S. farmers and food

manufacturers cannot supply all the foods American palates now desire.

Ironically, farm policy may be partially responsible for the inability of U.S agriculture to meet all these consumer demands. Subsidies encourage farmers to mono-crop rather than diversify, as Tim Nissen's neighbor found. A ride around any Midwestern state where program crops are raised confirms that mono-cropping is the order of the day. Iowa farmers grow lots of corn and soy beans, for example, and very little else. USDA reports that Iowa farmers plant about 12 million acres of corn and another 10 million acres of soybeans each year. Iowa is in the heart of farm country, and in many people's minds, the word Iowa signifies farming. Yet almost all of the food eaten by Iowans comes from out of state. Less than 10 percent is produced on farms in Iowa.

It is not that the soil in Iowa is incapable of producing other foods. In the past, Iowa farmers produced many other commercial crops. In the early part of the twentieth century, southeastern Iowa was one of three primary sweet potato growing regions in the United States.[26] But

today, sweet potato production levels are negligible. Once a top apple-producing state, Iowa currently ranks near the bottom among states that produce apples commercially. The most popular brand of apple sold in the United States, the Delicious brand, was first introduced to Americans from orchards in Iowa. But driving today on Iowa's interstates, the views are nearly identical on both sides of the road, traveling north, south, east or west—acre upon acre of corn and soybeans.

Myth Three: Subsidies have made the United States "the breadbasket of the world."

The Great Plains has been called the breadbasket of the world because of its prodigious grain production. Is this due to subsidies? While it is true that some production decisions, such as how much rice and soybeans to grow, are shaped by the size of government subsidies, the real abundance in U.S. agriculture comes from the rich soil, good climate, hardworking farmers and technical innovations that have long been the hallmarks of American farming. Many people around the world enjoy food produced in the United States.

But U.S. farmers do not, by themselves, feed the world. Other countries compete with the United States for a share of world commodity markets. U.S. wheat exports, for example, are rivaled by those from Canada, Australia, Argentina and Russia. Thailand and Vietnam are the world's largest rice exporters, and India

is expected to overtake the United States for third place within the next decade. Brazil is the second largest exporter of soybeans. The United States continues to lead the world in corn exports, though it is not yet clear how much the expansion of the ethanol industry will impact exports.

One reason these countries can compete with U.S. exports is that they are lower cost producers. The paradox of the remarkable efficiency of U.S. agriculture is that it comes with extraordinarily high production costs—for renting land, buying farm equipment and paying farm workers. Land and labor are simply cheaper in many other countries.

When taxpayers see U.S. farm products sent to other parts of the world as food aid, they may assume that the food is being made available under commodity programs. The United States is the most generous donor of food aid—food intended to meet emergency nutrition needs in poor countries—and in this way we are indeed helping to feed the world. But U.S. food aid programs are authorized and funded under a different title of the farm bill, and changes to the commodity programs would have no direct effect on U.S. food aid. Although both involve partnerships between the government and farmers, they are entirely separate programs.

Myth Four: Ending subsidies will be devastating for rural communities.

All the evidence shows that the U.S. counties receiving the most farm supports are stagnating economically and losing population. What poor rural areas need is an alternative to farm programs, not more of the same.

Yet within this myth is the real possibility that reducing subsidies would cause land values to spiral downward in areas dominated by subsidized crops. Since most farmland is not easily convertible to other uses, the value of the land is determined by what can be produced on that land. If there is a history of subsidized crop production, the value of each acre increases because of the anticipated federal farm payments.

Reducing those subsidies might harm farmers who own their own land, especially those who receive the highest farm payments. For this reason, it is necessary to proceed with caution and build an alternative farm safety net to ensure that farmers who currently receive payments are not put out of business by a sudden change in the structure of farm subsidies.

But this real concern should not stop the government from making reforms. There may be significant advantages for many people in rural America if the existing set of farm payments is modified. One large group which stands to benefit is aspiring farmers who cannot afford to get into farming because of its high startup costs. Many young people would farm if they could afford to rent land, but without significant incentives and assistance, it is unclear who will replace the current generation of farmers, one third of whom are 65 or older.[27]

Rather than relying on farm subsidies to support rural communities, as was done in the era when many people worked in the agricultural sector, government must forge a more direct relationship with rural America. For example, money saved by limiting subsidy payments could and should be used to fund rural development initiatives that will help to diversify and sustain rural economies.

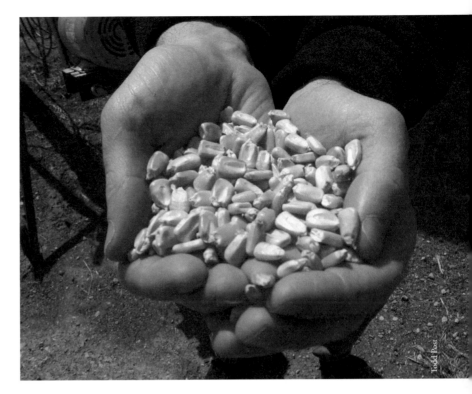

Where To Go From Here: Reforming An Unsustainable System

There is no shortage of innovative ideas about how to reform U.S. farm policy, ranging from minor modifications to major overhauls. Which reform proposals to pursue depends on what we want to accomplish with them. Farm policy must effectively support farmers—those like Kevin Miskell who want to continue farming program crops as well as those like Tim Nissen who prefer to diversify their farming operations. Farm policy should also do a better job of supporting rural development. Devising a farm safety net that encourages innovation, diversification, and good environmental practices is crucial for American farmers and for the majority of rural residents who do not farm (and, as discussed in Chapter 3, for farmers in developing countries). Equally important, farm programs can be designed so as not to encourage

further farm consolidation.

One possible change to farm programs has been proposed by Senators Charles Grassley (R-IA) and Byron Dorgan (D-ND). In the first serious attempt to address the issue of subsidies in more than two decades, the two introduced a bill during the 2002 farm bill negotiations that would have capped

Figure 1.6   **Subsidies Soak Up Funds**

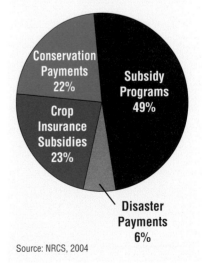

Source: NRCS, 2004

Pesticide Poisoning and Farmworkers

– Shelley Davis, Farmworker Justice

An estimated 10,000 to 20,000 hired farmworkers are poisoned by pesticides on the job each year, according to the U.S. Environmental Protection Agency (EPA). To compound the problem, poverty keeps many farmworkers from seeking medical treatment when they are ill or injured. Despite the risks, federal law provides few pesticide safety protections for agricultural workers.

Farmworkers and their children face an increased risk of leukemia, non-Hodgkin's lymphoma, brain cancer, infertility, birth defects and neurological disorders due to pesticide exposure. A recent Oregon study, for example, found that migrant farmworkers who had repeated exposures to neurotoxic pesticides scored far worse on tests of attention, memory, and intellectual functioning than did comparable immigrants who had no contact with pesticides.

Farmworkers have made several key proposals to safeguard their health, among them that growers be required to keep and make available pesticide application records and that the government fund long-term studies on the health risks to farmworkers of their pesticide exposure.

Pesticide application records are an essential component of a pesticide safety program. Using these records, health care providers can more accurately diagnose an episode of acute pesticide illness, since the records enable them to correlate the onset of symptoms with the time of a pesticide exposure. Similarly, researchers could use these records to determine if a link exists between exposure to particular pesticides and an increased risk of cancer, birth defect or other chronic health problems. Regulators could use application records to determine whether an employer complied with pesticide safety requirements or whether existing safety protections are adequate to prevent injuries.

Few studies have examined the long-term health effects of pesticide exposure on farmworkers or their children. Since 1995, the National Cancer Institute has been conducting a study of 90,000 growers, pesticide applicators and their families in North Carolina and Iowa. While this research

Celia Escudero Espadas

Farm bills have been used to achieve modest gains in pesticide safety.

sheds some light on farmworker risks, the situation facing farmworkers is far different than for the groups in the study. The National Cancer Institute conducted feasibility studies to determine if long-term research could be conducted with the hired farmworker community and concluded that it could. Unfortunately, no money has been set aside for this purpose.

The upcoming farm bill affords an excellent opportunity to increase pesticide protections for farmworkers. Farmworker advocates, working with environmental, labor, faith-based and other groups, will be pressing Congress to incorporate such measures into the new legislation.

Shelley Davis is the Deputy Director of Farmworker Justice (www.fwjustice.org), an organization helping migrant and seasonal farmworkers to improve their wages and working conditions, labor and immigration policy, health and safety, and access to justice.

subsidy payments at $250,000 per individual farmer rather than the current limit of $360,000. The bill would also have eliminated loopholes that now allow producers to collect subsidies from multiple farming operations. Limiting the size of farm payments could help keep large farming operations from getting even bigger. The bill has been reintroduced every year since 2002.

A much more ambitious proposal has been offered by David Orden, an agricultural economist with the International Food Policy Research Institute.[28] He suggests that gradual elimination of program crop subsidies could be achieved through a buyout program that would provide decreasing lump sum payments to farmers over a number of years to help them make the transition. Congress has already agreed to eliminate peanut and tobacco subsidies using a buyout option. The farmers participating in these buyouts feel they are getting a good deal because they have been guaranteed income support for several years, providing them ample time to retool.

A buyout program that includes some or all currently subsidized commodities would be costly in the short run, but it would likely save the government billions of dollars over the long term. Independent of a system of government support for commodities, farmers would be better able to respond to new and emerging market demands by growing the crops that have the highest return on their investment. Money saved through the reduction of subsidies could be used for other rural development initiatives. Because many farmers earn a substantial portion of their household income from off-farm jobs, investment in rural entrepreneurship could significantly strengthen and diversify rural economies. In the long run, this would increase the incomes of both farm and non-farm rural households.

Reducing or eliminating current subsidy programs would not necessarily mean that farmers would receive no government support. Several proposed alternatives would strengthen conservation efforts. Half of all the land in the United States is used for farming and ranching, so the environmental impact of how land is farmed or ranched is an issue that affects everyone.

Agriculture accounts for more than 80 percent of water consumed in the United States, according to USDA. The overall environmental performance of the agricultural sector has become a much bigger issue in recent decades.

Payments to farmers for good environmental practices can contribute to a wider public good while also helping farmers cope with a difficult economic climate.

For an example of the importance of conservation, look no further than the 5,000-8,000 mile "dead zone" that forms each summer in the Gulf of Mexico—suffocating all marine life in the area. Fertilizer used to raise subsidized crops has been identified as one of the main culprits; run-off washes down the Mississippi River from as far away as Michigan and Minnesota.[29] Conversely, through sound management practices, farmers can provide important environmental benefits that improve the quality of life for all. For example, farmers using no-till planting techniques trap carbon in the ground instead of releasing it into the atmosphere where it could contribute to global climate change.

Public concern over the loss of natural resources has been responsible for many of the most substantive changes in farm policy over the last 20 years. The Conservation Reserve Program, included in the 1985 farm bill, was the first program to provide farmers with financial incentives to take land sensitive to erosion out of production. Other programs were added in later farm bills, such as the Conservation Security Program (2002) and the Environmental Quality Incentives Program (1996), which provide financial and technical assistance for soil, water, air and energy enhancements.

When compared with funding levels for commodity programs, however, these and other conservation programs are woefully underfunded. "That leaves everyone

A Farm Bill in the Name of Stewardship

– Robert Gronski, National Catholic Rural Life Conference

The 2002 Farm Bill made significant strides for farmland stewardship by increasing the overall funding level of conservation programs. The major achievement was congressional approval of the Conservation Security Program and the creation of comprehensive stewardship incentives for working lands. The Conversation Security Program is designed to support conservation farm operations of all types, crops and enterprises; it is a natural-resource, outcome-based program that comprehensively addresses soil, water, wildlife and other resources of a healthy agricultural industry.

The implementation and funding of the farm bill's conservation title has had its ups and downs in the intervening years, but as we transition into the next farm bill cycle, conservationists should feel generally positive about the progress made. The 2007 Farm Bill should continue to promote and reward stewardship of the land by placing a high priority on working lands and fostering a new generation of conservation-minded farmers and ranchers.

Therefore, one of the most important challenges of the next farm bill will be consolidating and strengthening the Conservation Security Program and integrating it more closely with both farm programs and the other conservation programs. Reforms to commodity programs, namely payment limits, do not automatically translate into dollars for conservation or other farm programs. In a period of large budget deficits, proponents of a farm safety net based on conservation and stewardship need a sound argument for both congressional consideration and public support.

As a start, subsidizing environmental stewardship instead of commodity production will certainly help clean up the rivers, lakes and streams. Taxpayers are less likely to object to the cost of farm programs if they get a cleaner environment in the bargain.

Joe Moton, a farmer in Alabama, grows fruits and vegetables. Farmers who are ineligible for subsidies because they grow fruits and vegetables can still receive government support through conservation programs.

Supporting environmental stewardship is also likely to encourage more diversification and entrepreneurship in rural America. In breaking away from conventional commodity production, farmers and ranchers will have the opportunity to expand into new ventures under the protection of a stewardship safety net.

The next farm bill offers an opportunity for a change from commodity subsidies to "green payments." The guiding principle is to devise an income safety net that rewards farmers and ranchers for sustainable land use.

The next farm bill should subsidize farmers according to their stewardship of the environment, expanding on the concept of the existing but inadequately funded Conservation Security Program. The government's new farm safety net should be made available to all types of farmers and farming systems while allowing

All of us, especially those closest to the land, are called to a special reverence and respect for God's creation. Nurturing and tilling the soil, harnessing the power of water to grow food, and caring for animals are forms of this stewardship. The Church has repeatedly taught that the misuse of God's creation betrays the gift God has given us for the good of the entire human family. While rural communities are uniquely dependent on land, water, and weather, stewardship is a responsibility of our entire society.

— For I was Hungry, Catholic Reflections on Food, Farmers and Farmworkers, U.S. Conference of Catholic Bishops, 2003

market influences to encourage innovation and entrepreneurship in rural America. Farm programs currently favor intensive commodity production, placing more diverse, extensive and resource-conserving systems at a competitive disadvantage. Besides the enormous cost of commodity programs, there is evidence that the subsidies foster a culture of dependence, discourage risk-taking among farmers and hinder rural economic development.

Stewardship and "Bioenergy Crops"

In the corn belt of the country, farmers talk about a coming agricultural revolution tied to energy production in the form of corn ethanol, biodiesel and other biomass fuels. Some believe farm programs should be rewritten to coax this along. Although "bioenergy" and the call for a "bioeconomy" may sound environmentally friendly, it is essential to have a set of principles or criteria to manage biomass.

Renewable bioenergy, like any energy development,

should go through individual site and environmental review to insure that ecological impacts are minimized. Indeed, biomass energy should be grown or produced in a sustainable way that provides net environmental benefits. Biomass energy crops should be grown and harvested in a way that embodies best stewardship practices to maintain or improve air, water and soil quality.

Development of new energy sources should not only be ecologically sound but socially responsible and, when possible, locally managed. A farm-based sustainable energy system has great potential to respond to the economic needs of rural communities and family farmers as a matter of course. The public good of a farm-based energy system must meet the same criteria as a sustainable agriculture system: economically viable, locally managed, ecologically sound and socially responsible.

The Next Farm Bill

It is possible that the next farm bill will include a conservation title with improved stewardship programs and increased funding. However, given budget deficits, it is also possible that the next conservation title will not make any significant strides and will perhaps lose ground. If the American public allows an erosion of conservation programs, they will have missed an opportunity to improve the quality of life for farmers and farming communities, improve the environment, and improve the delivery and effectiveness of federal dollars. The next farm bill should not be a "farm bill" at all, but rather a farm/stewardship/conservation bill that will be remembered as landmark legislation.

Robert Gronski is a policy coordinator with the National Catholic Rural Life Conference in Des Moines, Iowa. He also serves as Conservation and Stewardship committee chair for the Sustainable Agriculture Coalition.

Through the Conservation Reserve Program, Nebraska farmer Jerry Kobs has had an incentive to take highly erodable land out of production.

worse off: the public, farmers, ranchers and the environment," writes American Farmland Trust (AFT).[30] Recognizing the paucity of funding available to reward good environmental stewards, AFT has proposed an ambitious agenda to shift much of the current funding for commodity programs into conservation ("green" payments) and rural development.

The green payments program proposed by AFT would be available to all agricultural producers who manage land and provide environmental benefits, including specialty crop producers and ranchers, without respect to the size of operation, crops produced or geographic location. Payments would be based on performance outcomes rather than on specific practices, so farmers could choose how to achieve the environmental goals. Payments would be made on a graduated scale to encourage continual improvement

in environmental stewardship.[31]

Government payments that reward farmers to use land in environmentally sustainable ways are also much more likely than program crop subsidies to be in compliance with U.S. obligations to the World Trade Organization (WTO). Several WTO members have made the case that U.S. commodity programs distort world trade and increase hunger in the developing world. Hundreds of millions of people in the developing world who live on $1-$2 per day earn their living in agriculture. The difference between a meal and hunger might well be defined as market access. But commodities subsidized by the U.S. government can be "dumped" into the world market at artificially low prices which undercut lower-cost producers in developing countries. The WTO has already ruled that the U.S. cotton subsidy program is trade-distorting and must be modi-

fied to conform to WTO standards. Other subsidized commodities could be subject to similar rulings. A longer discussion of the relationship between farm programs and the WTO follows in Chapter Three.

In addition to the move towards green payments, the AFT proposal calls for a farmer safety net based not on price, as with the current set of farm payments, but on total farm income. This "revenue insurance" plan would combine government protection against nationwide risks with private insurance to protect farmers against individual risk. At the beginning of each year, the government would set a per-acre revenue projection based on national averages for price and yield. After harvest, the revenue insurance program would then pay the difference between the projection and actual revenues. Private insurers would make up the difference if an individual farmer experienced a loss greater than the national average. Some farm groups, such as the Iowa Corn Growers Association, have begun to look favorably on revenue insurance proposals.

Another possibility that is based on farm revenue rather than commodity prices is Farm Savings Accounts (FSAs). Each farmer would contribute to an FSA and the government would match each farmer's contribution up to a specified amount. Under one version of the

FSA, all farmers would be eligible. Since most farmers do not receive subsidies now, FSAs would be a way of distributing government support more equitably.

While the creation of revenue insurance programs or FSAs would be a step in the right direction, it is important that the design of these programs support other public policy goals, such as encouraging rural economic development and promoting sound environmental practices. The bottom line: restructuring farm programs has the potential to revive rural areas and support young people who want to stay in or return to rural America to farm and work. Older farmers now reliant on commodity subsidies would also benefit from a way to diversify their incomes.

Despite the benefits that these alternatives could yield, 70 years of farm policy cannot be reversed in one farm bill. Over the years, many good ideas have been proposed but failed to make it into legislation. FSAs have been a subject of farm policy reform proposals since before the 2002 farm bill. Farm and Ranch Risk Management (FARRM) Accounts, for instance, were brought before Congress in 1998 by Senator Richard Lugar (R-IN) and later championed by Senator Charles Grassley (R-IA). Counter-Cyclical Accounts (CCAs), another version of the FSA, were included in the version of the 2002 farm bill that passed the Senate but dropped from the final bill.[32] These two programs, following the FSA model, were designed to encourage farmers to save in high-income years to cover shortfalls in lean years. Both included matching contributions from government.

Though these and other proposals show that significant reforms are being taken seriously by members of Congress known for their stalwart supporters of U.S. farmers, bringing real change to farm programs will not be easy. To be fair to middle-aged and older farmers, a majority of U.S. farmers today, reform will need to be phased in over time. To farmers who have always planned their work in accordance with commodity subsidy policies, change that is too rapid could threaten their livelihoods and savings. Yet the necessary safety-net programs must be designed to serve a wider group of farmers than those who now benefit from farm subsidies.

The farm payment programs that absorb much of the farm bill's Commodities Title funding are outdated. They do not benefit most farmers or the public, nor do they sustain today's rural communities. Moreover, they contribute to hunger in the developing world. The farm bill reauthorization is a new opportunity to begin making the needed changes to U.S. farm policy, and reform should start with the Commodities Title.

Mainline Recommendation

The United States should phase out the current system of farm subsidies which link higher payments with higher production levels. There should be no financial incentives to overproduce, because this leads to greater farm consolidation, drives up land prices, and distorts trade, making it much harder for small and medium-size farmers in this country and around the world to compete.

Other Recommendations

- Federal farm policy should offer farmers tools for managing financial risk, assistance during times of catastrophic crop failure, and support for adopting sound environmental practices. All farmers should be eligible. These types of assistance should go to people actively engaged in farming but not to absentee landlords. Federal farm policy needs to support the creativity and entrepreneurial spirit in farming and encourage farmers to plant the crops that make sense to them.

- The significant financial savings that will result from restructuring U.S. farm policy as outlined in this chapter should be redirected mainly to strengthening rural development and reducing hunger in the United States and around the world. As shown in the rest of this report, key improvements in the rural development, trade and nutrition titles of the farm bill could significantly reduce hunger and poverty.

Ethanol:
A Convergence of Farm and Energy Policy

The United States has been producing ethanol for decades, but not until recently has there been a surge of interest in stepping up production. Now many policymakers want to give the fledgling U.S. ethanol industry a boost. Supporting it will reduce U.S. dependence on foreign oil, they argue—plus the ethanol industry is good for rural America.

In the United States, corn is the crop of choice for making ethanol. The natural sugars from the corn are distilled into alcohol, which can then be used for fuel. Corn is not the only natural resource that can be converted into ethanol, but the United States grows so much of it—nearly 12 million acres in Illinois alone—that the corn is literally there for the picking. The areas of the country that grow the most corn today are Iowa, Nebraska, Minnesota and other Midwestern states—but if the industry takes off as expected, you can bet that farmers from around the nation will be producing a lot more corn.

Ethanol production has increased to 4 billion gallons in 2005, up from 1.8 billion gallons in 2001. Production could reach 7 billion gallons in 2010, if the current trend continues.

As the farm bill comes up for reauthorization, we are urging Congress to reform farm policy by eliminating subsidies that encourage farmers to overproduce. Since Midwestern corn farmers are also some of the largest beneficiaries of farm subsidies, it may make sense to promote ethanol as a way of expanding available markets for corn producers. Increased demand for corn would raise the market price for this commodity, and higher prices mean lower government payments for commodity subsidies. With continued high prices for corn, farm programs to support corn production could be scaled back or possibly even eliminated.

Developing the domestic ethanol industry is sure to help farmers, but how much it will benefit the rest of rural America remains to be seen. In this report, we take a hard look at how U.S. farm policy has neglected most rural communities. Current policies encourage the consolidation of farms, which has contributed to the exodus of people from rural communities. With fewer farmers in a community, there are fewer customers for other businesses too. No matter how the ethanol industry develops, it is important that the wealth created remain in rural communities.

Policymakers can ensure that rural communities benefit from the ethanol boom by supporting local ownership of new plants. Currently the two largest processors of ethanol in the United States are Archer Daniels Midland and VeraSun Energy. ADM and VeraSun's ethanol plants create jobs in the communities where they're located, but rural communities stand to gain a lot more if a larger share of the profits stay within the community instead of leaving for corporate headquarters. In the 1990s, more than half of all new ethanol plants were established as farmer-owned

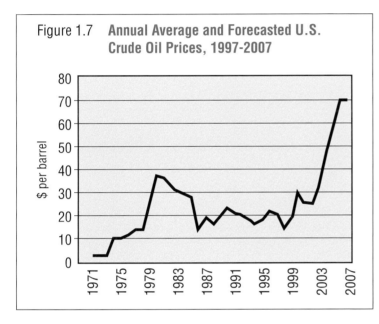

Figure 1.7   **Annual Average and Forecasted U.S. Crude Oil Prices, 1997-2007**

co-ops, but by summer 2006, just one in eight plants under construction was farmer-owned, according to the Renewable Fuels Association.

Rural communities where ethanol is produced need policies to ensure that the industry is not just another permutation of the "boom-and-bust" cycle that has plagued rural America for generations. Whether it is gold, coal, oil shale or the manufacturing of clothing and textiles, there is a long history of rural communities being left high and dry by outside developers. Resting a community's hopes on any one industry is a perilous development strategy; ethanol is no substitute for efforts to promote diversified economies in rural areas.

Two other caveats should be noted. First, the development of a corn-based ethanol industry may affect the amount of corn grown for food uses. Corn

is a cheap commodity that supplies feed to domestic as well as international livestock producers. Some have already expressed concern that stepping up U.S. ethanol production may exacerbate food insecurity and hunger. Second, the extensive monocropping of corn for ethanol may have adverse environmental impacts. Through the Conservation Reserve Program (CRP), farmers receive government support for taking highly erodable land out of production. CRP has been a successful program that supports farmers at the same time it provides wider environmental benefits to the public. If the price of corn remains strong, however, the temptation to pull environmentally sensitive land out of production may be too great for farmers to resist. The ensuing environmental degradation could cause serious and permanent harm to that land.

It makes good sense for the government to pursue diverse energy sources to help fuel the American economy. But if policymakers truly want to reduce the country's dependence on foreign oil—and team energy production with rural development—then an initiative to increase the production of corn-based ethanol is just one of several options worth attention. Plants, trees, grasses and even waste have potential to be converted into fuel, perhaps in ways that are more efficient than current production methods for ethanol. The U.S. government should invest heavily in research to refine other biofuel technologies so that rural areas not producing corn can also participate in efforts to diversify our nation's energy sources.

The United States has met previous technological challenges, but each of them has required a significant investment in research and development. Without these efforts, ethanol production alone will not be able to end U.S. dependence on foreign oil.

Rural Development:
Strengthening Communities

Chapter 2

Phaedra W...

Charis Combs-Lay, a pastor at the Zion Lutheran Church in Olewein, Iowa, knows many families in her community who depend on the federal nutrition programs to get by from month to month. Olewein has just less than 7,000 people, and is located in the northeast end of the state. Nearly half of the children qualify for federally subsidized school meals, and several are Charis's neighbors. She knows them personally and knows how their parents have struggled to put food on the table.

Last Memorial Day, my family had a cookout in the yard. I went over to chat with Geri [a neighbor] for a minute. I noticed she was holding eight hot dogs, two for each of her children. She said she was not hungry but she knew the kids would enjoy the grilled wieners. Then another neighbor walked up to us with a wrapped, foot-long sub sandwich. He just smiled and said, "Hey, I couldn't eat another bite but I hate to let this go to waste. Would you like it?" I glanced up at Geri's face and saw her eyes as she reached for the sandwich. At that moment, I knew my neighbor was facing the end of the month without sufficient food.[1]

Charis's neighbor Geri and her children rely on the Food Stamp Program. The children receive free school meals, and over the summer they participate in the Summer Food Service Program. Without this help, the family would have little more than the kindness of their neighbors to help fill their cupboard. Strong communities and helpful neighbors are perhaps as common to rural life as tall trees and blue skies, but still, in a community where half of the children qualify for free school meals, it is hard to imagine that just kindness could provide for everyone.

The federal nutrition programs are an important safety net that stretches across the entire United States. Rural America benefits especially from a strong nutrition safety net. In a report released in 2005, researchers at the University of New Hampshire used U.S. government data to show that 7.5 percent of nonmetropolitan (rural) residents participated in the Food Stamp Program compared to 4.8 percent in metropolitan (urban) areas.[2] In the most recent government data available on food insecurity, 12.0 percent of households in rural America were food insecure compared to 10.8 percent in the rest of the country.[3] One in five children in rural America lives in a food insecure household, and 48 of the 50 counties with the highest child poverty rates are rural.[4] Seniors in rural America are poorer and more at risk of hunger than their peers who reside in metropolitan regions.[5] Among most groups of people, food insecurity is highest in rural areas.

Lisa Morrison lives in Dewey County, South Dakota, on the Cheyenne River Indian Reservation. Dewey County is one of the 20 poorest counties in the United States. Lisa and her four children rely on the Food Stamp Program. Summertime is hard for Lisa and her children. She has to make the food stamp benefit stretch further. The schools her children attend do not sponsor a Summer Food Service Program. Most of the stores on the reservation carry a limited selection of foods. Lisa has to travel

USDA

40 miles to find good deals on food. Not everyone on the reservation can travel as far; unlike some of her neighbors, Lisa has a car.

Nationwide, 90 percent of people who receive public assistance do not own a car.[6] In an urban area,

Rural communities with high rates of carless residents are characterized by persistent poverty and have high concentrations of Black, Hispanic or Native American residents.

this may not be such a problem because public transportation, while sometimes unreliable, is generally available. In rural areas it is far less common for low-income areas to be served by public transportation. Less than 60 percent of South Dakotans, a predominantly rural state, have access to public transportation.[7] In 2005, when Hurricane Katrina barreled into the Gulf Coast, many people could not escape the destruction because they did not own cars or have access to public transportation. The focus of the media attention was on New Orleans, but people in surrounding rural areas were also unable to escape.

Transportation is one of many challenges facing low-income households in rural America. It would take awhile to list them all, but a

few significant details get right to the point. Nonmetro poverty rates have exceeded metro poverty every year since poverty was first officially measured in the 1960s.[8] The most recent data on poverty shows an overall nonmetro poverty rate of 14.2 percent compared to 12.1 percent for metro areas.[9] Compared to their urban counterparts, rural incomes are lower, education levels are lower, unemployment is higher and employment is more concentrated in low-wage industries. A 2005 government report, *An Overview of USDA Rural Development Programs*, found that rural areas have a disproportionate share of the nation's substandard housing,[10] and rural households also pay more of their income for housing than their urban counterparts.[11]

Rural areas are not only disproportionately poorer than metropolitan, they are more likely to be severely poor. "Persistent poverty"

is a term used to describe areas of the country with extremely high poverty rates (20 percent or higher) lasting for several decades. Presently, 88 percent of persistent-poverty counties in the United States are in rural areas.[12] One of these is Perry County in Alabama, where 35 percent of the population lives below the poverty level.[13] "The unemployment rates, infant mortality rates, the number of elderly and children who lack support—you name the indicator and it's heartbreaking," said Mart Gray, regional coordinator for the Cooperative Baptist Fellowship. In 1998, Perry County lost its one remaining hospital. Meanwhile, diabetes, cardiovascular disease and other conditions common in poor communities are all present in Perry County at alarming levels.

USDA defines urban and rural areas by county. An urban county has a population of 50,000 residents or greater. A rural county has a population of less than 50,000 residents, and its economy is not tied to an urban area.[14] Rural America is home to less than 20 percent of the U.S. population, but accounts for 80 percent of the country's land area.[15]

Four rural areas of the country stand out as having especially high

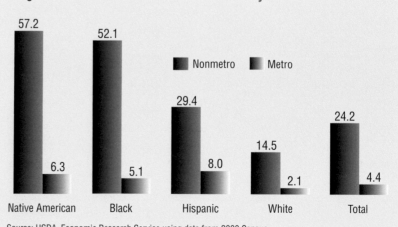

Figure 2.1 **Percent of Poor in Persistently Poor Counties**

Nonmetro ■ Metro

Native American: 57.2 / 6.3
Black: 52.1 / 5.1
Hispanic: 29.4 / 8.0
White: 14.5 / 2.1
Total: 24.2 / 4.4

Source: USDA, Economic Research Service using data from 2000 Census

For much of the 20th century, most rural communities experienced out-migration and population loss as millions of rural residents left for opportunities in booming cities."

— Carsey Institute, University of New Hampshire

concentrations of poverty: Central Appalachia, the Deep South, the Rio Grande River Valley, and the Great Plains. In each of these regions, the poverty is concentrated most heavily among particular groups: whites in Appalachia, blacks in the South, Hispanics in the Rio Grande, and Native Americans in the Great Plains. Poverty rates are higher in the South than in any other major region of the nation. Of the 10 states with the highest rates of food insecurity, 6 are Southern states: Texas, Mississippi, Arkansas, South Carolina, North Carolina and Tennessee. It is no small coincidence that 34 percent of southerners reside in rural areas.[16] Three out of every five rural residents who receive food stamps live in the South.[17]

Of course, the fact that there is extreme poverty in rural America is hardly news. Rather, the question is why so little has been done to address this state of affairs. The persistence of poverty leads to the inevitable question: What accounts for the persistence of neglect? In the 1960s, Robert Kennedy led a delegation from the U.S. Senate into the Mississippi delta to investigate the extreme poverty and malnutrition that existed there. The images they brought back shocked the nation and led to hearings and a great many improvements in nutrition programming. Many people in rural America were helped as a result, but far too many rural Americans experienced only nominal improvements or none at all. Today, it is possible to visit areas of rural

America and find life has changed very little since the 1960s.

Why Does America Need A Rural Policy?

Until the middle of the 20th century, rural policy and farm policy were essentially one and the same. What was good for farming was good for the majority of people who lived and worked in rural America. But that is not true anymore, and has not been for some time.

In the early years of the 20th century, agriculture was clearly the fulcrum of the rural economy, if not the national economy. At the turn of the 20th century, farming employed nearly half the workforce.[18] But within a few decades the number of people working in agriculture was cut in half. In 1970, it had decreased to only 4 percent of the U.S. population.[19]

A number of factors contributed to this decline, some of which have already been covered in this report. Above all, government farm-income support programs and dramatic advances in farm technology have encouraged the consolidation of small farms into bigger farms. Inelegant as it may sound, "Get Big or Get Out," the famous advice of former Secretary of Agriculture Earl Butz, succinctly describes what U.S. farm policy was about for most of the 20th century. Between 1900 and 2000, the number of farms in the United States declined by 63 percent, but the average farm size grew by 67 percent, with no

change at all in the amount of land being farmed.[20]

As full-time farming became untenable for those who could not or would not grow bigger with their competition, many families left the farm and rural America altogether to seek greater financial security in the metropolitan areas of the country. The rural population shrank steadily during the 20th century, declining by two-thirds from 60 percent of the country's overall population in 1900 to 20 percent by 2000.[21]

Farming's changing role in the nation's economy

1900
41 percent of workforce employed in agriculture

1930
21.5 percent of workforce employed in agriculture

Agricultural GDP as a share of total GDP, 7.7 percent

1945
16 percent of the total labor force employed in agriculture

Agricultural GDP as a share of total GDP, 6.8 percent

1970
4 percent of employed labor force worked in agriculture

Agricultural GDP as a share of total GDP, 2.3 percent

2000/02
1.9 percent of employed labor force worked in agriculture (2000)

Agricultural GDP as a share of total GDP (2002), 0.7 percent

Source: Compiled by Economic Research Service, USDA. Share of workforce employed in agriculture, for 1900-1970, Historical Statistics of the United States; for 2000, calculated using data from Census of Population; agricultural GDP as part of total GDP, calculated using data from the Bureau of Economic Analysis.

Empowering Change in Rural Arkansas

— Carla Wynn, Cooperative Baptist Fellowship

A little hope can go a long way. Cooperative Baptist Fellowship (CBF) field personnel Ben and Leonora Newell are trying to bring hope to Helena-West Helena, Arkansas.

Since 2001, the Newells have been in Helena-West Helena working with Together for Hope, CBF's rural poverty initiative. The initiative seeks to address poverty in 20 of the poorest counties in the United States, including the Newells' site of Phillips County, Arkansas.

In Helena-West Helena, a community of about 15,000, more than 28 percent of the population lives below the federal poverty line. Poverty has been a problem in Phillips County for a long time, affecting generations of residents.

"Their dreams have been cut down so many times that they don't dream anymore," said Leonora Newell.

The Newells did not come armed with a pre-packaged development strategy and expect the community to implement it unquestioningly. They believe that community development begins with what residents want their community to be. This approach, called local assets-based community development, "is the backbone of what we do," said Ben Newell.

Fifty local organizations came together to develop the strategic poverty-alleviation plan for Phillips County. The Newells serve as catalysts in the community, helping residents identify their existing and potential resources and seeking ways to empower change.

Early on, the Newells established credibility by bringing in volunteers to help restore the community center, which now houses an art and creativity lab called the Imagination Station. It gives local children "space to create and therefore dream and hope for something," Leonora said.

Volunteers from within the Helena-West Helena community participate in activies with the children.

Not every child can come to the community center, so through the "Stories on Wheels" bus, the community center comes to them. "Stories on Wheels" is a traveling arts station and library which even offers nutrition classes for children and exercise activities like yoga.

For children in Helena, the main emotional and physical escape from poverty is sports. A sports academy teaches children leadership skills through playing sports, usually basketball or baseball. The Newells are constantly trying to broaden the kids' horizons by introducing new sports. This year's summer sports camps included soccer, tennis and golf.

By providing stimulating social interaction, a learning environment and positive relationships, the Newells hope to improve the lives of local children while at the same time slowly changing the entire community. "Reaching kids at an early age is more effective for their long-term development," said Ben. "If you do some positive things at an early age, their development will be so much better and will allow them to be better leaders."

Economic development is also a major focus. Through a partnership with the Good Faith Fund of Southern Development Bank Corps, residents can come to the community center to do laundry. The money they spend is applied toward a savings program in which the bank contributes $3 for every $1 contributed by a resident.

Another project is Kingdom Enterprises, a new effort that will focus on attracting small and large businesses to rural areas like Helena. "If you can bring 100 new jobs to the community that pay livable wages, benefits and child care, you're offering something very valuable…that can change the whole outlook of the community," Ben said.

The Garden of E.D.E.N.—Empowering Development through Education and Nutrition—is an opportunity for residents to grow and sell produce. Created by local and outside volunteers in one of the town's most rundown areas, the garden has been a symbol of hope and an educational opportunity for children at the neighboring Knowledge is Power Program (KIPP) school, a national charter school.

Together for Hope seeks to provide resources to fulfill residents' hopes and dreams. One of the key resources is a steady stream of volunteers, particularly during the summer. All Church Challenge is an annual two-week summer mission blitz that attracts hundreds

Cooperative Baptist Fellowship

During the summer 2005 All Church Challenge, 200 local children participated in activities that included swimming lessons and a basketball tournament. Volunteers came from as far away as North Carolina.

of volunteers. So far in Helena, they have helped with community gardening, construction, a children's camp and more.

At the municipal pool, volunteers have also organized a swimming camp for local children, many of whom did not know how to swim despite living next to the Mississippi River. The success of the swimming program led to a partnership between Helena-West Helena and two Cooperative Baptist Fellowship partner churches to build a new pool house.

As helpful as volunteers are and as many improvements as they can bring, the Newells consider carefully the extent of volunteer contributions. "Our major goal in our community is to provide for things that are community owned and community driven, not driven by outside volunteers," said Leonora.

The secret, according to Ben and Leonora Newell, is forming relationships and inspiring residents to create their own change.

Carla Wynn is a communications specialist with the Cooperative Baptist Fellowship. For more information on Together for Hope, visit www.ruralpoverty.net.

Manufacturing jobs have also decreased as a percentage of overall rural employment. By the mid-20th century, manufacturing was regarded as the most promising source of rural employment. In recent decades, many low-skill manufacturing jobs have left the United States, with businesses searching for (and finding) cheaper labor in developing nations and taking with them an important source of stable rural income. The South has been hurt more than other areas by the disappearance of low-skill manufacturing work. Areas whose residents have higher levels of education and where higher skilled manufacturing is more prevalent, for instance the Great Plains region and parts of the West, have done better in withstanding the exodus of companies seeking cheaper labor overseas.[22]

While many families continued to farm (and still do), it has gotten ever more difficult to make farming pay without government support. Those who reap the most from government support payments are the biggest and most industrialized farms. From 1995-2004, 74 percent of farm subsidies went to 10 percent of recipients, and most U.S. farmers received no subsidies at all.[23] The average farm family cannot get by on just their farm earnings. Nine in ten farm households earn income off the farm.[24]

But what ails rural communities runs much deeper than the vagaries of family farming. "Today, 96 percent of the income in rural counties is from non-farm sources, and that percentage is going to stay strong,"[25] explained Tom Dorr, Under Secretary of Rural Development at USDA, to a 2005 conference on National Economic Rural Development.

The majority of rural Americans make their living in the service economy. This is true of the nation as a whole, but it is a greater challenge to rural areas than elsewhere because higher-paying service sector jobs generally depend on conditions harder to secure in rural areas, such as well-developed communications and transportation infrastructures and, perhaps the greatest challenge of all, high population densities.[26]

Population loss, or outmigration, erodes the quality of life in communities. Vital services are reduced or vanish when there is a lower tax base to support them. It means there are fewer libraries open, fewer police and fire fighters, fewer people to drive ambulances and repair aging infrastructure. It means that hospitals close, as the one in Perry County did. School systems may have to consolidate, meaning children have to travel farther to learn and parents may have to drive them because there are no longer bus services.

Between July 2003 and July 2004, more than 900 counties out of a total of 2,052 lost population. The greatest concentration occurred in the Great Plains, Corn Belt, Mississippi Delta and Appalachia, some of the same areas we identified earlier where there is persistently high poverty.[27] This is a snapshot of one year, but the picture over time is much the same. In Perry County, a class reunion of 50s-era high school graduates brought together many people who'd gone on to college and received advanced degrees. But most of them had left the area. In 50 years, the county's population had shrunk from 30,000 to 11,000. The failure of communities like Perry County to establish sustainable employment alternatives gives people no choice but to leave, while those who remain are stuck there, lacking the means or skills to capitalize on better opportunities that may exist elsewhere.

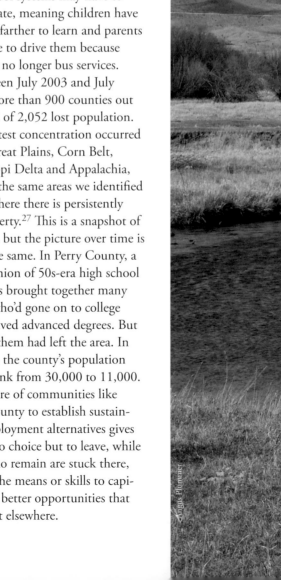

Angus Plummer

Not all rural areas are losing ground. Those that are flourishing tend to be located where natural amenities are abundant—meaning a good climate with nice scenery and easy access in and out of the area. These areas have become popular with retirees, attracted by lower living costs than in metropolitan areas as well as by the amenities.

Rural counties that rely on recreation as their main industry are growing almost three times as fast as other rural counties.[28] Americans are increasingly spending their disposable income on activities that take them into the outdoors. Whether to fish, hunt, hike, cycle, bird watch, apple pick, rock climb or just rest, those who come to enjoy the outdoors eat at restaurants, stay in motels, spend money on local arts and crafts and shop for groceries to fill their backpacks. The Florida Fish and Wildlife Conservation Commission estimated in 2004 that hunting, fishing and wildlife viewing alone generated a $10 billion economic return and supported more than 100,000 jobs.[29] According to the Washington State Department of Fish and Wildlife, "Wildlife watching creates an economic boost to the state's economy that is nearly double that of the state's biggest agricultural commodity, apples."[30]

The rural economy turns on a much different set of assumptions today than when Congress established the Commodity Credit Corporation in 1933 to support farmers with subsidies. Farm payments, or subsidies, seem to be providing very little help to the rural economy, even in the counties that depend on them most. Some of the highest poverty counties in the country are found in the Great Plains, the area of the country that receives the greatest percentage of farm payments. "Per capita income in the farm-dependent counties of Iowa, Kansas, Minnesota, Nebraska and the Dakotas is less than three-fourths of income in the region's metropolitan counties," said the Center for Rural Affairs in 2005. "Poverty rates are more than half again as high."[31]

Nor do current farm programs appear to ensure the long-term survival of rural communities dependent on farming. A study conducted by the Center for the Study of Rural America found that farm payments do not yield population gain. "If anything, the payments appear to be linked with subpar population growth."[32] This finding is confirmed by USDA research of the period from 1998 to 2003, during which high-payment counties experienced population losses of 9 to 10 percent.[33] What seems to be occurring in these regions as a result of farm consolidation is a broader form of economic consolidation. There are fewer jobs for all associated businesses.

Reshaping Rural Policy for the 21st Century

It is much more difficult to formulate a rural policy today than when rural America was mostly about farming. Today, what we call "rural America" is a complex amalgam.

"Besides farming communities, there are factory towns, resort towns, wide-open unsettled mesa land, casino towns in the desert, small mountain communities, fishing and logging villages, "whistle stops," commuter communities and more. Across rural America today we can find predominantly black communities and predominantly white, recent immigrants and families who have occupied the same land for generations. With such variety, it is difficult

Rethinking Rural Development: A New Yardstick to Measure Success

– Dr. Florine P. Raitano, I-70 Coalition

For far too long, rural communities have competed against each other for large manufacturing plants, call centers, big box stores and other "knights in shining armor" to provide jobs in their communities. Some of these jobs pay barely above minimum wage, and in misguided attempts to attract employers, communities often tout a workforce that is willing to work for lower wages than their urban counterparts. The old saw that "a rising tide floats all boats" is apparently forgotten in the rush to grow the numbers of jobs.

There is a reason why small rural communities feel compelled to do this. Every major federal and state agency "economic development program" uses an identical measurement of success—number of jobs. Why such uniformity? The truth is that it is much easier to count noses than to measure real economic impacts. Using the number of additional jobs as a measure of economic development success requires very little time and paperwork.

Measuring the creation of wealth in a community, on the other hand, may tell quite a different story. Benchmarks of community wealth include the number of residents with checking and savings accounts, the average balance in savings accounts, the percentage of residents who own property, the average age of vehicles owned by local people, rates of foreclosure, loan default and denial rates, the number of families with adequate health insurance coverage… and other statistics that paint a much clearer picture of community wealth and vitality.

Of course it is far more challenging to identify and track the growth and development of wealth in a community than it is to count jobs. When one uses jobs as the yardstick, the opening of a new store or plant facility gives an immediate measure of comparison: on Friday community X had 378 jobs; on Monday, when the plant opened, it had 432. Never mind that ten months later, the community had only 368 jobs because the new box store resulted in the closure of 12 local stores. Measuring the growth of wealth allows for more meaningful comparisons because it uses a longer time frame.

How Communities Can Generate Real Wealth

Cultivating a solid base of local entrepreneurs is an integral component of a wealth-generation strategy. The Center for Rural Entrepreneurship, part of the Rural Policy Research Institute, has researched the impacts of locally grown entrepreneurs on small rural communities. The initial results are promising, indicating that unlike large employers coming from outside a community, local entrepreneurs have deep roots and a strong sense of community. They often pay higher wages. The wealth created by local entrepreneurs also remains in the community and helps to underwrite prospects for other entrepreneurs to flourish.

The irony is that at a time when significant numbers of rural entrepreneurs are finally beginning to emerge, their access to venture capital and even traditional loans is evaporating. Financial institutions need incentives to make available in rural areas the venture capital that is essential to emerging markets and entrepreneurial endeavors. The central bank of the United States, the Federal Reserve, should recognize that monetary policy that encourages mergers, acquisitions and increased centralization of banking works against the economic interests of rural communities, and adjust the policy accordingly.

Rural development policy must also be expansive enough to include regionalization, which means that communities have to reach across long-standing geo-political boundaries to forge new alliances and partnerships. At the state and federal level, there must be an effort to encourage and support a move toward regionalization of commerce and economic growth, while still recognizing and protecting the uniqueness of that intangible sense of place and community spirit that makes rural America the touchstone of the American Dream.

Even as rural communities mourn the loss of their young people who move to the cities, many fail to

James Hines

offer opportunities for that ambitious and creative next generation to come back home and play meaningful roles as leaders of the community. Too often, successful young professionals who are seeking to return to their roots, to give their children the same type of small town upbringing they had, are looked upon with suspicion and dismissed as having been contaminated by big city ways and holding big city ambitions. But rural communities should view these returning "expatriates" as assets, not threats to the status quo. These could well be the future leaders of their communities.

Perhaps most important of all is the need for a new and more rational national policy that supports rural wealth generation. This would include new benchmarks of success that encompass more than the one-size-fits-all category of jobs. What is sorely needed at both the state and federal levels are programs that are not "Father knows Best" in their approach. Instead of creating more of the all-too-common rural community welfare programs, state and national government should make a coordinated effort to work with rural communities as full partners. This requires empowering communities to assume responsibility for their own future and giving them the skills needed to identify creative new ways to meet their needs.

Change comes slowly and painfully for many rural communities. But there are communities that have found their way in the world, often without—and sometimes in spite of—state and federal assistance. These places should be celebrated, acknowledged and rewarded for their efforts, and most of all studied. They are the leaders from whom to learn. The more progressive rural communities have learned that if they aren't growing, they are falling farther and farther behind. In the meantime, the rest of the world is not waiting for them to catch up.

Dr. Florine P. Raitano is Director of the I-70 Coalition and has been awarded former Vice President Al Gore's "Hammer Award" for reinventing government for her work on the Colorado Ecosystem Partnership. She has more than 20 years of experience working on a variety of rural development issues.

to make general statements. There is simply no one-size-fits-all description of rural America."[34]

One thing we can say is that rural development has not been a federal priority. In 1972, Congress authorized the Rural Development Act, and a year later the farm bill included a rural development title. Though rural policy had not yet been formally decoupled from farm policy, this was still a watershed, heralding a change in attitude about rural America and making it clear that rural policy was more than what was good for farmers. Unfortunately, the federal spending aimed at making life better for the rest of rural America has not given up on the old way of thinking.

Federal spending priorities remain firmly on the side of commodity producers. From 1995 to 2004, commodity subsidies totaled more than $113 billion.[35] While the rural development budget looks good on paper, roughly $12 billion annually, the overwhelming majority of that comes in the form of loans made for such things as utility services and housing. Only about $1 billion is direct spending, according to an analysis by the Center for the Study of Rural America, and 70 percent of all government spending in rural areas comes in the form of transfer payments such as Social Security, the Food Stamp Program, Medicare, and Medicaid.[36]

The next farm bill offers a chance to address the challenges faced by rural America and develop the potential that exists there to step outside the shadow of farm programs. The expansion of a rural development title is essential. A number of strong programs are already in place. With the reductions in farm payments called for earlier in this report, there would be substantial resources to reinvest in rural development, targeting programs that are already working effectively but on a smaller scale than they could be. The following sections of this chapter will identify the best opportunities to reshape rural development policy in the next farm bill. The time has come to end the neglect of rural America and redirect payments from commodity growers into rural development.

Rural Development and Non-Farming Small Business Development

It was clear by the middle of the twentieth century that there were no longer enough farming jobs to support everyone in the rural workforce. First on the scene to fill this void was low-skill manufacturing jobs. The firms started arriving in force with the end of World War II. In recent decades, meatpacking houses, call centers, and even prisons have been heralded as the next engine of rural economic growth. In each case, the source of the development is recruited from outside the community.

For a time these initiatives seem to work, until the industry either exhausts the natural resources it came to extract or discovers cheaper labor elsewhere. Mining companies, for example, are notorious for the former. In the case of the latter, the manufacturing firms and call centers have figured out that the cheapest labor is overseas, and there they are going. Boom and bust cycles have been a way of life in rural America, and the phenomenon shows no signs of abating.

Today, it is the behemoth retailer Wal-Mart that represents the latest incarnation of this economic development model. The Arkansas-based company has expanded across rural America at a staggering pace in the last decade. But Wal-Mart brings with it some other concerns that rural leaders must pause to consider before rolling out the red carpet. While its stores bring low-cost items to consumers, as well as jobs and tax revenue to communities, a new Wal-Mart in town also makes it difficult for smaller local businesses to compete. Ultimately, this may

An increasingly common feature of rural landscapes is the big "box store," most notably Wal-Mart. Seventy percent of Wal-Mart supercenters are in rural areas.

result in the death of a town's small business sector. This has happened in a number of rural towns across the United States.

To develop sustainable models of economic development, rural communities would do far better to look within rather than without to seek their fortune. Entrepreneurship provides such a model. Rural residents themselves are the agents of economic development. According to the Center for the Study of Rural America, "Entrepreneurs add jobs, raise incomes, create wealth, improve the quality of life of citizens and help rural communities operate in the global economy."[37]

Of course there is nothing new about small business creation in rural towns. What has changed is the amount of emphasis this sector gets in rural development strategies. Local entrepreneurship has not been the traditional economic model.

Local entrepreneurs are more than just financially invested in the community. It is not incidental when business owners live in the community where they establish their enterprise. Having roots in a community gives one an altogether different sense of a place. Here is where they send their children to school and rely on the police and fire departments and other services. They also care about their neighborhoods and are ready to take on leadership roles as needed.

Unemployment, depopulation and the spiraling cycle of poverty that plagues persistently poor rural areas are all exacerbated by the lack of opportunities for people who possess the business acumen but lack the resources to achieve business success. A rural development model based on entrepreneurship strengthens rural communities.

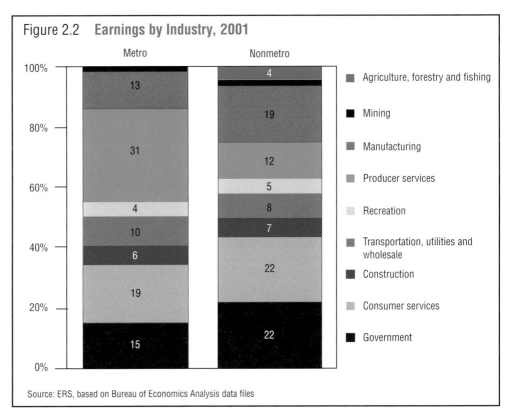

Figure 2.2 **Earnings by Industry, 2001**

Source: ERS, based on Bureau of Economics Analysis data files

Several programs are in place to stimulate small business creation in rural communities. The problem is that these programs are scattered widely across many government agencies. Some consolidation of programs makes sense, but more importantly, the rural development title in the farm bill needs to place greater emphasis on small business creation in the non-farm sector. As this report has already shown, most rural counties are no longer agriculturally dependent. The demand for business services is coming from other sectors of the economy.

In the version of the 2002 Farm Bill adopted by the U.S. Senate,[38]

a provision creating a new rural microenterprise program was included. Unfortunately, this provision was dropped in House-Senate conference negotiations; however, it did represent a significant step in making non-farm rural economic development a greater focus of the farm bill. This bit of progress in 2002 makes the debate on the next farm bill (2007) crucial for all of rural America.

The rural microenterprise provision would have created and funded a program within USDA specifically for the development and expansion of small businesses within rural communities. It would have provided capital for business development and resources for technical assistance to such businesses. It also recognized that rural small business development is vital to the sustainable development of rural communities and that rural development is no longer synonymous with agriculture.

REAP, a statewide program operated by the Center for Rural Affairs in Nebraska, is a wonderful example of what such a national program might well look like. REAP has helped hundreds of rural small businesses get started or improve by providing loans, technical assistance, and training.[39] Rusty and Bob Zeigler, a father and son partnership from Salem, Nebraska, started a lumber milling operation in 2004 after obtaining a loan from REAP. Keri Chamberlain of Kimball, Nebraska, dreamed of owning her own restaurant. She received help from REAP in developing a business plan and putting together the financing to open her restaurant on Main Street in Kimball. These are just two of the new entrepreneurs who have been helped by this program.

The federal government has an important role to play in promoting economic development in rural regions. Rural development policy must help communities develop their human capital by expanding opportunities to establish new business enterprises. Communities grow stronger as ownership expands to more local people. The capital created by this new development stays in the community rather than returning to corporate headquarters or into shareholders' pockets.

Rural Development and Infrastructure

Appalachia, one of the poorest regions of the country, made a stunning impression on John F. Kennedy while he was campaigning for president in 1960. At the time, one in every three Appalachians was living in poverty and per capita income averaged 23 percent less than the rest of the United States.[40] Soon after he was elected, Kennedy appointed a commission to look at the region and come up with recommendations on economic development. In 1964, the commission reported that economic growth was tied directly to ending the region's isolation from the rest of the country. The Appalachian Regional Commission (ARC) was formed in 1965. For more than 40 years, the ARC has focused on improving the physical infrastructure of the region, predominantly by building roads. By 2005, nearly 3,000 miles of roads had been completed or were under construction.[41]

Appalachia includes all of West Virginia and parts of 12 other states from Mississippi up to New York. Not every part of the region has benefited equally—Central Appalachia remains one of the poorest areas of the country—but there is no question that overall the ARC has been a tremendous boon to scores of Appalachian communities. The highway projects alone have created thousands of jobs and led to billions of dollars in economic development. The success of the ARC illustrates how crucial infrastructure development is to setting up a long-term economic development strategy.

Another area of the country facing terrible poverty is the Delta region of the South. Appalachia and the Delta once had similar degrees of poverty, but no longer, said Dr. Amy Glasmeier, Professor of Economic Geography at Penn State University and an expert on the relationship between poverty and place. "Now they are very far apart. Standards of living, quality of life, levels of education, square miles of road—you name it. The Delta is still way behind."[42]

In 2000, Congress established the Delta Regional Authority (DRA) to help distressed communities in this region leverage federal and state programs to stimulate economic development. Fifty percent of the funding must be used for transportation and other basic infrastructure needs. Similar to the challenges faced by Appalachia, transportation has been identified as critical to rural

US Highway 90 in Mississippi, damaged by Hurricane Katrina.

Scott Leigh

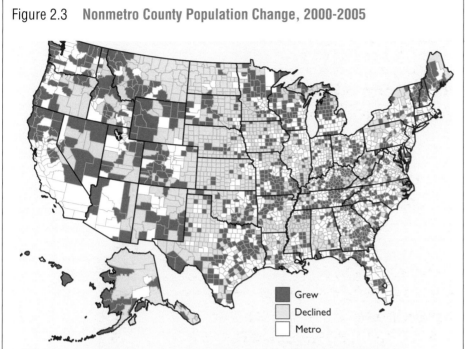

Figure 2.3   Nonmetro County Population Change, 2000-2005

Grew

Declined

Metro

Source: Prepared by Economic Research Service using Census Bureau 2005 population estimates, available on the ERS website at www.ers.usda.gov/data/population/.

either. "There is a paucity of mental health professionals in rural areas and even fewer who are culturally competent to serve farmers and ranchers," reports the Center for Disease Control and Prevention.[43] Farming is associated with a high risk of mental illness and depression. "The suicide rate of farmers and farm workers is well above average during normal economic conditions," the CDC report adds, "and rises to between two and three times the national average during economically stressful times."[44]

USDA rural development funding is available for communities to improve infrastructure, and projects targeting infrastructure have always been part of federal rural development programs. But too many communities in areas like the Delta and Central Appalachia

economic development in the Delta. Most rural communities in the Delta have limited public transportation services at best. Transportation links rural residents with jobs and services and connects rural industries to markets. Lack of transportation options also isolates rural poor people from government services and programs designed to help them climb out of poverty.

The Delta butts up against areas of the Gulf Coast. The destruction caused by Hurricane Katrina exposed some of the worst examples of poverty in the United States. The destruction along the coast in particular was a result of neglected infrastructure. Levees that were long overdue for repair were breached. Public transportation was not available to people in the poorest neighborhoods. Substandard housing crumbled under the weight of years of neglect. With federal resources now being directed to areas hit the hardest, policymakers

must not neglect other parts of the South that managed to escape the destruction but are still struggling nonetheless, such as those in the poorest rural areas of the Delta.

Rural areas cannot prosper without a solid infrastructure. It is literally the foundation of their community. A solid infrastructure includes good roads and schools, clean air and water, quality housing, reliable telecommunications services and access to affordable healthcare. Farmers in rural areas rely on these services as much as anyone. For example, thousands of farmers are injured or die every year in work-related accidents. An entire community is at risk when hospitals shut down. Barriers to effective mental health services should not be overlooked

Richard Lord

represent "the last mile"—consumers located there are the ones who remain unconnected to a service, whether it be Internet or power or roads or sewers or some other vital service needed in the development of that community.

In the 21st century, policymakers need to think broadly about infrastructure. So far we have discussed physical infrastructure. Physical infrastructure is important, but just as important is a community's knowledge infrastructure. Rural areas that have experienced depopulation have also undergone a brain drain. Programs that provide training and education to compete in a modern knowledge economy should be a priority. The school system is a critical institution in a community. Good schools can be a catalyst for economic development, just as bad schools can be the bellwether of a community's demise. Especially in smaller communities, the school is an even more critical factor in a community's economic and social well being. "For many rural communities, the school is not only the social hub of the village, but the school setting also contributes to the sense of survival of adults in the culture," argued Professor Thomas Lyson of Cornell.[45] "[Schools] serve as places that nurture participation in civic and social affairs and as such can be viewed as nodes that anchor people to place."[46]

In a study of upstate New York schools, Lyson found that communities with schools experience less population loss, and some even posted a gain in population.

Communities with schools were better developed in terms of their physical infrastructure. They were likely to have better municipal water and sewer systems than communities that did not have schools. Communities with schools had appreciably higher housing values and employment rates than those without.

Through USDA's Rural Utilities Service, $8.9 million in grants for broadband service were awarded in 2006 and an additional $20 million for distance learning and telemedicine.[47] The distance learning program is designed to bring educational resources to disadvantaged rural schools, the telemedicine program to improve health care delivery for communities outside the reach of specialty services. These are the kinds of programs that can mitigate some of the physical isolation rural communities have felt. Again, though, policymakers must make sure they reach all the way out to "the last mile."

Rural Development and Agriculture

"Getting started [in farming] is an issue," explained Steven Haroldston, a beginning farmer from Georgia, at a farm bill listening session in October 2005. He was telling this to the Secretary of Agriculture, Mike Johanns. Haroldston was speaking from his experience in Georgia, but beginning farmers are saying the same thing in Nebraska, Arkansas, Florida, Vermont, California and elsewhere. This is what Secretary Johanns heard as he attended listening sessions across the country: just about anywhere that people want to enter farming, getting started is an issue. "You've got people farming 10,000 acres and drawing

Richard Lord

Let me suggest to you…instead of a Farm Bill with a Rural Development title, we have a Rural Development bill with a Farm Policy title."

— *Thomas Dorr,*
USDA Under Secretary for Rural Development

over $1 million worth of government payments and you can't compete with that," Haroldston said finally, putting it as succinctly as anyone else has.[48]

The steepest barrier for beginning farmers is the cost of buying or renting land. One of the unintended consequences of current farm policy has been the capitalization of program benefits into land values. Nationally, farmland values have been rising at record rates. Escalating land values may be a terrific windfall for the current generation of farmers, but it has had a tragic effect on a younger generation of farmers. The cost of owning or renting land has priced younger farmers right out of the market, and the result has been the aging of the country's farmers. Nearly half of all farmers are over 55, and there are now twice as many farmers over 65 as there are under 35.[49] Farmer replacement rates have fallen below 50 percent, meaning that as older farmers retire there is no longer a one-to-one ratio of new farmers coming onto the land.

For much of this chapter, we have focused on the depopulation of rural communities. There is a direct connection between the inability of new farmers to become established and the depopulation of rural communities, especially in communities of the Midwest and South with agriculturally dependent economies. Current farm policy rewards big producers and neglects smaller and medium-sized ones.

Beginning farmers are far more likely to be among the latter than the former. Farm programs which have encouraged consolidation and a "get-big-or-get-out" business model are forcing these would-be young farmers to leave their communities in search of more viable economic opportunities elsewhere. No community can survive without people —after all, it is people that sustain the life of a community. It does little good for the health of agriculturally dependent communities if more commodities can be produced with less people.

Nor can this bode well for the future of U.S. agriculture. Who are the future farmers of America and where are they going to come from? The problem has much broader ramifications than the preservation of rural communities. U.S. agriculture suffers by encouraging a system that makes it untenable for beginning farmers to get started. No industry can restrict the ambitions of a younger generation of aspirants and expect to be healthy in the long run.

New farmers need help getting started. First they need access to credit and other financial supports. USDA's Farm Service Agency (FSA) is required to target a portion of funds to lower income, lower equity beginning farmers unable to get a

loan elsewhere. "FSA loan criteria is set up so that you have to be so small and have so few financial resources that you would have a tough time getting a commercial bank or Farm Credit Services loan," explained Dan Looker, editor of *Farm Business.* "Yet you have to have cash flow and be profitable enough to pay the loan back. Needless to say, that's a pretty small group of people."[50]

One solution suggested by the Center for Rural Affairs is for

Continuity of the family farm sector depends on a successful transition when older farmers retire and pass on land and knowledge to their heirs.

Congress to consider Individual Development Accounts that would provide a matched savings account to new farmers.[51] Account proceeds could be used to finance purchases of land, equipment and livestock. California has already developed a similar program to target new farmers of disadvantaged means. Why not a national program along these lines in the next farm bill?

Farm Beginnings™: Creating a Path to Sustainable Rural Communities One Farm at a Time

– Amy Bacigalupo, Land Stewardship Project

Four years ago Mark and Wendy Lange started farming together. They hoped that farming could provide the independence and quality of life that no job in town had. But from their home near the western Minnesota community of Milan, the couple didn't have to look far to see that even the most experienced farmers often succumb to rock-bottom commodity markets, sky-high production and land costs, and changing markets. Enrolling in Farm Beginnings™ was the first step toward their goal of creating enough income from the farm to support them both.

Farm Beginnings graduates Mark and Wendy Lange have launched a meat goat enterprise on their farm near Milan, Minnesota.

Farm Beginnings, a community-based, farmer-led initiative of the Land Stewardship Project (LSP), is one of the most successful beginning farmer training programs in the country. It combines classroom instruction with on-farm mentoring and provides graduates with equity-building opportunities. The region's successful, sustainable farmers are the teachers and mentors in this farmer-to-farmer training program.

Farm Beginnings started in the mid-1990s when a group of southeast Minnesota farmers called the "Wabasha County Give-A-Damns" approached LSP with a desire to provide training and support for the next generation of sustainable farmers. These farmers and their peers throughout the region are the backbone of an extensive support network.

For the Langes, having a farmer support network proved critical as they launched their farming operation soon after completing Farm Beginnings in 2002. The couple owns 80 acres that were homesteaded by Mark's

great-grandfather in 1910. Through the class, they were able to research and compare alternative enterprises for their farm, ultimately deciding to raise meat goats. In November 2002, they acquired 60 does through the Farm Beginnings no-interest livestock loan program. Within a year of completing Farm Beginnings, Wendy quit her town job to work with the goats at home, bringing the Langes halfway to their goal of making a living from their farm.

Farm Beginnings is not just about getting new farmers started working on the land. It is about helping new and transitioning farmers realize that over the long run, their profitability is directly connected to the quality of their soil. And the message is definitely taking hold—a recent survey of Farm Beginnings graduates found that 92 percent use conservation practices on their farm. Through Farm Beginnings, many graduates are connected to federal farm programs like the

Environmental Quality Incentives Program (EQIP). EQIP provides technical, educational and financial assistance to eligible farmers and ranchers to enable them to address soil, water and related natural resource concerns on their lands in environmentally beneficial and cost effective ways.

Not only are Farm Beginnings farmers working for environmental sustainability, they are also key members of successful rural communities. Farm Beginnings graduates are creating economic opportunity by starting up their own on-farm entrepreneurial businesses and walking away from town jobs. This kind of job creation is critical to strengthening rural communities.

Mark and Wendy Lange have been creating the path toward sustainable farming by walking it. In 2004 they acquired two used stone flour mills to add value to the organic grains they raise. In May 2006 they broke ground on their third enterprise: a goat dairy. All along, they have been making it easier for others who want to farm. For example, theirs is one of the first goat dairies in the state to be financed through the USDA's Farm Service Agency's Beginning Farmer and Rancher loan program. The business planning and research skills they learned through Farm Beginnings were essential to educating Farm Service Agency officials about the viability of this novel enterprise and persuading them to grant a loan.

The Langes are not the only sustainable farmers challenged to prove to lenders the viability of their farm enterprises. A 2003 LSP survey of farmers, lenders and educators in Minnesota and Wisconsin found that while 89 percent of the sustainable farmers surveyed viewed sustainable farming as equally or more profitable than conventional farming, only 35 percent of the lenders shared their view. A second finding was that an additional 35 percent of lenders did

Farm Beginnings began in Minnesota, but recently it has served as the model for similar programs in Illinois, Missouri and Nebraska.

not have enough experience or knowledge to assess the profitability of sustainable farming. Although Farm Beginnings prepares farmers to participate fully in the fastest-growing sector of today's food market, they can nonetheless find themselves with limited options for financing.

Like many beginning farmers, Mark and Wendy Lange feel called to the land and the trade of farming. The Langes' success stands out in contrast to the general public opinion of the future of agriculture. But a growing group of farmers like the Langes are in fact making a go of it. And they aren't just surviving— they're thriving. Even with the struggles and hardships they have faced so far, they are actively encouraging and mentoring other beginning farmers. "If you do your research and homework, there's no reason you can't make it," says Wendy. These forward-looking sustainable farmers are already planning how to work a beginning farmer into their operation when they retire. Now that's sustainable.

Amy Bacigalupo coordinates Farm Beginnings™ for the Land Stewardship Project in western Minnesota. Farm Beginnings was started in 1998 and developed in part with a USDA Sustainable Agriculture Research and Education (SARE) grant to help disadvantaged farmers. Amy is also a beginning farmer.

Conservation programs also provide a means of helping beginning farmers. Conservation programs should be structured to provide all farmers with a steady level of support if they agree to practice conservation. Federal support could be extended to beginning farmers who develop a conservation plan and agree to practice good stewardship.

good judgment comes from experience, but gaining experience includes making plenty of mistakes. Too many mistakes and a farmer may quickly find him- or herself out of business.

There are other ways to build relationships between older farmers and beginning farmers. For example, the next farm bill can encourage retiring

(VAPG) program, authorized in the 2002 rural development title of the farm bill, is intended to help farmers and ranchers to diversify their operations and is another means of support for beginning farmers. "Value-added" refers to how agricultural products are marketed, processed and/or grown. Organic produce, for instance, is a form of value-added production—although the VAPG program is by no means restricted to organic products. By targeting small and medium-sized farmers, the program is good for U.S. agriculture and good for rural communities, encouraging small business creation and serving as a catalyst for further economic development. It is exactly the kind of program rural communities need, promoting a model of rural economic development based on entrepreneurship.

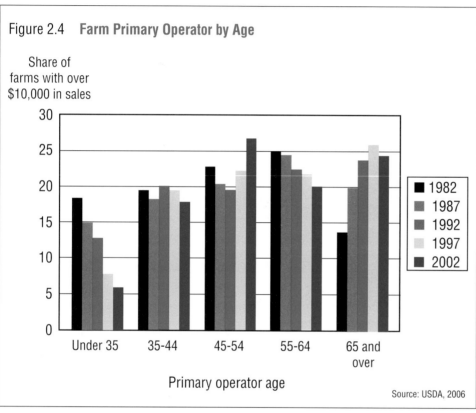

Figure 2.4   **Farm Primary Operator by Age**

Share of farms with over $10,000 in sales

Legend: 1982, 1987, 1992, 1997, 2002

Primary operator age: Under 35, 35-44, 45-54, 55-64, 65 and over

Source: USDA, 2006

Beginning farmers need help managing risk. Farming is an inherently risky business. There is no substitute for learning from one's own experience, but the next best thing may come from people who have lived through their periods of inexperience and can pass on valuable lessons learned. New farmers, like any professional, stand a better chance of not making costly mistakes at the beginning of their careers if they can be mentored by experienced farmers. As anyone who has had a career long enough will tell you,

farmers to transition their land to a younger farmer by providing tax breaks on the sale of the land. The Beginning Farmer and Rancher Development Program (BFRDP) was authorized in the 2002 farm bill. The program was aimed at providing training, education and mentoring opportunities to beginning farmers and ranchers. Unfortunately, funds were never allocated. The BFRDP should be reauthorized and funded at the level needed to meet current demand.

The Value-Added Producer-Grant

Farmers who can provide value-added products also need support bringing these products to market. It is far more difficult for a farmer of non-program crops to find markets for what he or she grows than it is for commodity producers. The American Farmland Trust (AFT), in its sweeping vision for farm policy reform released in 2006, has suggested a new Farm and Ranch Profitability Grant program [FARP] "for states to encourage innovative marketing strategies, new business ventures, product promotion and consumer education and on-farm improvements or diversification related to any of the state's agricultural products."[52] The AFT program would use state agriculture or development agencies or councils who are closer to the communities in need to determine priorities for funding, rather than setting these priorities at the federal level.

There's a great disparity between the funding that currently exists in the federal budget and what reformers like AFT say is needed. The FARP proposal asks for a $1 billion investment, but the VAPG program is now funded at just $15 million per year. Meanwhile, polls have been conducted that show public support for small and medium-sized farmers. Much education is still needed to correct misperceptions about who is and who is not helped by the current farm programs.

Clearly, there are ways to bring farm policy closer in line with rural development policy and nutrition policy. The most important step federal policymakers can take in this direction is to lower payments on commodities programs. The savings would be significant and the money could be used to improve programs for rural development. Support for small and medium-sized farmers through programs like those described above will strengthen rural communities. The next farm bill needs to make sure that these farmers, and the rural communities where they live, receive the support they need.

Mainline Recommendation

Savings from cuts to commodity payments should be redirected to rural development. Commodity payments, or subsidies, seem to be providing very little help to the rural economy, even in the counties that depend on them most. With the reductions in farm subsidies called for earlier in this report, there would be substantial resources to reinvest in rural development, targeting programs that are already working effectively on a smaller scale.

Other Recommendations

- Rural economic development policy should put a heavy emphasis on small business creation and support for local entrepreneurs, especially in the non-farm sector. Communities grow stronger as ownership expands to a greater number of people, and the capital created by local business stays within the community. Targeting the non-farm sector is critical because most rural communities do not depend on agriculture.

- Persistently poor rural areas should be guaranteed a long-term commitment to infrastructure development. Investments in infrastructure such as better transportation systems, broadband and Internet access, education and health care, water and sewage treatment form an essential foundation for economic development. All of these are equally necessary to creating the kind of communities where families want to put down roots.

- U.S. farm programs should provide more help to beginning farmers and ranchers, including better access to credit and better opportunities to learn from older farmers. It has become extremely difficult for a new generation of farmers to afford to get started in farming, particularly given the high cost of purchasing or renting land. The future of U.S. agriculture depends on the ability of a new generation of farmers to take their place on the land as older farmers retire.

The 2007 Farm Bill and Rural Development: A Time to Address All of Rural America

—Jon Bailey, Center for Rural Affairs

Rural development policy in the United States is not working for many rural communities. Declining populations, high poverty rates, low incomes and earnings—the defining conditions of many rural communities—are the result of a failure of public policy at all levels to develop and implement a specific rural development agenda that corresponds to evolving rural economies.

Any development model for rural communities that seeks reform must begin with the philosophy that rural communities are important: a significant portion of the nation in terms of culture, geography and population that is worthy of policies that enhance the long-term economic and social well-being of the people who live there. The 2007 farm bill provides an opportunity to correct mistaken premises about rural development and adopt an efficient, comprehensive and sustaining rural development policy.

Currently, rural development within the U.S. Department of Agriculture (USDA) is too narrowly defined. It provides primarily funding to maintain and upgrade community infrastructure and housing, with a relatively minor amount for economic development. The current model of rural development generally favors program delivery across multiple agencies rather than a comprehensive, efficient federal rural agency. Most important, rural development policy does little to address rural poverty or other rural socio-economic challenges.

Both the FY 2006 and FY 2007 presidential budget requests proposed a significant restructuring of the federal role in economic and community development. The Strengthening America's Communities Initiative (SACI) was first included in the administration's

FY 2006 budget. It proposed eliminating 18 federal community and economic development programs, including several rural development programs in USDA and the Department of Housing and Urban Development (HUD), and replacing them with a new block grant program with one-third less funding. The FY 2007 version of SACI again proposed to eliminate several rural development programs, while reforming the Economic Development Administration (EDA) within the Commerce Department and the Community Development Block Grant program within HUD. To date, Congress has rejected all SACI-related appropriation initiatives.

While these reform proposals were introduced with the explicit goal of addressing the inefficiencies in the federal multi-agency approach to economic and community development, they are also based on false premises. Eliminating rural programs, cutting available funds and placing all economic and community development needs—rural, urban and suburban—in the same competitive pot would not generally serve the needs of rural places and rural people. Furthermore, reform proposals to date do not specifically address the socio-economic challenges of rural communities and rural residents; they have a certain "rearranging the deck chairs" mentality.

True reform that addresses these socio-economic challenges must give rural development the high priority that the 60 million people living there deserve. A real rural development reform agenda should:

■ Change the name of USDA to the United States Department of Agriculture and Rural Affairs (USDARA). While this may appear symbolic, it would carry real meaning for the vast majority of rural people who are not farmers or ranchers. USDA was created in the 1860s when most rural people were farmers; a name change and a corresponding adjustment in focus would acknowledge the reality of rural life in the 21st century United States.

■ Transfer most rural programs into the new USDARA. Using the model of the Texas Office of Rural Community Affairs, programs focused on rural housing, rural economic development and rural healthcare belong in a federal agency with a specific focus on rural communities and rural people. For example, there seems to be no logical rationale for rural housing and rural economic development programs to exist in both USDA and HUD; all rural housing and economic development programs should be in one rural-focused agency. Further, these programs should be consolidated within the rural-focused agency. For example, HUD rural housing programs should not be simply transferred to the new USDARA, but should be consolidated with similar, existing USDA programs.

■ Focus current rural development grant programs on regional needs. Federal rural economic development funding is too often focused on funding specific local needs through local governments or non-profit intermediaries. Due to the limited size and capacity of most rural communities, most rural development literature now emphasizes regional initiatives and partnerships to enhance efficiency. Reforming rural economic development programs to focus on regional needs, partnerships and initiatives will give more "bang" for the federal buck. The 2002 Farm Bill included the Rural Strategic Investment Program, a new program that would have funded rural development planning on a regional basis.

However, this program was not funded because of concerns that it would infringe on funding for other rural development programs.

■ Target rural development funding to entrepreneurial development, asset-building and poverty alleviation. Spurring innovation and job creation through entrepreneurship in rural communities is the key to ensuring the long-term future of rural America. Federal rural policy must begin to recognize the importance of entrepreneurship as a rural development strategy and provide the necessary resources. The goals of rural development programs should be rural repopulation, attacking the root causes of rural poverty, and addressing the continuing and growing economic disparity between rural and urban areas of the nation. Meeting those goals will require a focus on entrepreneurial development and asset- and wealth-building that complements efforts to enhance the physical infrastructure of rural America and receives equivalent resources. A commitment to rural asset- and wealth-building strategies can lead to sustainable communities and stronger individuals and families.

Good rural development conserves the best in people: the resources they live on, the values that nourish them, the institutions that sustain them. It secures the future of rural people and rural communities. Reforming rural development policies in the ways described here will begin to build an ethic of sustaining rural communities and rural people in an efficient manner. The 2007 farm bill provides an opportunity to improve the nation's rural development efforts in ways that meet all of these complementary goals.

Jon Bailey is Rural Research and Analysis Program Director with the Center for Rural Affairs in Lyons, Nebraska.

Trade:
Farm Policy in the Global Economy

Chapter 3

Martin Lueders

U.S. farm policy has profound effects around the world. The subsidies provided to U.S. farmers encourage overproduction and drive down world prices for agricultural commodities. The spiral of increasing production and falling prices hurts farmers everywhere.

In the United States, shrinking profit margins make farmers ever more reliant on government support to ensure they are not forced off their land and out of business. In the developing world, billions of people live on less than $2 per day, the vast majority dependent on agriculture for their survival. Even if most farmers in developing countries never sell their grain on the world market, they may still be hurt by policies in the United States that distort trade in their home markets.

Chapters One and Two discussed why rural America needs farm policy reform. This chapter will address how international trade and economic development objectives are also driving the need for reform. It is possible to develop reforms that benefit both U.S. farmers and farmers in developing countries: there is a win-win situation, and with it comes the opportunity to make dramatic gains in reducing world hunger.

How U.S. Farmers Stand to Gain from Reform

One of the first things very poor people do when they have additional income is increase their food consumption. Once people satisfy their basic caloric needs, they begin to look for new and varied foods to upgrade their diets. Often this will include the addition of fruits and vegetables, animal protein or edible oils—many of the products where U.S. agriculture is most competitive.

China and India are examples of how this works. Fifty years ago these countries were economic basket cases; their people suffered the worst famines of the twentieth century. Today, both China and India are on track to achieve the first Millennium Development Goal (MDG) of cutting hunger in half by 2015, and both are important customers for U.S. agricultural exports. "The emergence of China as a freer market and expansion of the middle class in India have been important factors in increased exports to Asia," noted USDA in analyzing the growth of agricultural exports from 1976 to 2002.[1]

There are nearly 3 billion people in the world living on less than $2 per day. Raising their incomes to $5 or $9 per day could give a substantial boost to U.S. farmers by expanding the available markets for agricultural exports.

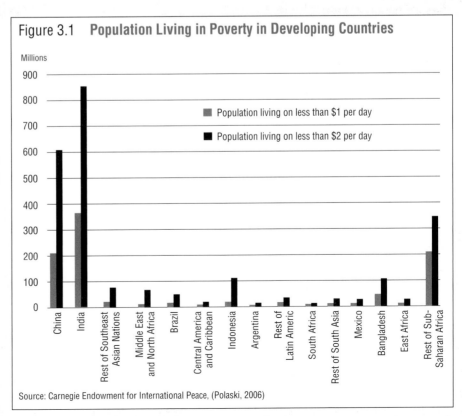

Figure 3.1 Population Living in Poverty in Developing Countries

Population living on less than $1 per day

Population living on less than $2 per day

Source: Carnegie Endowment for International Peace, (Polaski, 2006)

Africa's share of world agricultural trade has fallen by more than half since 1965.

Richard Lord

only potential growth market for world agriculture. But only if they experience broad-based economic growth will they have the purchasing power to translate need into market demand, and trade is one of the most important drivers of economic growth."[2]

The acceleration of economic growth in low-income countries should be a concern to U.S. farmers, but so far farm groups have not used their powerful influence on Capitol Hill to press policymakers to understand the relationship between global poverty reduction and emerging markets for U.S. agriculture. Maybe the catch is that reducing poverty in the developing world depends largely on increasing agricultural productivity there. Three-fourths of the poorest people in the developing world make their living in agriculture. Among the world's poorest nations, farming employs more than half of the work-

Midwestern producers, particularly corn and soybean growers, have a great deal to gain from poverty reduction in the developing world. The demand for animal protein will quickly outstrip these countries' own productive capacity. U.S. producers of feed grains are well positioned to capture some of these markets.

Robert Thompson, former World Bank economist and now Gardner Chair of Agricultural Policy at the University of Illinois, is one of the most articulate voices on this subject. For years, Thompson has argued that the greatest potential for U.S. agricultural products is in the developing world. The populations of the European Union, Japan and other industrialized countries are not growing quickly, and new markets are already tapped out.

"The (almost) three billion people to be added to the world's population in the first half of the 21st century plus the three billion people (almost half of the world's

present population) who live on less than two dollars per day are the

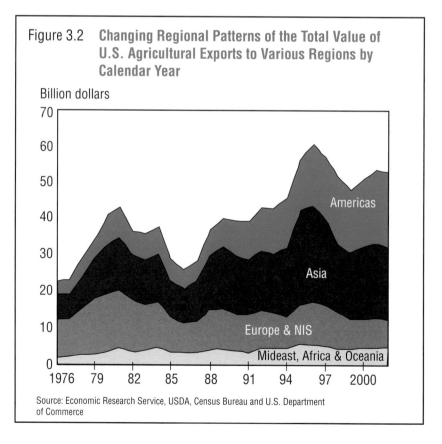

Figure 3.2 **Changing Regional Patterns of the Total Value of U.S. Agricultural Exports to Various Regions by Calendar Year**

Billion dollars

Americas

Asia

Europe & NIS

Mideast, Africa & Oceania

Source: Economic Research Service, USDA, Census Bureau and U.S. Department of Commerce

"Is our present farm policy designed for the age of globalization and are our policies assisting the maximum number of our farmers and rural residents to compete and win in the international marketplace? My answer is No."

– Cal Dooley
President of the Food Products Association and
former Member of the U.S. House of Representatives

force and accounts for at least 14 percent of GDP.[3]

It may sound counterintuitive that U.S. farmers should be rooting for farmers in other countries, but without large-scale growth in the agricultural sector of these countries, broad-based economic development will not occur and potential new markets for U.S. agricultural products will continue to go untapped.

A new study by Marcelle Thomas and Antoine Bouët at the International Food Policy Research Institute (IFPRI) finds that U.S. agricultural exports to Africa and Asia could rise substantially if low- and middle-income countries in these regions were to achieve broad-based economic growth. The study, commissioned by Bread for the World Institute, presents some of the most compelling evidence to date to show how much the U.S. farm sector stands to gain if these regions can achieve sustainable growth rates.

IFPRI simulated annual growth rates of 7 percent in Gross Domestic Product (GDP) for three groups of developing countries in Africa and Asia. This level of GDP growth is a sharp increase from recent growth rates in most countries in these regions, but it is clearly within the range achieved by such fast-growth economies as China and India. Figure

3.3 shows how U.S. agricultural exports would climb between 2006 and 2020 if low- and middle-income countries in Africa and Asia grow at 7 percent versus baseline forecasts of between 3 and 4 percent according to the World Bank. The complete IFPRI study is included in the Appendix, starting on page 118.

How Farm Policy Contributes to Global Hunger and Poverty

For developing countries, economic development and sustained poverty reduction will be much more difficult without reform of the international trade rules, espe-cially those governing agriculture. Policies that unfairly disadvantage farmers in the developing world are, quite simply, policies that under-mine their ability to escape poverty.

The world trading system in its current form favors developed coun-tries. Not only do they produce a greater variety of products than low-income countries, but government policies in industrialized countries create unfair advantages, especially for products where developing coun-tries enjoy a competitive advantage. By one estimate, farmers and entre-preneurs in developing countries lose $24 billion per year in agriculture and related business due to the poli-cies of industrialized nations.[4]

Each year the Organization of Economic Cooperation and Development (OECD), a group of 30 industrialized nations with shared economic interests, docu-ments the amount of support its farmers receive. In 2005, farmers in OECD countries, including the United States, received $279 billion in support, mostly through

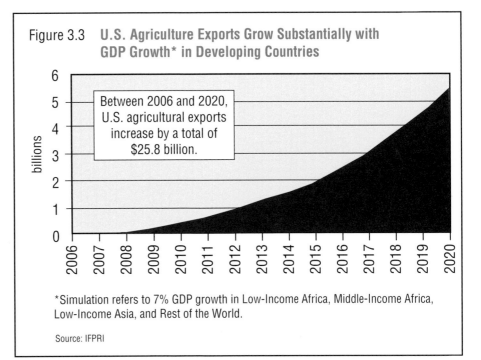

Figure 3.3   **U.S. Agriculture Exports Grow Substantially with GDP Growth* in Developing Countries**

Between 2006 and 2020, U.S. agricultural exports increase by a total of $25.8 billion.

*Simulation refers to 7% GDP growth in Low-Income Africa, Middle-Income Africa, Low-Income Asia, and Rest of the World.

Source: IFPRI

subsidies and tariffs.[5] These payments are at the core of farm policy in most industrialized countries. The support—most of it trade-distorting—is equivalent to 63 percent of the gross domestic product of sub-Saharan Africa.[6]

The impact of subsidies

Consider the case of cotton. A heavily subsidized commodity in the United States, cotton is also grown in sub-Saharan African countries, particularly Mali, Chad, Benin and Burkina Faso. Since 2000, U.S. cotton subsidies have averaged $2.3 billion per year.[7] This amounts to approximately half the GDP of each of these African countries.

As with other subsidies tied to production, cotton subsidies affect

U.S. cotton subsidies cost sub-Saharan Africa $302 million in 2001-2002, according to Oxfam International.

production levels and market prices. This has a direct negative impact on income generation in the developing world. Each year, cotton-growing countries like Burkina Faso lose between 1 and 2 percent of their gross domestic product because of the depressed market price of cotton. These lost earnings directly impact poor people. Between 2000 and 2002, a drop in world cotton prices caused a sharp spike in rural poverty in Benin. According to the World Bank, "The incidence of poverty among cotton growers in the short run rose from 37 percent to 59 percent while the average incidence of rural poverty (i.e. including cotton growers and other farmers) rose from 40 percent to 48 percent."[8]

The international NGO Oxfam has used the example of cotton to draw attention to the linkages between trade policies in rich countries and poverty in the developing world. One of its most effective strategies has been simply to provide a venue for farmers in the developing world to tell their own stories. Seydou Coulibaly, a Malian cotton farmer, visited the United States in 2006 to discuss the challenges he and his community face because of subsidized cotton in the United States.

It's getting close to planting season on my farm back home in Mali, in West Africa. But I postponed my preparations and came to America with Oxfam America for a week. . . . I spent a couple days in Virginia, talking to other farmers and to students, journalists, leaders of faith communities, and people just like you. . . . They were
stunned to hear that my village has no doctor or nurse. Or that we don't have a single tractor for the entire community. Or that many of us live on less than $1 a day. Most of them seemed shocked to find out that certain U.S. agricultural policies developed for farmers here in America actually hurt us on the other side of the globe. . . . For about six years now, I have struggled to make enough money to feed and clothe my family. It's not because of drought, or war—it's because of the price of cotton on the world market. Prices have dropped sharply because of the dumping of subsidized, surplus American cotton.[9]

Cotton is perhaps the most visible example of the high cost that farmers in the developing world pay for agricultural subsidies in industrialized countries, but it is not the only commodity which distorts world markets. In economics, the practice of exporting goods at a price less than their normal value—sometimes even less than the cost of production—is known as dumping. The Institute for Agriculture and Trade Policy (IATP), an independent research organization based in Minneapolis, MN, sought to determine the extent of U.S. dumping of agricultural products. IATP found evidence everywhere it looked. For five highly traded commodities—wheat, soybeans, rice, corn and cotton—the cost of production ranged from 10 to 47 percent *above* the export price received for the commodity.[10]

The impact of tariffs

Subsidies are only half the story—quite possibly the lesser half—of how trade policies in the developed world cause harm to farmers in the developing world. The gains that would come from reductions in subsidies could be lost if export markets are not opened to products from developing countries. Tariffs (also called duties) are taxes levied on exported goods when they enter an importing country's market. Tariffs distort trade and deny developing countries equal access to markets where their products could have a competitive advantage over domestically produced goods.

U.S. sugar policy illustrates how tariffs distort trade. In the United States, the price of sugar is controlled by a complex set of quotas, tariffs and price supports. Together, these three mechanisms keep the domestic supply of sugar at an arbitrary (high) price while effectively blocking developing countries from exporting their cheaper sugar to the United States. The sugar program shields U.S. sugar producers and refiners from competition.

Reform to U.S. sugar policy could lead to new market opportunities for farmers in countries such as South Africa and Guatemala. According to one scenario, global policy reforms to agriculture, including changes in U.S. sugar policy, would raise world sugar prices by up to 24 percent.[11] A price increase of this magnitude could make an important contribution to reducing poverty in developing countries where sugar is a major export crop. It is true that some current U.S. producers of cane sugar and sugar beets would have to alter their farming operations if U.S. sugar policy were reformed. But changes to sugar policy would not necessarily mean a net loss to the U.S. economy. "For each sugar growing and harvesting job saved through high U.S. sugar prices," reported the U.S. Department of Commerce, "nearly three confectionery manufacturing jobs are lost."[12]

Sugar is perhaps the most egregious example of how the United States uses tariffs to distort trade in agricultural products. But sugar is

an unusual case in some ways, since most raw products imported into the United States from developing countries are subject to low tariffs, especially when compared to the tariff rates of other industrialized nations. A more widespread and damaging market barrier faced by developing countries is "tariff escalation," a process whereby raw goods may be subject to one set of low tariffs, while the same goods in processed form are subject to higher tariffs. For example, most developing countries can export soybeans to the United States without facing any tariff, but the tariff for soybean oil is 20 percent. Raw cocoa beans can be exported tariff free to the European Union, but intermediate cocoa products such as cocoa paste or cocoa butter face a 10 percent tariff, and chocolate imports are subject to a tariff of 21 percent.[13]

The practical effect of tariff escalation is to discourage entrepreneurs in developing countries from producing and exporting value-added products, tethering them to the export of cheap raw goods that are processed and sold in rich countries.[14] Given an opportunity, entrepreneurs in developing countries demonstrate their willingness to trade up to value-added products. Paul Mugambwa, a Ugandan coffee farmer, explains how trading up can benefit an entire village.

Each family only owns half an acre to an acre and produces two or three bags of raw coffee beans on average. Currently, one kilogram of coffee at the

farm level is $1, but the value of one kilo of coffee at the roaster level is $14; and at retail it is worth $20. My idea is to add value by collecting the coffee from as many farmers as can supply it at high quality, process it on their behalf, sell it in the United States in the finished form at the $14 export price, and then plow the money back to the farmers themselves. This will go a long way in meeting the objective of reducing poverty of African farmers.[15]

Trade rules are used to exclude poor farmers from selling high value-added agricultural products. Chocolate is an example of a product worth much more in processed form than in its raw state.

Mugambwa and his fellow villagers are free to pursue their plan to export value-added processed coffee to the United States, because Uganda and other developing countries receive duty-free access for a number of value-added products exported to the United States. But not all products receive duty-free access. Most textiles, watches and electronics, and certain agricultural goods deemed import sensitive, such as dried milk, are still subject to high tariffs. Duty-free access for all products exported to the United States and other industrialized nations could provide entrepreneurs in developing countries with a strong incentive to increase production of value-added goods.

Farmers Learn the Value of Diversification

– Emily Sollie, Lutheran World Relief

"Without coffee, there is no life." This quote, spotted on a T-shirt in Managua, Nicaragua, eloquently sums up the role of coffee in Nicaragua's culture and economy.

For more than a century, coffee has been one of Nicaragua's chief exports and a primary source of income for its farmers. But in recent years, extreme fluctuations in the world market price for coffee have made coffee farming an extremely insecure source of income. When prices were at their lowest, many small-scale farmers could not even cover their production costs and were forced to sell their farms. Hundreds of thousands of coffee farm workers were unemployed.

Nicaraguan coffee farmers producing for the Fair Trade market have weathered the coffee crisis better because of the premium prices consumers pay for specialty coffee. Lutheran World Relief has worked both

with coffee farmers in Nicaragua, to help them improve their coffee crops and gain access to the growing Fair Trade market, and with constituents in the United States, to educate them about the benefits of Fair Trade and increase the demand for Fair Trade Certified coffee.

Lutheran World Relief is also working with coffee farmers in Nicaragua to diversify their sources of income so that they and their families and communities are no longer dependent on a single cash crop for their livelihoods. Some of these initiatives are: forming women's cooperatives to make and market natural products like herbal teas and fruit jams; introducing cocoa as an alternate income-generating crop; and establishing eco-tourism programs in coffee farming communities.

These diversification efforts have been quite

Nicaraguan coffee farmers sort beans in the sun. Lutheran World Relief is working with coffee farmers in Nicaragua to diversify their sources of income.

successful: by December 2005, just 14 months after the project began, the women's cooperatives were earning an average of $500 a week selling their herbal products and jams at local fairs and markets. Farmers not only grew cocoa, but learned to process it as well, and they easily found a market for their initial cocoa crops.

In one eco-tourism program, families in the La Reyna community in Nicaragua's Matagalpa region began to receive visitors eager to learn more about coffee farming and Fair Trade. For a modest fee, the tourists stay in homes with host families, discovering the ins and outs of growing, picking and processing coffee while getting to know the farmers and their families, forming bonds of friendship that transcend language and cultural differences.

"Before, I never had the opportunity to meet people from other places," said Valeria Ochoa, one of the eco-tourism hosts in La Reyna. "All the visitors have been so interesting. . . . When you start talking to people and getting to know them you feel like they are part of your family."

"We meet, we become friends, it's beautiful to have those relationships with other people," said Bertalina Lopez, another La Reyna host. "I hope that the people who come here do not forget us; that they come to visit us more, and tell other people to come."

In addition to the economic benefit to the community of hosting visitors, the farmers are eager to show their guests the improvements they've made in their community thanks to the extra income they receive

Coffee farmers in La Reyna have invested their Fair Trade income in a school for their children. Now these boys have access to education right in their own community.

Lutheran World Relief

from Fair Trade. They know that the visitors will go home and spread the word about the very real benefits of Fair Trade for small-scale farmers and increase the demand for their product.

"We have used the earnings to invest in a school for our kids," explained Bertalina. "Before, the co-op didn't have a school. Now the kids go all the way to fifth grade. I never went to school, but thanks to God, my kids will be better off than me."

Emily Sollie is the Director of Communications and Media Relations for Lutheran World Relief.

To help achieve wide-scale economic growth in the developing world, developed countries must demonstrate their commitment to reforming trade-distorting farm policies. The United States and other industrialized nations have shown an interest in using trade as a tool to promote economic development, but so far there have been no firm commitments.

Agriculture and the World Trade Organization

In 2001, the member nations of the World Trade Organization (WTO) opened the latest round of trade talks. The talks were christened the Doha Development Round for the city in which they began. Agriculture, so important in the developing world, received special emphasis. Lowering the overall level of trade-distorting support in agriculture was put front and center as a major goal of the negotiations. Officials reasoned that this would help to better align trade policies with economic development goals.

According to the WTO Ministerial Declaration that set the framework for the Doha round, "International trade can play a major role in the promotion of economic development and the alleviation of poverty… The majority of WTO members are developing countries. We seek to place their needs and interests at the heart of the Work Program adopted in this Declaration."[16]

The Doha Round has not evolved as intended. Bickering between the United States, the European Union and other countries that are large agricultural producers brought the negotiations to a halt in July 2006. Achieving an outcome that satisfies everyone has been a challenge. With so much to be gained from a successful completion of the round, it would be tragic if countries are not able to resolve their differences about how much each must adjust to satisfy the interests of the others.

A Doha deal: what is at stake?

A recent study undertaken by the Carnegie Endowment for International Peace demonstrates just how much there is to be gained from a new trade deal. Several scenarios were investigated, including one with lower levels of domestic support payments, lower tariff levels, and flexible measures to protect the interests of developing countries. The specific provisions of this model mirrored proposals under consideration by

WTO members in the summer of 2006. The Carnegie model showed that a new trade deal with these provisions would generate $58 billion in real income (see Figure 3.3).[17] A relatively small number of industrialized countries would reap roughly half of the benefits, with the other half of the real income gains distributed among a larger group of developing countries.[18] Among low- and middle-income nations, China would see the largest increase in real income, with India, Vietnam and other Southeast Asian countries also capturing a large share of the gains.[19]

It may seem unfair that nearly half of the benefits of a new trade deal would accrue to a small group of industrialized nations. After all, low- and middle-income countries make up a majority of WTO membership, and the Doha round is supposed to focus on development. But for smaller economies, a modest increase in real income has a proportionally greater impact. A successful Doha deal will bring several developing countries greater than a 1 percent increase in real income as a percentage of GDP, while developed countries will gain no more than a .45 percent increase.[20] Developed countries come out ahead in absolute terms because of their larger economies, but that shouldn't prevent negotiators from seeing how much developing countries stand to gain in relative terms from a successful outcome of the Doha round.

It is worth asking if the current proposals represent the best possible outcome. A study by IFPRI suggests the answer is no.[21] Before negotiations were halted in July, it was proposed that Least Developed Countries (LDCs) would receive duty-free, quota-free access on 97 percent of all products exported to OECD markets. Under this scenario

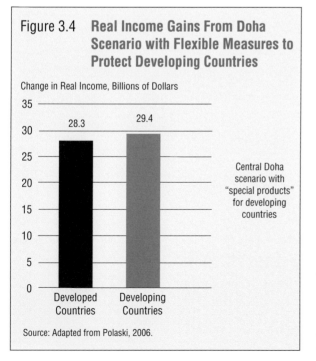

Figure 3.4 Real Income Gains From Doha Scenario with Flexible Measures to Protect Developing Countries

Change in Real Income, Billions of Dollars

Developed Countries: 28.3
Developing Countries: 29.4

Central Doha scenario with "special products" for developing countries

Source: Adapted from Polaski, 2006.

the 32 LDC member countries of the WTO would achieve only a modest increase in economic prosperity.[22] But moving from 97 to 100 percent duty-free, quota-free access could improve the outcome for LDCs sevenfold, from a $1.1 billion increase in real income to a gain of $7 billion.[23] A better deal for developing countries is possible; when the negotiations resume, 100 percent duty-free, quota-free access for the poorest countries should be at the top of the agenda.

A world trade agreement is not a zero-sum game in which the gains made by some countries are measured against losses experienced by others. As economic models suggest, a successful Doha round could help to spur economic growth and increase wealth in developed and developing countries alike. Countries are in vastly different stages of development, so the gains in absolute terms will be different. Dealing with these differences adds to the complexity of the WTO negotiations.

As we approach the 2007 Farm Bill, we may discover that all of our traditional commodity programs are in jeopardy because of their inherent trade distortions."

— *Clayton Yeutter,*
U.S. Trade Representative, 1985-89;
Secretary of Agriculture, 1989-91

U.S. farm programs in violation of trade rules

The Doha Round may yet be completed successfully, realizing the goals set in 2001, because it is in the interests of all countries for the round to reach its goals. But the uncertain status of the talks should not prevent U.S. policymakers from pursuing reforms to farm programs in the absence of a final agreement.

U.S. policymakers are already under international pressure to reform farm policies. In one of the first cases of its kind, Brazil challenged the legality of U.S. cotton subsidies under the rules of trade formulated within the WTO. (One of the core functions of the WTO is to resolve disputes between member countries regarding which

trade practices are acceptable under existing WTO rules.) The case concluded in 2005 with a major victory for Brazil. The WTO found that U.S. subsidies distort markets for cotton and cause economic harm to Brazilian cotton farmers.[24] As a result of the WTO ruling, the United States is obligated to modify its cotton support programs.[25]

The outcome of the cotton case sets a precedent that increases the likelihood that subsidies for other U.S. commodities will face similar challenges in the WTO. "There now is a high probability that a series of WTO cases will be brought against the United States for other commodities with support programs similar to those for cotton," says economist Robert Thompson. "With the precedents set by the cotton dispute, it is hard to see how the United States would win those cases."[26]

It makes little sense to let litigation set the pace of reform. It is costly to defend these programs and seems like a frivolous expense if reform is inevitable. Plus, it leaves U.S. farmers in a continued state of uncertainty as to whether the programs they rely on will be available to them in the coming months or years. A slow, piecemeal process of reform would not provide the best outcome for farmers—in the United States or in developing countries. Without a comprehensive reexamination of U.S. farm programs, it is difficult to see how anyone will come out ahead.

USDA

Dealing with adjustments

The success of a new WTO trade deal should be measured by the contribution it makes to economic growth, poverty reduction and food security. Meeting these goals requires that developed countries phase out trade-distorting agricultural subsidies and open their markets. A trade deal must also strike a balance between getting developing countries to lower their own tariffs and offsetting the cost of adjustment to their economies.

This market in Bwaise, Uganda is a typical scene in many developing countries. Some of these women have traveled great distances to secure a spot to sell their goods.

A new trade deal could result in increased world prices for agricultural products. While this is good for farmers, it could also bring higher food prices for consumers. A steep rise in food costs would force poor people to cut consumption or spend a larger share of their income on food. Neither outcome is desirable, particularly in countries with large populations of people already malnourished or at risk. At the national level, the small economies of net food-importing developing countries (NFIDCs) are further weakened by more money flowing out of the country to pay for food.[27] This leaves less money to invest in productive enterprises. A World Bank study estimated that higher food prices as a result of a Doha deal would cost net food importers at least $300 million.[28]

Developing countries need flexibility in adapting to this new trading environment. "Special-and-differential treatment" has been discussed as one way to address the challenges they will face. Special-and-differential treatment might allow developing countries to make graduated cuts in tariffs over longer transition periods, raise tariffs to protect special products as needed, and limit their cuts to domestic supports (though many developing countries do not have high levels of domestic support to begin with).

The assistance developing countries will need in adjusting to a new trade climate extends beyond special-and-differential treatment. Many developing countries currently enjoy preferential access to markets in developed countries. A new trade deal could extend these benefits to a larger group of countries, resulting in "preference erosion" for some countries. Individuals and sectors that have taken advantage of preferential trade opportunities may be pushed out of markets as a result of the increased competition. The poorest countries—the ones that most rely on these preferences—may have an especially difficult time adjusting. It is a concern negotiators must be willing to address.

The obstacles developing countries face in trying to adjust to a new trade environment are not new. Similarly, this is not the first time developed countries have promised to help low- and middle-income nations deal with adjustment costs. As part of the WTO's Uruguay Agreement on Agriculture in 1996, developed countries agreed to provide additional food aid in cases where developing countries faced higher food import bills because of increases in world agriculture prices. Thus far, high-income countries have not followed through on this pledge, though they have recommitted to providing this assistance as part of a Doha deal.

The WTO must ensure that trade reforms ultimately lead to greater prosperity for all, rather than causing even deeper poverty for some. Anything less would mean that the Doha round has been a broken promise. Assisting developing countries with adjustment costs is one important piece of a new trade deal. As the next section will explain, aid for trade is another.

Aid for Trade: Development Remains Central

For farmers in developing countries to compete in local, regional, and even global markets, they need access to open markets in developed countries; they need protection from cheap imported commodities that flood into world markets from highly subsidized farmers; and they need help in overcoming other barriers. In the developing world, these barriers come in many forms. Examples include poor energy and transportation infrastructure; inadequate credit and financial resources for business development and expansion; and a lack of technical expertise to negotiate, interpret and enforce complex trade rules. It is unlikely that most low-income countries can commit sufficient resources to overcome these barriers without international assistance.

Trade ministers from developed and developing countries agree that "aid for trade" is a critical component of a successful Doha Round. "Aid for Trade should aim to help developing countries, particularly LDCs, to build the supply-side capacity and trade-related infrastructure that they need to assist them to implement and benefit from WTO Agreements and more broadly to expand their trade."[29]

Developed countries need to do their part by providing targeted aid packages that address trade-related capacity building in several of these key areas. With or without a final Doha deal, the United States should increase aid for trade funding. Aid for trade should encompass three broad areas: assistance in planning and financing major trade-related infrastructure projects such as roads and ports; technical assistance to help countries negotiate and comply with international trade agreements; and support for programs to develop small and medium-sized businesses that can expand and diversify exports.

Infrastructure

Large-scale investment in infrastructure is essential for low-income countries to take advantage of increased opportunities in international trade. Roads and railways, communications networks, ports and airport facilities, as well as electricity, water, and sanitation systems, are often barely developed in low-income countries. When farmers are ready to harvest a product, for

Roads are vital to the development of rural areas. Farmers depend on them to reach markets that would otherwise be inaccessible.

example, often no storage facilities are available.

"The problems of small and medium-sized business enterprises stem from insufficient human resources and inefficient physical infrastructure. If you want to compete in a global market place, you have to deal with these problems and the government must help to address these issues," says Shade Bembatoum-Young, a business consultant in Nigeria.[30]

In its development plan for the World Bank in 2002, the government of Ethiopia argued that major investment in road construction was a prerequisite to reviving the country's stagnant economy, since only 30 percent of the country was serviced by a functional transportation system.[31] In Uganda, more than half the roads are in poor condition, and the associated higher transportation

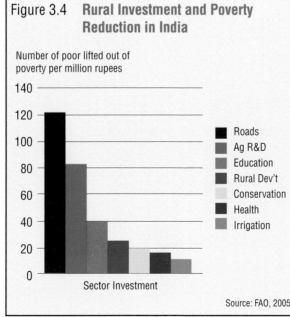

Figure 3.4 **Rural Investment and Poverty Reduction in India**

Number of poor lifted out of poverty per million rupees

- Roads
- Ag R&D
- Education
- Rural Dev't
- Conservation
- Health
- Irrigation

Sector Investment

Source: FAO, 2005

Food Aid and World Trade Negotiations

– Charles Uphaus and Eric Muñoz, Bread for the World Institute

Since the 1950s, the United States has been the most generous food aid donor, often providing half or more of all annual food aid donations. Almost all of this food aid is provided in-kind, in both bulk and processed forms.

Food aid is used for a variety of purposes. It may be a humanitarian response during emergencies or a component of long-term development programming. The McGovern-Dole International Food for Education and Child Nutrition Program, a U.S. food aid program that guarantees children a meal if they attend school, is a good example of how food aid is used for development purposes. When McGovern-Dole food aid is used to support school feeding initiatives, children receive a hot breakfast, snacks or lunch. In addition to addressing hunger and nutrition issues, school feeding programs using U.S. food aid can increase school attendance and improve children's educational outcomes. Food aid is undoubtedly an important resource in the fight against hunger.

During the current Doha trade round of negotiations, WTO members have reached a tentative agreement on rules to govern food aid:

On food aid, we reconfirm our commitment to maintain an adequate level and to take into account the interests of food aid recipient countries. To this end, a "safe box" for bona fide food aid will be provided to ensure that there is no unintended impediment to dealing with emergency situations. Beyond that, we will ensure elimination of commercial displacement. To this end, we will agree to effective disciplines on in-kind food aid, monetization and re-exports so that there can be no loophole for continuing export subsidization.

Though the Doha Development Round is currently stalled, any new disciplines on food aid reached as part of a final trade deal must be carefully designed. For example, creating a "safe box" for emergency food aid will require agreement on what constitutes an emergency and when emergency food aid is an appropriate response. Poorly defined terms of reference could lead to an unenforceable agreement and, worse, slower response to emergencies.

Commercial trade and local production together constitute the only sustainable way out of chronic food insecurity. There is evidence to show that food aid deliveries, if not properly structured and correctly timed, can sometimes crowd out commercial food sales and discourage local production. If aid agencies and recipient governments are to have continued access to food aid for use in social safety net programming, these programs must be designed and implemented so as to minimize trade distortions. One way to do this is to replace in-kind food aid donations with cash assistance, which can then be used to procure food through existing market channels, preferably from local sources so as to encourage production in food aid recipient countries.

In previous years, the United States sold food aid to recipient countries on concessional terms. The European Union (EU) contends that such sales amount to an export subsidy. The EU, which has already pledged to eliminate its export subsidy programs, is using this argument to pressure the United States to eliminate food aid programs that contain any element of export subsidization, or another trade distortion such as displacement of commercial sales.

A move by the United States toward at least partial substitution of cash for in-kind food aid (as the Canadian government has already done) would go a long way toward addressing EU objections and would

Following the 2005 Pakistan earthquake, a boy receives high energy biscuits and cans of vitamin A-fortified vegetable oil at a distribution point run by the Pakistani army and the American Refugee Committee. The earthquake killed more than 73,000 people and left more than 3 million people homeless, many without their regular sources of food.

undoubtedly help minimize the likelihood of commercial displacement. However, there is some resistance to such a move on the part of U.S. food aid implementing partners in the NGO community, who fear that any reduction in in-kind aid would not be replaced with equivalent cash assistance.

Whatever WTO disciplines are ultimately imposed on food aid, it is critical that this tool remain available in the fight against food insecurity and hunger. During humanitarian emergencies, when local food markets have been disrupted, the direct provision of food aid may be necessary to prevent hunger or starvation. Direct feeding activities ensure adequate nutrition for vulnerable populations, especially people who are elderly or ill, mothers, infants, and young and school-age children. For example, fortified foods donated as

food aid and not available on local markets can meet the specific nutrition needs of people on anti-retroviral drugs. Such critical health and nutrition benefits will be lost if food aid is subjected to overly strict WTO policies—causing incalculable harm to the world's hungry and poor people.

Charles Uphaus is a senior analyst with Bread for the World Institute on aid effectiveness. Before joining BFWI he spent 30 years as an agricultural and economic growth specialist with USAID.

Eric Muñoz is the lead analyst for Bread for the World Institute on Healthy Food, Farms & Families.

Uphaus and Muñoz are the authors of a longer study on food aid, Feeding a Hungry World: A Vision for Food Aid in the 21st Century, *available at www.bread.org.*

costs amount to an estimated 80 percent tax on exported goods such as textiles.[32] One study found that, "Poor trade-related infrastructure such as dysfunctional ports, roads, and telecommunications can add up to 40 percent to the cost of overseas-bound products in some African countries."[33]

Technical assistance and human resource development

The physical constraints posed by poor or nonexistent infrastructure are matched in many cases by a lack of expertise in trade that makes it

Richard Lord

In sub-Saharan Africa, women produce 80 percent of the food supply.

difficult for developing countries to effectively navigate the international trade system. A good example of this appeared in Bread for the World Institute's 2003 Hunger Report, *Agriculture and the Global Economy*. Nicholas Sabwa, a trade analyst for the Kenyan government, wrote about his experience participating in WTO agriculture trade negotiations. "Most African countries have not been able to send negotiators to Geneva [where the WTO is located] regularly, if at all. Even when negotiators are sent, sometimes countries can afford to send only one negotiator who cannot attend concurrent negotiating sessions. Many times, I missed key Geneva meetings due to lack of funds for travel."[34]

Aid for trade programs must include more than just getting developing country negotiators to the table at the WTO. Once trade agreements are negotiated, many countries will need assistance in building the technical expertise to implement new trade rules and export regulations. Farmers wishing to export fresh or prepared foods, for example, face significant challenges in adhering to international sanitation standards. The Codex Alimentarius is an internationally accepted set of standards governing the production, preparation, packaging, labeling and shipping of food products. It contains well over 4,000 separate provisions. Mastering this maze of technical regulations should not be the sole responsibility of individual farmers or agro-processing companies. They should be able to obtain help from extension agents, trade specialists, food technologists, and a range of other partners, functioning as a trade-related knowledge network. This is critical to developing countries struggling to participate in the global economy,[35] but building such networks takes time and money, and key investments are needed to spur their development.

Entrepreneurship and business development

In addition to providing technical and financial assistance for infrastructure and human resource development, a comprehensive aid for trade package must promote the growth of small and medium-sized businesses.

The entrepreneurial spirit is not unique to the United States. But people in the developing world face much higher hurdles when trying to start a business. Strategic assistance to small and medium-size enterprises would help to expand and diversify opportunities in areas where producers and service providers can be competitive, but lack the finance capital to start a business.

Despite all the challenges to business development, some developing countries are demonstrating that they have the capacity to compete. Kenya is a fine example. Most Kenyans live in rural areas and participate in small-scale farming enterprises. Processing and exporting horticultural products has become a major economic activity for small farmers in Kenya. As an LDC, Kenya enjoys duty-free and quota-free access to U.S. and European markets for horticultural exports, and it has taken advantage of this opportunity. Exports generate about $46 million annually for small-scale farmers.[36]

Several factors contribute to Kenya's success, especially in the highly profitable but labor-intensive area of fruit, vegetable and flower production. First, Kenya has an extensive infrastructure including a good road network and several airports to efficiently move products from field to market. Second, the government supports fruit and vegetable production by funding research and development, providing advisory services and disseminating regulatory and market information. Such policies have nurtured a stable business environment conducive to investment.[37]

Support from donor countries through multilateral institutions such as the World Bank and other international development banks can help accelerate development and cultivate the potential that clearly exists in Kenya. In consultation with the World Bank and the International Monetary Fund, Kenya has identified a need to improve credit and financial services to stimulate business development. Kenya's forthrightness in naming and discussing these shortcomings is a strong signal of its commitment to supporting entrepreneurs. But Kenya remains a deeply impoverished country and presently is not on track to meet the Millennium Development Goals.

Agriculture and the Millennium Development Goals

The Millennium Development Goals (MDGs) are a set of targets to improve the health and welfare of the world's poorest people. The MDGs were adopted formally in 2000 at the United Nations by nearly every country in the world, and they are to be achieved by 2015. It was also agreed through the United Nations that all countries share a "collective responsibility" in the development of countries that need the most support. Not all countries are on track to achieve the MDGs. The poorest countries face enormous challenges, especially in rural areas.

The first MDG is to cut hunger and poverty in half. That this is the first goal is not an accident; it recognizes the overall importance of reducing hunger and poverty in order to achieve the other goals, which include decreasing child mortality, increasing the number of children receiving primary education, improving maternal health, promoting gender equality and combating HIV and other diseases.

Reducing hunger and poverty is tied directly to improving the pros-

Richard Lord

pects of farmers. For desperately poor families living off the land, farming is not only a way to make a living, it is a matter of survival. There are many direct and indirect linkages among agriculture, health, economic development and poverty reduction—linkages that all depend on increasing agricultural productivity and the prices farmers receive for their products.

Growing more food and more varied food items can lead to better health and nutrition, both because more food is then available and because profits increase for producers. Each of these factors can help reduce hunger and lead to lower food prices. In Ethiopia, poor households spend 50 percent or more of their income on food, while non-poor households spend less than 30 percent of their income to meet their nutritional needs.[38]

Improvements in nutrition also have a positive effect on a country's overall economic health. Improved nutrition is associated with higher labor productivity. A one percent loss in adult height resulting from childhood stunting has been associated with a 1.4 percent decrease in labor productivity. In sub-Saharan Africa, better nutrition could contribute up to 4 percent per year in increased economic growth.[39] In India, malnutrition may cost the country more than $2.5 billion in lost income; in Sierra Leone, anemia associated with malnutrition costs the country at least $2 million each year in lost agricultural productivity.[40]

Increasing agricultural productivity and the economic returns to farmers can have ripple effects throughout a country's economy. The extra income may be used to purchase other agricultural and non-agricultural goods, which, in turn, encourages the growth of related industries. This is an especially important result if the goods can be produced locally. Greater agricultural productivity often creates demand for farm inputs such as seeds, fertilizer, and other basic supplies, while also increasing opportunities for agro-processors to process raw goods into high-value food products. According to a recent IFPRI study, "The consumption linkage generated by increased rural incomes is agriculture's most important linkage in the development process."[41]

Perhaps nowhere are the linkages between increasing agricultural

A vendor sells grapes at the Laad Bazaar in Hyerabad, India. India produces one million tons of grapes each year.

productivity and reducing poverty more apparent than in East and South Asia, where a dynamic synergy between agriculture, economic diversification and industrialization has catalyzed substantial economic growth and helped to lift many millions of people out of poverty. The gains in agricultural productivity made possible through the Green Revolution, for example, resulted in a 90 percent rise in the average real income of small farmers in India between 1973 and 1994. Success in reducing poverty rates among small farmers goes a long way toward explaining why the region is on track to meet the first MDG.

The United States has declared its commitment to the MDGs. U.S. policymakers can take a big step towards honoring that commitment by doing all they can to support the livelihoods of the many millions of hungry and poor people around the world who depend on farming. This includes reforming domestic farm programs that encourage overproduction and distort world trade, since these practices harm smallholder farmers in developing countries. U.S. farm policy reforms alone will not guarantee that poor countries achieve the MDGs, but without them, the task will be more difficult by orders of magnitude.

Developing countries must increase agricultural productivity in order to achieve gains in trade that will help to lift large numbers of people living in rural areas out of poverty. Trade-distorting policies in the developed world simply make it harder for developing countries to end hunger and poverty among their people.

Mainline Recommendation

The United States should support the development objectives of the Doha round by phasing out the current system of farm subsidies which link higher amounts of payments with higher production levels. Current farm programs distort trade and worsen world hunger by making it harder for farmers in developing countries to escape poverty.

Other Recommendations

■ The United States should show leadership in pushing for a swift and successful conclusion to the Doha round of the World Trade Organization (WTO) negotiations. While negotiations continue, the United States must be prepared to act independently by using the 2007 farm bill to reform trade-distorting farm programs.

■ The United States should provide Least Developed Countries (LDCs) with 100 percent duty-free, quota-free access to U.S. markets. This change could provide LDCs with billions of dollars of additional income while costing the United States little to implement.

■ The United States and other developed countries should provide assistance to developing countries to build their trade capacity. Developing countries need "aid for trade" to improve their physical infrastructure, develop trade-related knowledge networks, increase their capacity to negotiate and implement trade rules, and support small and medium-sized businesses.

A Green Revolution for Africa?

– Charles Uphaus, Bread for the World Institute

India in the 1950s and early 60s, like Africa today, was mired in poverty. Overall economic growth barely kept pace with population growth. Agricultural productivity was stagnant. Massive food imports were the rule, not the exception.

Then, in the late 1960s and 70s, India launched its version of the Green Revolution, already underway in Latin America and in other Asian countries. The Green Revolution was based on technologies developed by international agricultural research centers in partnership with the Rockefeller Foundation. It emphasized the use of improved varieties of wheat, rice and hybrid maize in combination with increased fertilizer use and irrigation development.

National leaders in India committed the human and financial resources—and their own political reputations—to the task of agricultural transformation. Green Revolution innovations were augmented by supportive policies at the national level and by upgrading agricultural research and education systems. The technologies that were promoted could be adopted by farmers regardless of their scale of operations, but they were particularly well adapted for the prevailing smallholder farmers.

As a result of these investments and policies, overall cereal production in India doubled between 1970 and 1999, with wheat production increasing threefold. India is now a net rice exporter, and wheat imports are an insignificant share of the country's overall food availability. Despite what many viewed as nearly insurmountable obstacles—heavy population pressures against available arable land, poorly educated and overwhelmingly rural populations, widespread and deep poverty—India was able to decrease its poverty rate, from 55 percent in 1970 to 35 percent by the end of the 20th century, largely due to growth in agricultural production.

Over this same period, Africa has regressed in terms of food security. Per capita cereal production was lower in 1997 than it had been 30 years before. The number of people suffering poverty and hunger has steadily increased. Reliance on food aid, both emergency and ongoing, has increased.

Africa's Challenge

Why didn't Africa benefit from the first Green Revolution? Unlike India, which was a single country with an established identity and administrative capability, sub-Saharan Africa in the 1960s comprised 40 countries—most in the immediate aftermath of independence—with relatively poorer administrative capability, infrastructure and educational systems. In addition, the Green Revolution focused on field crops and production technologies that were not appropriate for Africa's diverse and predominantly rainfed agricultural conditions. Pastoralism, which serves as the basis for much of the African rural economy, was bypassed completely.

On top of this, many African countries have been characterized by pervasive strife and a lack of political commitment to development in general and broad-based agricultural development in particular. Internal and external economic policies have been conflicting or counterproductive. Investment in agricultural research, education, irrigation and other crucial infrastructure has lagged.

Agriculture-driven development in Africa faces further difficulties not confronted by India 40 years ago. One impediment is posed by the very success of the Green Revolution—prevailing low prices for agricultural commodities. Since the 1960s, world prices for the most important agricultural commodities have steadily fallen. The low prices and increasingly integrated global market make it more difficult for farmers to transition from largely subsistence farming to market-oriented production.

A second hurdle is posed by a stagnant shelf of technologies appropriate for African agriculture. Relatively little research has been directed at the diverse, low-input cropping systems and "orphan crops" that typify African agriculture. This problem is complicated by Africa's agro-climatic diversity and near-total reliance on rainfed farming and pastoralism. There have been some successes: Hybrid maize and sorghum work well where appropriate inputs are available, and production of high-value crops such as green beans, flowers, coffee and cocoa for export is expanding. However, the number of African farmers who can participate in such high-value, export-oriented production is still quite small because of the general absence of efficient supply chains and market support infrastructure.

A third impediment is posed by rich countries—trade restrictions and subsidies. Such protectionism has two pernicious effects. By maintaining production levels well above those that would prevail in a free market, global agricultural supplies are increased and prices lowered, making it difficult for African farmers to compete. Also, in protecting their farmers, rich countries restrict the markets available to African farmers. In 2003, the International Food Policy Research Institute estimated that protectionism and subsidies by industrialized nations cost developing countries about $23 billion annually in lost income.

Africa's Opportunity

While the "Green Revolution" as commonly understood may have been a product of a specific time and set of circumstances, it is possible for Africa to achieve sustained agricultural growth. The emerging Alliance for a Green Revolution in Africa (AGRA), which brings the Gates and Rockefeller Foundations together in partnership with African leaders and scientists, holds real promise for stimulating the kind of research and policy reform that will lead to sustainable, pro-poor economic growth.

Sub-Saharan Africa is clearly too large, politically divided and agro-climatically diverse to deal with as a whole. New strategies and interventions will need to be tailored to a number of specific conditions and implemented in close collaboration with local researchers and farmers, many of them women. Still, gains are likely to be incremental and hard-won. A smallholder-based development model, akin to India's, may work in areas with relatively high population densities that are well-connected to markets for inputs and products, but will not apply in the pastoralist economies that predominate in large parts of the continent.

It's important at this juncture to recall that many experts at the time were skeptical that India could ever emerge from chronic food insecurity. For Africa to do so will depend on the following:

1. Political commitment, over the long term, on the part of both African and donor governments.
2. Sustained focus on the top priority—economic growth that benefits poor people. In most countries this means smallholder agriculture.
3. Significantly increased investments, through partnerships like AGRA, in agricultural science and the development of technologies appropriate for African farmers.
4. Global trade reforms to make agriculture more profitable for developing countries, combined with reasonable "development space" and aid for trade to enable African agriculture to become more productive and competitive.
5. Significantly increased investment in rural infrastructure (irrigation, roads, electricity and communications).
6. The integrated deployment of all available resources, public and private—including trade liberalization, food aid, agricultural research, education and infrastructure development—in support of broad-based economic growth.

Charles Uphaus is a senior analyst with Bread for the World Institute on aid effectiveness. Before joining BFWI he spent 30 years as an agricultural and economic growth specialist with USAID.

The Obesity Challenge:
Poverty and Malnutrition

Chapter 4

CAPACITY
330 LBS

In 1967, Senator Robert Kennedy set out to visit one of the poorest regions of the country, the Mississippi Delta. Warned by civil rights workers beforehand, he was still shocked and mortified (as was much of America) by the scale of poverty in the Delta. "I've seen bad things in West Virginia," Kennedy told reporters accompanying him, "but I've never seen anything like this anywhere in the United States."[1] They visited communities where there were people so poor they did not own a pair of shoes. Food was scarce and hunger pervasive. A two-year-old child Kennedy tried to caress stared at him blankly, head limp and attention dulled by severe malnutrition.

In the years that followed, Congress took up the challenge of reducing hunger and poverty. Despite the sudden loss of Robert Kennedy and his leadership, it was the strongest commitment to an anti-poverty agenda since the Great Depression. Images like those from Mississippi created the impetus for a host of policy reforms in the late 1960s and early 70s that included improvements to the Food Stamp Program, improvements to the National School Lunch Program, and the creation and expansion of other nutrition programs like the Special Supplemental Nutrition Program for Women, Infants and Children (WIC) and School Breakfast programs.

In the summer of 2006, the National Public Radio (NPR) show *All Things Considered* traveled to the Mississippi Delta and retraced some of the same steps covered by Robert Kennedy. The NPR report described, once again, high rates of poverty and rampant malnutrition. But in 2006, the story was about another form of malnutrition: obesity. In Belzoni, Mississippi, the focus of the NPR report, obesity was described as an epidemic by medical experts interviewed on the show. "They have food in the cupboard," said Dr. Aaron Shirley, who chronicled hunger in the Delta during the 60s. "Unfortunately, it's the wrong kind of food."[2]

Health Consequences

The United States has the highest rates of obesity in the developed world.[3] Words like "epidemic" and "crisis" are frequently used to describe the problem. In 2004, 16 percent of Americans ranked obesity as the most important U.S. health problem, with only cancer (24 percent) ranked higher.[4]

Obesity is distinguished from overweight using a measure known as Body Mass Index (BMI), obtained by dividing a person's weight in kilograms by height in meters. Figure 4.1 illustrates the difference between normal weight, overweight and obesity. Neither overweight nor obesity is good for one's health, but obesity is by far the greater threat.

Obesity is most prevalent in high-poverty areas, but people in all income groups are affected. Sixty-six percent of Americans are considered overweight, and thirty percent are obese according to the latest data.[5] It's clear that the problem affects people from all walks of life.

For decades Americans have been gaining weight, but in recent years the pounds have been piling up faster. From 1994 to 2004, obesity in adults rose from 22.9 to 32.2 percent.[6] Rates of overweight and obesity among children have also been climbing alarmingly. The data on

Figure 4.1 Measuring Obesity

A sample range of weights measured in lbs.

Height	Normal Weight	Overweight	Obese
5'6"	115 to 154	155 to 185	186 or more
5'9"	125 to 168	169 to 202	203 or more
6'	137 to 183	184 to 220	221 or more

Source: RAND Corporation

children has triggered many people's resolve to pay serious attention to obesity. Since 1974, there has been a fourfold increase among children between the ages of 6 and 11 and a threefold increase for adolescents 12 to 19.[7] The percentage of children between the ages of 6-19 who are overweight stands at 17 percent. If current trends continue, it will be 20 percent by 2010.[8]

Obesity is associated with increased risk of high blood pressure, high cholesterol, coronary heart disease, stroke, osteoarthritis, some cancers, and type 2 diabetes. As rates of obesity and overweight have gone up, so has the prevalence of many of these conditions. The number of Americans with type 2 diabetes almost tripled from 1980 to 2004.[9] Previously known as adult-onset diabetes and usually found in people over 40, type 2 diabetes is now appearing in children and adolescents. It is associated with poor nutrition, lack of exercise and a family history of the disease. If left untreated, type 2 diabetes can lead to cardiovascular disease, loss of vision,

kidney disease and nerve damage.

The consequences of overweight and obesity should be of concern to all Americans. Added pounds translate into poor health and higher mortality rates—and extra strain on the federal budget. Because people living in poverty have higher rates of overweight or obesity, they are more susceptible to health problems like type 2 diabetes that accompany obesity.[10]

Individuals with diabetes have been shown to have medical expenditures and out-of-pocket expenses that are two to five times higher than those of people without diabetes.[11] Often, the only way for poor people

America's Second Harvest

Children who live in areas where fruits and vegetables are expensive gain significantly more weight than children who live where fruits and vegetables are cheaper.

to cope with the high cost of health care is to turn to federal assistance. Of the $78.5 billion in medical expenses attributed to overweight and obesity in 1998, about half of it was paid for through Medicare and Medicaid. This was approximately 8.8 percent of all Medicaid spending and 11.1 percent of Medicare spending.[12]

Hunger, Poverty and Obesity

A poor diet and lack of exercise are the most direct causes of overweight and obesity. Data are widely available to show that Americans consume too many calories and do not get enough exercise. In a recent government report, it was found that 89 percent of all Americans fall short of the U.S. Healthy Eating Index.[13] Less than half get the recommended levels of moderate physical activity.[14]

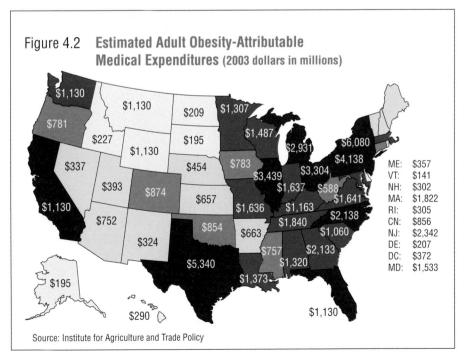

Figure 4.2 **Estimated Adult Obesity-Attributable Medical Expenditures** (2003 dollars in millions)

$1,130 · $1,130 · $209 · $1,307 · $781 · $227 · $195 · $1,487 · $1,130 · $2,931 · $6,080 · $337 · $454 · $783 · $4,138 · $393 · $874 · $3,439 · $3,304 · $657 · $1,637 · $588 · $1,130 · $1,636 · $1,163 · $1,641 · $752 · $854 · $1,840 · $2,138 · $324 · $663 · $1,060 · $5,340 · $757 · $2,133 · $1,320 · $195 · $1,373 · $290 · $1,130

ME: $357
VT: $141
NH: $302
MA: $1,822
RI: $305
CN: $856
NJ: $2,342
DE: $207
DC: $372
MD: $1,533

Source: Institute for Agriculture and Trade Policy

Clearly there are plenty of Americans who are not eating the right foods or exercising enough. But why are overweight and obesity so much more prevalent in low-income communities? Can nutrition programs play a role in solving this problem? The answer to the second question is yes, and will be explored later in this chapter. Answering the first question is more complicated—there is no simple response that applies to everyone.

The answer might seem clear at first: people are obese because they eat too much and are not burning enough calories. But often there are other, less obvious factors that contribute to a problem. Consider the work of Amartya Sen, a Nobel Laureate in economics who has studied the relationship between famines and poverty. While it seems obvious that famines are caused by a lack of food, Sen (and others) argues that it is more accurate to say they are caused by poverty.[15] In many documented cases, people have been starving in one region of a country while other areas had food surpluses. Poverty may affect only certain families, who are unable to buy even enough food to survive, or it may undermine an entire region or country—there may be, for example, a lack of passable roads or working vehicles to ship food from harvest areas to people who are starving. The point is that sometimes the root causes of a problem—whether famine or obesity—are obscured by a factor that seems obvious.

The fact is that in high-poverty areas where obesity levels are highest, hunger is also lurking. It may sound like a paradox, but hunger, poverty and obesity can and do coexist. Severe hunger in the United States—bone-thin hunger like what Robert Kennedy found in the Delta—has been cut sharply since the 1960s, but the more common form of hunger today, "food insecurity," affects a startling number of people. Government statistics show that more than 35 million Americans are food insecure,[16] defined as having "limited or uncertain access to nutritious, safe foods necessary to lead a healthy lifestyle."[17]

Food insecurity and obesity are connected in several ways. For example, women living in poverty have higher rates of overweight and obesity than other women.[18] Researchers have observed that in food insecure households, mothers skimp on their own food, or miss meals altogether, in order to feed their children when food supplies and money are running out. When food is again available, they may seek to catch up on eating. Scientists know that this "feast or famine" cycle is a factor in weight gain.

There is no question that food insecurity plays a role in the choices women make about how, when and what to eat.

The very poorest people in our country do not have high rates of overweight or obesity, but there are many people living in poverty who do. They are the group most vulnerable to obesity, according to economist Darius Lakdawalla of the RAND Corporation and the National Bureau of Economic

Among U.S. adults, black women have the highest prevalence of overweight and obesity.

Eugene Meebane, Jr.

Research.[19] Too poor to afford healthy foods, they stock their cupboards with cheap foods high in fats and sweeteners. Choosing high-fat, low-nutrient foods saves money.

We frequently hear in the media that U.S. consumers pay less for food than people in other industrialized countries. Indeed, calories are cheap—it's the nutrients that are expensive. Healthy foods cost significantly more than foods of lesser nutritional value.[20] Compare the price of a half-gallon of milk to a half-gallon of cola, or orange juice

Diets of low income consumers for whom food price is the most important consideration may be high in sugars and fat simply because these are the cheapest sources of dietary energy available."

– Adam Drewnowski
Center for Public Health Nutrition

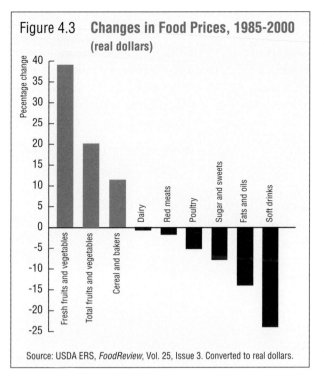

Figure 4.3 Changes in Food Prices, 1985-2000
(real dollars)

Pecentage change

Fresh fruits and vegetables
Total fruits and vegetables
Cereal and bakers
Dairy
Red meats
Poultry
Sugar and sweets
Fats and oils
Soft drinks

Source: USDA ERS, *FoodReview*, Vol. 25, Issue 3. Converted to real dollars.

to orange drink. Between 1985 and 2000, when overweight and obesity rates started to soar, the cost of fruits and vegetables increased by 40 percent.[21] Over the same period, the cost of fats and sugars actually went down.

In low-income households, where food insecurity is an ever-present danger, cost is a primary factor affecting shopping decisions. Studies comparing grocery prices in poor urban and rural communities against prices in wealthier suburban areas have found that the urban and rural communities paid more for food.[22] The importance of shopping with cost in mind is magnified by the declining value of low-income wages. In the last ten years, the minimum wage has been stuck at $5.15. When adjusted for inflation, this is the lowest level since the United States created a minimum wage.[23] With choice at the grocery store dictated by purchasing power, low-income households have little power to choose groceries with their family's health in mind.

Not only do low-income households have difficulty affording a consistent diet of healthy food, they may also have trouble getting their hands on it. "I was in a Tunica, Mississippi, Piggly Wiggly food market," explained researcher Amy Glasmeier, author of *An Atlas of Poverty in America*, "and what I found there was a lot of normal products, except for the vegetables and the meat counter. The vegetables were wilted lettuce and dried apples, or even tomatoes with black spots. At the meat counter, I found mostly chicken wings and ham hocks…and they're 90 percent fat. That's the sum of what's available for people to buy. Low-income communities support retail operations that sell low-cost goods."[24]

Studies also show that low-income communities have fewer grocery stores than higher-income areas. In one study of the Mississippi Delta, 70 percent of the food-stamp eligible population lived more than 30 miles away from a supermarket.[25] In Chapter 2, Lisa Morton, a resident of the Cheyenne River Indian Reservation, explained that she and her neighbors carpool to the

nearest supermarket—more than 40 miles away. Transportation is less of a problem in urban areas, but access may be complicated by security issues. Often in high-crime neighborhoods, trips to the grocery store must be planned according to the safest routes and times.

Thus, economics and environment are important factors in selecting foods. So is education; there is a well-documented relationship between poor nutrition and low levels of education. Overall, the members of households below the poverty line have fewer years of schooling than people in households above the poverty line. Nutrition education programs exist to help introduce people to foods they may not be familiar with, but a story told by a nutrition educator in Hartford, Connecticut, sheds light on one of the challenges faced by low-income families. The mother in a food-insecure household admitted that

As a country, the United States spends more than half of every food dollar on ready-prepared, ready-to-eat food.

she was reluctant to prepare a meal with ingredients she had never used before. Given her precarious financial position, she could not afford to experiment with new foods and fail and then have nothing to feed her children.

Overweight and obesity are societal problems. Many other factors which play a role in the obesity problem are shared by everyone in our culture. For example, every day a quarter of all adults eat at a fast food restaurant.[26] Fast food, despite its widely publicized role in contributing to overweight and obesity, remains extraordinarily popular with Americans.[27] And as a society, Americans are putting in more hours on the job than they did 20 years ago, so there is less time to prepare nutritious meals at home. This is as true for low-income families as for everyone else. One of the celebrated accomplishments of welfare reform has been the number of low-income adults who have returned to the workforce.[28] Other poor adults have second and third jobs. The concept of "time poverty" resonates with many Americans—poverty, after all, is often about limited choices.

Another societal factor in rising obesity rates is the current system of commodity subsidies. Highly subsidized corn and soybeans have meant an abundance of high-fructose corn syrup and hydrogenated vegetable oil produced from soybeans. In the 1970s, the Secretary of Agriculture exhorted farmers to plant fencerow to fencerow, and they did, boosting their output with the aid of marvelous advances in agricultural technologies. But what were they to do with all the extra products? One option was to dump them into world markets, as described in Chapter Three; the other was to sell corn and soybean products domestically, mostly in the form of fats and sweeteners. U.S. consump-

tion of high-fructose corn syrup—a product that did not exist before the 1970s—has increased 1,000 percent in the last 30 years.[29] Consumption of added fats went up 35 percent in the same time period.[30]

Nutrition Programs and Obesity Prevention

The federal nutrition programs represent an investment in the health and welfare of the country. But we must be careful not to overstate the role of the nutrition programs in

Fast food, which perhaps epitomizes unhealthy eating, is a deal when value is measured by the calorie. Generally, the healthiest items on the menu are the most expensive.

solving the obesity problem. Obesity must be confronted by a broad anti-poverty agenda. Nutrition programs should not be expected to shoulder the entire burden or even most of the burden. A comprehensive approach should deal with wages, transportation and other barriers, as discussed above. Nutrition policy is only one front in the battle.

The nutrition programs are already engaged in obesity prevention. None, including the Food Stamp Program, cause obesity.[31] But

what more could they do? A logical place to start would be with child nutrition. Since poor eating behaviors established at a young age are hard to break, childhood is a critical time to cultivate an appreciation for healthy foods.

Obesity Prevention in Schools

Obesity is the most common nutritional disease of children and adolescents in the United States.[32] For the first time in history, the life expectancy of this generation of U.S. children is lower than their

parents' generation.[33] The reason, say medical experts, is obesity.

Outside the home, the best place to expose children to healthy foods on a regular basis is in school. The National School Lunch and Breakfast programs, the two pillars of school nutrition, do not come up for reauthorization in the farm bill, but the bill provides many opportunities to improve them.

The DoD Fresh Program, for example, is an innovative partnership between USDA and the Department

Growing Power: Providing Children with Fresh Fruits and Vegetables

– Margaret Munroe, Bread for the World Institute

Sean Bowie

It's an inviting scene: watermelons piled up outside, mounds of recently picked produce and shelves of organic goods, all in a storefront on the grounds of the last functional farm in Milwaukee.

Just past the storefront lie six greenhouses full of blooming flowers, patches of cilantro and basil, a rustic red barn, and a number of goats munching happily on greens in pens out back.

This is the environment that kids need in order to change their eating habits, says Will Allen, the director of Growing Power. A former professional basketball player who grew up on a farm in rural Maryland, Allen left a career in the corporate world to take up farming in 1992. He founded Growing Power with the idea of providing good, healthy food to the surrounding community and getting youth involved in the food production system. By learning how to farm, he reasoned, kids would gain an appreciation for the hard work that it takes to make things grow and at the same time would have the pleasure of eating fresh food—which was often in short supply in the north side of the city. One of his hopes was that this would lead children to a more nutritious diet. What he found was that introducing kids to wholesome food is just a beginning.

One of Growing Power's major youth initiatives is through the Youth Corps program. Each summer, Growing Power accepts a small group of local children to work on the farm throughout the year. Youth Corps was originally envisioned as an unstructured program focused on giving participants basic knowledge about farming. Most of the kids hear about the program through friends or community organizations, or simply because they live in the neighborhood where Growing Power is located.

Often they stay with the program for many years. Sophie Brown first began working at Growing Power in high school, after hearing about it through an internship program at her church. Now in college, she comes back in the summer to work in the storefront and help run workshops on composting and aquaculture. Working at Growing Power through the Youth Corps program has given her an opportunity to develop leadership skills and gain experience working with kids, which has influenced her goal of becoming a teacher. It has also given her the conviction that getting locally-grown food to people in the surrounding community can make an impact on how healthfully they are eating. "We [gotta] make changes and make people see how much work it takes to grow food that actually tastes good and not just looks good on a shelf," she comments.

It also takes a lot of work to help the kids see this reality. Allen learned early on that getting participants involved in all aspects of the food production system is an essential part of changing unhealthy attitudes towards food. Participants perform tasks ranging from planting and harvesting, to getting market baskets ready for sale and delivery, to preparing recipes. Allen makes a special effort to introduce new dishes to the children. Many kids had their first fresh salad at one of his classes—and it was made with greens and vegetables they had grown themselves. On Saturday mornings before they began work, Allen would fix a breakfast of fruit and organic eggs. The kids began to look forward to these small treats, and one Saturday when Allen was out of town for a conference they complained loudly when told they wouldn't get their usual breakfast. "That's when I knew I was going in the right direction," he remarks.

As Growing Power's successes mount, Allen has been able to start other programs oriented toward local youth. One program, with the local Boys and Girls Club, helped establish another farm at the club's building in the countryside outside Milwaukee. In the summer, the kids get to help plant and harvest; during the school year, Growing Power has partnered with the Milwaukee School of Engineering to create an after-school program, Eat Smart, that teaches kids how to adapt their family recipes to make them healthier. Once parents see that their children want to eat fruits and vegetables, they often begin to change the foods they keep in the house.

Getting kids to start thinking about food in new ways is an inherent part of Growing Power's mission. Allen says that teaching kids about farming is an essential part of teaching them about nutrition: "The missing link in all of this is that if we don't have the food production, we can't do any of this." By learning that food doesn't

just appear on a grocery store shelf, participants in Growing Power's programs begin to understand more about what they are putting in their mouths. They get the information they need to begin making changes in their own eating habits and inspiring changes in the people around them.

Margaret Munroe works at Bread for the World Institute as the Project Assistant on the 2007 Hunger Report. She volunteered at Growing Power during the summer of 2006.

Figure 4.4   Obesity Prevalence in Chidren

	Children (Ages 6 to 11) Prevalence (%)		Adolescents (Ages 12 to 19) Prevalence (%)	
Race	Overweight	Obesity	Overweight	Obesity
Black (Non-Hispanic)	35.9	19.5	40.4	23.6
Mexican American	39.3	23.7	43.8	23.4
White (Non-Hispanic)	26.2	11.8	26.5	12.7

Source: American Obesity Association

of Defense (DoD), which distributes fresh fruits and vegetables to schools and Indian reservations in 43 states, the District of Columbia, Puerto Rico, the Virgin Islands and Guam. USDA purchases the produce from DoD, which delivers it to the school districts while en route to deliver supplies to military installations and veteran's hospitals. DoD operates 10 regional buying centers around the country, acquiring produce directly from growers. The program began as a $3 million pilot in 1995 and grew to $25 million by 1999. The 2002 farm bill increased spending to the current level of $50 million. The next farm bill should continue to increase funding of this important program.

Improving school nutrition should mean offering children additional healthy foods, to counter the many forces pushing them towards unhealthy foods. In a 2004 study published by the Center for Science in the Public Interest (CSPI), 251 schools across the country were surveyed and the contents of nearly 1,500 vending machines examined. Of 9,723 total snack slots, only 26 contained a fruit or vegetable.[34] What researchers found was an assortment of hard candies, chips, chocolate products and other foods of minimal nutritional value.

CSPI, the American College of Preventive Medicine, and the United Fresh Fruit and Vegetable Association have suggested doubling the budget for the DoD Fresh Program to $100 million and expanding it to all 50 states. Given that most American children do not consume the recommended five servings of fruits and vegetables per day, and with vending machines offering so much junk food, a $100 million investment to bring fresh fruits and vegetables to the schools seems minimal.

Any investment in improving the quality of foods offered would be money well spent. Parents will appreciate it, especially parents hard-pressed to provide healthy foods at home due to poverty, and so will the children. Anyone who doubts that children appreciate healthy foods when they are offered in appealing ways might consider the following. In a study of

another USDA pilot program to increase fresh fruit and vegetable consumption in schools, researchers found that 95 percent of the 105 participating schools considered the pilot successful: it resulted in increased consumption of fruits and vegetables.[35] Children seem to prefer their carrot sticks accompanied by a low-fat dip or a smear of peanut butter, but doesn't this still sound better than a chocolate bar and a 20 oz. soft drink?

In 2006, proponents of better school nutrition had good reason to rejoice. Beverage giants Coke and Pepsi agreed to remove high-calorie soft drinks from all schools and limit the portion sizes of the remaining beverages. President Bill Clinton and Arkansas governor Mike Huckabee were instrumental in negotiating this agreement. Political leadership is always a critical ingredient in accomplishing reform, and this case was no exception.

Child nutrition is an issue that transcends politics for Clinton,

a Democrat, and Huckabee, a Republican. Both men have struggled with weight problems almost all of their lives. In 2003, Huckabee was diagnosed with type 2 diabetes, and Clinton has a heart condition that required a quadruple bypass in 2004. Since their conditions were diagnosed, they have been on a mission to raise childhood obesity to one of the top public health issues in the United States.

Removing soft drinks from the schools is an important step, but bolder measures than this are required. Schools should be junk food-free. Vending machines stocked with unhealthy foods undermine the message students hear that good nutrition matters. Congress and the administration have the responsibility to lead the way, but so far the strongest leadership seems to be coming from outside Washington, driven by private individuals who recognize the gravity of the problem and are frustrated by the pace of reform. For example, celebrity chef Alice Waters has been on a mission to improve the nutritional quality of foods served in American schools. Through her

private foundation, she has turned the Martin Luther King Junior Middle School (MLK) in Berkeley, California, into a laboratory of nutrition program reform.

Ten years into her work, Waters remains an idealist. Government commodities are tougher to chew than the foie gras at Chez Panisse, her signature restaurant a few miles away. At MLK, most of the students qualify for free and reduced-price meals. Waters says that you cannot fight obesity by mandating what types of food children eat or by scaring them with descriptions of health problems they can expect later in life—you have to transform their relationship to food. Through her 'edible schoolyard project,' she has sought to integrate the study of food into the whole curriculum, so that earth science class measures soil erosion in the school garden, math class calculates the dimensions of the garden beds, and history class grinds corn with a mortar and pestle as ancient cultures did.[36]

The school lunch program is the linchpin of Waters' strategy. To enhance the menus with plenty of fresh fruits and vegetables, she combines the government commodities the school receives from the federal meal program with fresh produce purchased from local growers with her foundation money. Farm-to-school programs like the one Waters started at MLK are another way to increase the amount of fresh, healthy foods available to students.

Farm-to-school programs

> ## "
> Learning is supposed to be a pleasure, and a food-centered curriculum is a way to reach kids in a way that is truly pleasurable."
>
> – *Alice Waters*
> *The Edible Schoolyard*

also provide a market for local producers. If policymakers are seriously interested in helping small farmers, here is a means to do it. Nutrition programs that help farmers to help schools fight obesity recall an earlier time when nutrition policy and farm policy were much more interdependent. As discussed in Chapter One, farm policy and nutrition policy were born of the same crisis in the 1930s. One of the first acts of the Roosevelt Administration when it took office in 1933 was to establish a federal food relief program to address the crisis in the cities and the crisis on the farms. "The Agricultural Adjustment Administration will put into operation as fast as they are developed, plans for supplying surplus farm products to needy and destitute people… This action will be taken in order to carry out the twofold purpose of stabilizing farm markets and feeding the unemployed."[37]

The National School Lunch Program uses government commodities obtained through another program established during the Great Depression and given the nondescript name Section 32. Today, Section 32 commodities are still used to support child nutrition programs, and these commodities all meet USDA's nutrition guidelines.[38] Section 32 is intended to support farmers of non-price-supported commodities, including fruits and vegetable

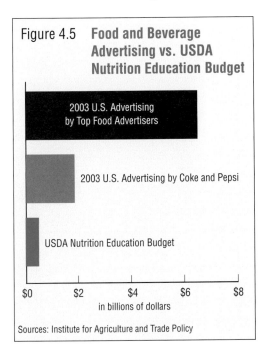

Figure 4.5 Food and Beverage Advertising vs. USDA Nutrition Education Budget

2003 U.S. Advertising by Top Food Advertisers

2003 U.S. Advertising by Coke and Pepsi

USDA Nutrition Education Budget

$0 $2 $4 $6 $8
in billions of dollars

Sources: Institute for Agriculture and Trade Policy

farmers, but the government has great difficulty moving fresh produce. Procurement, storage, distribution and coordination with school districts is complicated by the inefficiencies that come with government bureaucracies, making it impossible for schools to get a variety of fresh products through Section 32.

One of the goals of the National School Lunch Program is to improve children's fruit and vegetable consumption.

One way to circumvent the problem is to increase support for alternatives such as DoD Fresh. Improving the quality and choice of foods in school should be one of the highest priorities in addressing obesity. But reform mustn't stop there. The homes and communities to which students return at the end of the school day matter just as much; the food environment in the community also needs to change.

Obesity Prevention in Communities

At the same time as obesity rates have been skyrocketing, a much more hopeful trend has emerged in communities around the United States. Between 1994 and 2004, the number of farmers' markets increased by 111 percent. There are now more than 3,700 such markets across the country.[39] These numbers suggest that local producers have willing buyers for their products if they can reach these customers.

Establishing farmers' markets in low-income communities can help increase the availability of fresh fruits and vegetables where grocery stores are scarce or poorly stocked. The USDA Farmers Market Promotion Program is designed to "help improve and expand domestic farmers' markets, roadside stands, community-supported agriculture programs and other direct producer-to-consumer market opportunities."[40] The areas targeted by the program include urban and rural neighborhoods with limited access to fresh foods.

Two federal nutrition programs have been established to promote farmers' markets among at-risk groups—the Senior Farmers' Market Nutrition Program and the WIC Farmers' Market Nutrition Program. Low-income seniors and mothers in the WIC program receive coupons to purchase fresh fruits and vegetables. The idea is to link small local farmers with low-income consumers, providing the consumers with the freshest possible foods and offering the farmers the highest possible margins. But these are very small programs, providing participants with $20 in coupons to be spent over the course of an entire year, and obesity prevention is not an explicit objective.

Nutrition policy should be emphasizing obesity prevention. Thus, it would make sense to expand the farmers' market benefit to include the Food Stamp Program, the largest federal nutrition program at 25 million participants per month in 2005. To make healthier foods available to food stamp households, a farmers' market program as described above would be a start, but why limit such a good idea to farmers' markets? Most Food Stamp Program participants buy their produce, as they do other foods, at the grocery store. Not all food stamp participants have easy access to farmers' markets. If the objective is to encourage greater consumption of healthy foods, the place to do it is at the grocery store.

When purchasing foods at the grocery store, Food Stamp Program participants access their benefits with an Electronic Benefits Transfer (EBT) card. The cost of foods purchased with the EBT card is deducted from an account in the same way that funds in a bank account are accessed with a debit card. The EBT system has been in place nationally since 2004, and according to experts in this technology, it would be easy to program an EBT system to allow different benefit levels based on the foods selected. For example, every time a participant used food stamp benefits to purchase fresh fruits and vegetables, the EBT system could provide extra benefits—effectively reducing the cost of these healthy foods.

Offering families a chance to purchase healthy foods at a reduced cost would strengthen the Food Stamp Program in several ways. It would reinforce the gains made by improving the school nutrition programs, since half of all those who receive food stamp benefits are children. It would also help food stamp families stretch their monthly

Straight From the Farm: A Farmers Market Brings Something Fresh to the Inner City

– Cheryle E. Adams, Bread for the World Institute

The Anacostia Farmers Market, sponsored by the Capital Area Food Bank and the Chesapeake Bay Foundation, provides fresh produce at a reasonable cost to one of the poorest communities in the District of Columbia. The Anacostia community of the District is located in Ward 8, where 35 percent of the residents live in poverty.

The health problems associated with high rates of poverty and food insecurity, such as obesity, Type 2 diabetes and other diet-related conditions, are found at alarmingly high levels in the Anacostia community. Low-income communities in general, whether urban or rural, have the highest rates of obesity in the United States. It's not that people in these communities won't eat healthy foods, but it is difficult to afford them on a limited budget and often hard to locate them in poor inner-city communities.

The Anacostia Farmers Market was established to address the lack of access to fresh fruits and vegetables. A 2006 food security study by D.C. Hunger Solutions gave Ward 8 a grade of F for access to grocery stores. In a survey of the area, it was found that residents have to travel as far as three miles to get to a grocery store. Some people without a car must take three buses to reach a store where fresh produce is sold.

Customers who qualify for food stamps can use their Electronic Benefit Transfer (EBT) cards at the farmers market. According to Susan Topping, a program associate at the Capital Area Food Bank, "The use of the government benefits at the market shows that we are filling one of the needs of the community, not only providing a safe, clean, healthy venue to buy produce."

Customers have been asked if shopping at the market has made a difference in their diets. Most recently, 82 percent of the shoppers indicated that they now eat more fruits and vegetables every day, 35 percent are more health conscious, and 17 percent are trying new foods.

The Anacostia Farmers Market was originally located at the Union Temple Baptist Church. According to Vernon Hawkins, administrator of the church, "The market has allowed people to recognize the value of adding fresh vegetables and fruits to their diets."

Established in 1998, the market has received funding from USDA's Sustainable Agriculture Research and Education (SARE) Community Incentive Project Grant. The objective of the grant was to encourage farmers to invest their time and energy in a low-income community to provide a much-needed service. The SARE grant enabled the market to expand, which has increased the value to both the farmers and the consumers. Though the grant money has now run out, the Capital Area Food Bank and the Chesapeake Bay Foundation are committed to keeping the market open.

Access to nutritious food is a form of "health insurance," and for some families in Anacostia, it's the only health insurance they have.

Cheryle E. Adams is an administrative assistant with Bread for the World Institute.

More than half of all farmers' markets participate in WIC-coupon, food stamps, local and/or state nutrition programs.

allotment. Research shows that food stamps do not last the entire month in most households. In fact, a study analyzing food purchases found that 63 percent of food stamp households used more than half of their benefits within one week of issuance, and within two weeks most had already used more than 80 percent.[41] In a more focused study in California, researchers noted that grocery stores were making decisions on whether to carry healthy foods based on the monthly food stamp benefit cycle. At the beginning of the month, for example, stores stocked whole wheat bread; at the end of the month, when food stamp benefits were depleted, the stores switched to the cheaper white bread.[42]

Farmers would also benefit from an additional food stamp benefit for healthy foods, although these farmers would not be the same group of small local producers who sell at farmers' markets. The vast majority of the farmers whose products are sold on grocery shelves are the largest, most profitable producers. But there are other ways to strengthen the linkages

between local agriculture and food insecure communities. The Institute for Agriculture and Trade Policy (IATP) has suggested creating a program similar to the Conservation Security Program, an initiative which encourages farmers to practice good stewardship of the land and produces environmental benefits enjoyed by everyone. Under the IATP plan, farmers would be rewarded for dedicating areas of their land to growing fruits, vegetables, or other healthy foods and donating these products to food banks, schools, homeless shelters and other agencies that serve low-income people at risk of hunger.[43]

Josh Miner, a W.K. Kellogg Foundation Food and Society Policy fellow, has proposed using marketplace incentives to help food stamp recipients purchase more fresh fruits and vegetables. Under Miner's plan, every time a food stamp participant purchased a fruit or vegetable, he or she would receive a 50 percent discount. The USDA would pay the remaining cost so there would be no loss for grocers or farmers. To offset these costs, Miner suggests redis-

tributing money from commodity programs, and he justifies this on the following grounds: "Making healthful foods more widely available and less expensive to consumers would help bring agriculture and nutrition policies into accord with public health goals…There is no question that the food stamp and commodity support programs would distribute payments quite differently if the goals of both were explicitly to promote better eating habits among U.S. consumers."[44]

This report's underlying argument makes the same point: it is critical to bring agriculture and nutrition policies into accord with public health goals. This congruence of policies was the objective when federal agriculture and nutrition policies were established in the 1930s. Many years have passed, and agriculture does not look the same as it did 70 years ago. Nor does malnutrition in the United States. The obesity problem lends urgency to the task of strengthening the linkages between agriculture and nutrition policies to meet public health goals. We recommend a more gradualist approach than Miner has suggested, beginning with pilot studies on the effectiveness of a fruit and vegetable incentive program. It's important to understand how the incentives will affect people's food choices before adopting such a program on a large scale.

Several industry groups have called for marketplace incentives that would increase the availability of fruits and vegetables to food stamp families. The United Fresh Fruits and Vegetable Association (UFFVA) has asked Congress to "provide $10 million for states to develop and pilot test innovative programs that encourage increased consumption of fruits and vegetables…through use of electronic benefit transfer cards (EBT)."[45] Producers of fruit and vegetables, the so-called specialty crops, do not receive subsidies, but they are not averse to support through nutrition programs that encourage consumption of their products.

Many organizations agree that the Food Stamp Program should encourage families to purchase healthy foods, but not everyone agrees on how this should be done. For example, a task force sponsored by the Chicago Council of Global Affairs has suggested not only a marketplace incentive to encourage consumption of healthy foods, but also a complementary disincentive, basically a surcharge, applied to unhealthy foods "such as high sodium/low nutrient snack foods."[46] Presumably, which foods would be subjected to the surcharge would be determined by a body of experts such as the National Institutes of Medicine.

We believe, at this point, it would be counterproductive to restrict which foods families can purchase using their food stamps benefits. Until now, the Food Stamp Program has provided participants with freedom of choice when using their benefits, with the notable exceptions of hot foods; alcohol and cigarettes; vitamins and medicines; and other nonfood items. As discussed earlier, freedom of choice is at best a relative term for people living in poverty, and several factors beyond their control affect families' food choices in low-income communities. Until these are also addressed, the food choices available to food stamp participants should not be restricted.

A Challenge for Lawmakers

In the coming year, policymakers in Washington will reconsider the relationship that has existed between farm and nutrition policy since the 1930s. Changes to the commodities programs, as suggested earlier in this report, will free up resources to increase the healthy foods available to households participating in nutrition programs. Several nutrition programs come up for reauthorization in the farm bill. Through this legislation, lawmakers have a tool available to them to address the obesity challenge. Today's lawmakers should regard the obesity challenge with the sense of mission that policymakers in the 1960s had when they confronted severe malnutrition caused by lack of food. Today as in past decades, all Americans deserve access to healthy, affordable foods.

Mainline Recommendation

Federal nutrition policy and farm policy should be closely aligned to emphasize their linkages in promoting better public health. Programs that provide fresh fruits and vegetables to low-income communities create opportunities for small and medium-sized farmers who have traditionally been excluded from government farm support programs. Supporting these producers could also help low-income communities gain greater access to healthy foods. The time has come to reorient farm policy and nutrition policy toward priorities that help both groups.

Other Recommendations

■ Expand fresh fruit and vegetable access for children through school meal programs. Programs which do this include the National School Lunch and Breakfast programs, the DoD Fresh Program, and the School Fresh Fruit and Vegetable Program. The procurement policies for Section 32, which provides schools with USDA commodities, should be improved to make it easier for schools to obtain more fresh foods.

■ The Food Stamp Program should provide incentives for participants to purchase more fresh fruits and vegetables. Bonus coupons for farmers' markets are provided through some other nutrition programs. Healthy food incentives made available through the Food Stamp Program would also benefit local producers who sell at farmers' markets and stimulate the development of farmers' markets in communities where access to fresh foods is limited. An incentive program at grocery stores should begin with pilot studies.

Obesity Trends Among U.S. Adults

1996 ▶

In 1996, obesity rates across the country were still below 20 percent.

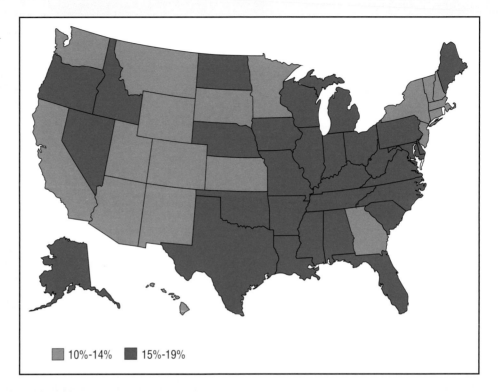

■ 10%-14%　■ 15%-19%

1999 ▶

By 1999, several states had climbed above 20 percent, with the greatest increases occuring in the South.

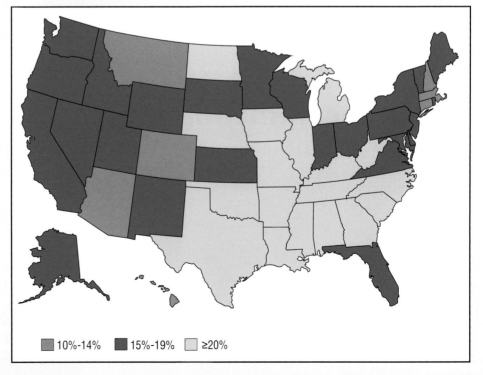

■ 10%-14%　■ 15%-19%　□ ≥20%

From 1996 to 2005

2002 ▶

In 2002, more than half the states were recording obesity levels above 20 percent and a few had climbed above 25 percent.

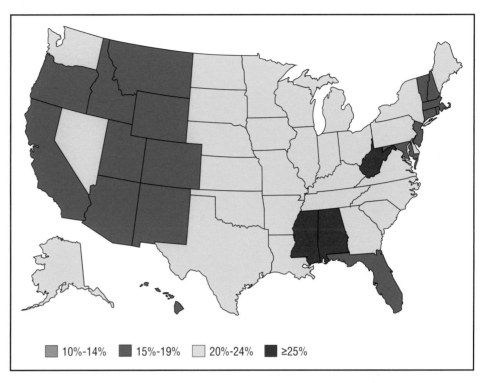

■ 10%-14% ■ 15%-19% □ 20%-24% ■ ≥25%

The data shown in these maps were collected through the Centers for Disease Control and Prevention (CDC) Behavioral Risk Factor Surveillance System (BRFSS). Color-coded maps showing obesity trends 1985-2005 are available on the CDC website.

2005 ▶

By 2005, the same three states that were at 25 percent in 2002 were now recording average obesity rates above 30 percent, and there were just 4 states left with rates below 20 percent.

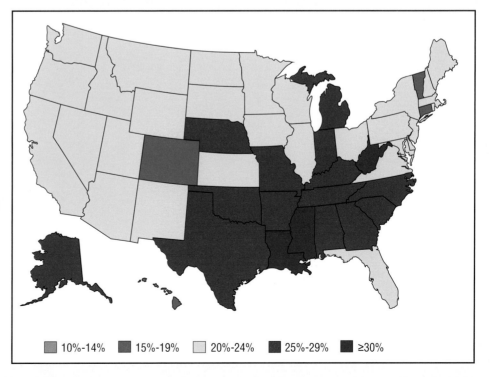

■ 10%-14% ■ 15%-19% □ 20%-24% ■ 25%-29% ■ ≥30%

Nutrition Programs:
Protecting Families From Hunger

Chapter 5

Margaret W. Nea

As recently as the 1960s, severe malnutrition on par with that found in the developing world existed in the United States. When this was brought to the attention of national policymakers, they declared unequivocally that the situation would not stand. During the late 1960s and the 1970s, there was a national commitment to developing and expanding federal nutrition programs. This commitment, combined with increased investment in other social safety net programs, sharply reduced hunger in the United States.

In 1977, physicians again conducted a study of some of the poorest communities in the United States. They reported, "Our first and overwhelming impression is that there are far fewer grossly malnourished people in this country today than 10 years ago. This change does not appear to be due to an overall improvement in living standards or to a decrease in joblessness… but in the area of food there is a difference. The Food Stamp Program, the nutritional component of Head Start, school lunch and breakfast programs… have made all the difference."[1]

Nutrition programs account for the greatest share of USDA spending. In 2005, spending on nutrition programs came to $52.2 billion, or 52 percent of USDA's budget.[2] The Food Stamp Program, the largest federal nutrition program, is due to be reauthorized in the next farm bill. Other programs, smaller but still important, are also reauthorized in the farm bill. The federal nutrition programs are the subject of this chapter.

The Food Stamp Program

The latest government statistics show that federal nutrition programs are still essential to combat hunger in the United States: more than 35 million people live in households struggling to put food on the table. Even more alarming, government figures show that a majority of the U.S. population will spend at least one year of their adult lives in poverty.[3] The United States needs an effective frontline program that addresses its high levels of food insecurity and hunger. The Food Stamp Program has fulfilled this role since it was established in the 1960s.

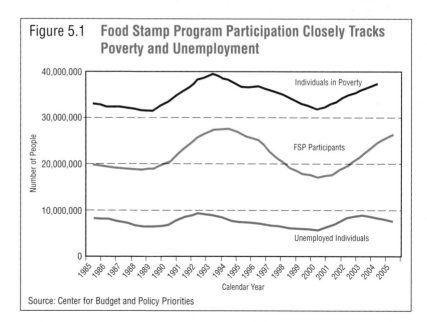

Figure 5.1 **Food Stamp Program Participation Closely Tracks Poverty and Unemployment**

Source: Center for Budget and Policy Priorities

In 2006, as the nation's largest nutrition program, the Food Stamp Program served an average of 25 million people per month. Thanks to food stamps, low-income people in communities throughout the country are receiving help to cope with one of the most debilitating effects of poverty: hunger.

Food stamps are used by an incredibly diverse group of people, nearly all of whom live below the poverty line. Many are working families struggling to get by on low wages. Mary and John Patterson [pseudonyms], both 23, and their

An estimated 4.5 million children in the United States are living in households headed by their grandparents, and the numbers are rising.[4] Many seniors live on modest fixed incomes which make it difficult to meet the needs of growing children. Food stamps, whether for the whole household or just the grandchildren, make a big difference.

Tamyra Lee and her three children, whose lives were literally turned upside down by Hurricane Katrina, survived on food stamps and her $93 monthly unemployment benefit.[5] In the months following the storm,

conditions faced by low-income households. The incomes of many families have remained flat; there has not been an increase in the minimum wage since 1997.

Today, the income earned by low-wage workers does not stretch nearly as far as it did a generation ago. The national minimum wage of $5.15 per hour, when adjusted for inflation, is worth just 85 percent of its value when it was last updated in 1997. Meanwhile, the cost of living continues to rise, increasing the gap between what low-wage workers earn and what is required to meet basic needs. Researchers using the actual costs of housing, food, utilities and other necessities found that in most areas of the country, families need about 200 percent of the poverty level to achieve "minimal economic self-sufficiency."[6]

Families are eligible for food stamps if their net incomes fall below the poverty line. People working 40 hours per week for minimum wage qualify for food stamps. But a salary increase of as little as one dollar may push them above the income cutoff for the program. With too much income to qualify for food stamps, but nowhere near the level of income needed to reach economic self-sufficiency, many low-wage workers find themselves trapped in or near poverty.

In many ways, the Food Stamp Program is a model program. A 2005 federal study found that payment errors are almost negligible—at their lowest levels since the program began.[7] Some of the errors included in the rates are underpayments—people receiving less help than they qualify for: See **Figure 5.2.** Americans used to hear frequent allegations of food stamp fraud, but the truth is that the Food Stamp Program has achieved a level of integrity that policymakers should want all federal programs to reach. Food stamp

More than 13 million U.S. children are living in food insecure households, or close to one in five of all U.S. children.

three-year-old daughter, Megan, live in Portland, Oregon. John works full-time in construction and Mary works part-time while attending college. Their combined monthly income puts them below the federal poverty line, and they worry about money on a daily basis. The family receives WIC and food stamps in addition to state supports. "The prices of everything aren't based on minimum wage," says John.

Other food stamp participants are grandparents raising grandchildren.

participation in the Food Stamp Program swelled. By November 2005, more than 29 million people were receiving food stamps.

The Food Stamp Program is not only the largest but also the fastest-growing of the national nutrition programs. Participation has increased by almost 50 percent since 2000. Although some of the increase is due to a government effort to reach out to people who were eligible but not participating, the primary cause is the increasingly difficult economic

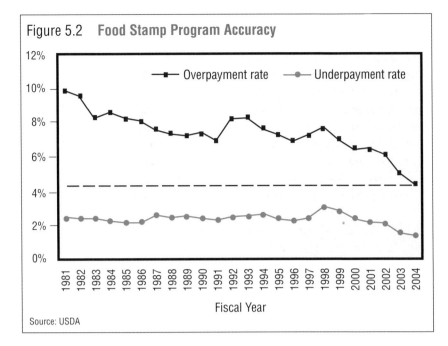

Figure 5.2   Food Stamp Program Accuracy

Source: USDA

participants are part of a remarkably efficient program.

Efficiency is important to policy-makers, who need to be able to assure voters that their tax dollars have been spent wisely, but what is important to Food Stamp Program participants? What can policymakers do to help them during their work on the next farm bill? Efforts should be made to ensure that the foundation of the Food Stamp Program remains strong, extend program benefits to a greater number of hungry and poor people, and increase food stamp benefit levels. The following sections of this chapter will explore how these goals can be met.

Protect Entitlement Status

In government parlance, the Food Stamp Program is an "entitlement" program, meaning that anyone who is eligible under program rules must be offered benefits. If food stamps were a "discretionary" program rather than an entitlement, participation would be determined by a predeter-mined budget line item. No matter how high the poverty rate rose or how many people needed food assistance,

the availability of food stamps would be limited.

Entitlement status for an urgent need such as food should be invio-lable. Yet in recent years, entitlement status for the Food Stamp Program has come under attack. In 2002, 2003 and 2005, the House of Representatives considered bills that would have allowed five states to turn the Food Stamp Program into a block grant, meaning that funding would be frozen at an amount tied to previous expenditures. "With funding levels capped under a block grant, states would no longer be able to provide food stamps benefits to families in need without cutting benefits or completely barring categories of people," wrote Cardinal Theodore E. McCarrick in a letter to members of the House.[8]

Cardinal McCarrick also criticized the expanded waiver authority in the proposed legislation, under which

"states could be allowed to put time limits on food stamps, reduce benefits… and then transfer the savings from such policies into other programs." According to the Center for Budget and Policy Priorities, "states could use superwaivers to shift federal resources into low-income programs previously funded with state resources and use the freed-up state funds for unrelated purposes, thereby reducing overall funding for low-income programs."[9] The superwaiver provision was defeated, but the fact that it came up at all is unnerving. It means that entitlement status for food stamps can never be taken for granted.

The single best example of why entitlement status should be preserved is Hurricane Katrina, which struck the Gulf coast in September 2005. In November, 29.6 million people received food stamp benefits, compared to an average of 25 million in the preceding 10 months.[10] "The foremost factor underpinning the Food Stamp Program's ability to act as an effective post Katrina 'responder' was and is its entitlement structure that lets it respond quickly and flex-ibly to changes in need," wrote the Food Research and Action Center (FRAC) to Secretary of Agriculture

Mike Johanns in December 2005.[11] Earlier, a coalition of 1,000 human services groups organized by FRAC told Congress: "We are confident that after Hurricane Katrina, Congress can build on proven successful programs, reject proposals to reduce such programs… and respond to the basic human needs Katrina has revealed."[12]

Following Hurricane Katrina, many people were hopeful that

Eugene Mebane, Jr.

The Food Stamp Program was one of the most effective "first responders" after Hurricane Katrina struck the Gulf Coast, enrolling more than 900,000 households in the first month.

protecting food stamps would now be easier. "We see people fleeing to all parts of the country who have no income and no food," said Terri Stangl of the Center for Civil Justice in Saginaw, Michigan. "This is a bad time to be looking at cuts when we see that this kind of program can make a huge difference."[13]

"Katrina may well be a fairly profound experience," said Ron Pollack, executive director of Families USA. "The images of two Americas in New Orleans may have a more lasting impression on the American public than other events. Or it may not. We'll have to see."[14]

Expand Eligibility

The response to Hurricane Katrina demonstrated that the Food Stamp Program is working. People saw for themselves who receives benefits: children, seniors, disabled people and low-wage workers. But both before and after Hurricane Katrina, the Bush administration's budget requests contained cuts that would have pushed approximately 255,000 people—mostly working poor parents and their children—out of the Food Stamp Program. Because entitlement status guarantees that all eligible people may participate, "cuts" in this case means that Congress changes the eligibility criteria so that people who once qualified can no longer apply.

Most of the adults who would have lost eligibility under the administration's proposal are people in low-wage jobs whose incomes hover below or slightly above the poverty line. Because they earn low wages, many are eligible for "non-cash" assistance funded by Temporary Assistance for Needy Families (TANF). The assistance might be subsidized childcare, transportation vouchers or other

supports that help parents keep their jobs. Welfare reform in 1996, which created the TANF program, made poor parents a deal: if you get a job, we will make sure that your family is not worse off than it was on welfare. You will still receive help while you are trying to qualify for a job with higher wages. The administration's suggested food stamp changes disregarded these promises. Fortunately, Congress rejected the proposals.

Cuts in eligibility take the Food Stamp Program in the wrong direction. The right direction is to expand eligibility to include categories of people who are currently excluded. Some legal immigrants fall into this group. Legal immigrants lost food stamp eligibility during welfare reform in 1996. The 2002 farm bill restored benefits to those who have lived in the United States for at least five years and to all immigrant children. But all legal immigrants should be eligible to receive food stamps—hunger does not wait five years to take a toll on one's health. According to the Urban Institute, there are currently between 700,000 and 900,000 legal immigrants who meet the income guidelines for the Food Stamp Program but have not been in the country long enough to qualify for food stamps.[15]

Another group of low-income people subject to strict eligibility rules is able-bodied adults without dependent children, many of whom are ineligible for food stamps. If they are not employed, they may not qualify for food stamps unless their states have been granted a waiver—regardless of the local unemployment rate. Many are unable to find work because of low skills, lack of education or some other challenge that adds to their difficulty in escaping poverty. In addition, a lifetime ban on people convicted of drug offenses keeps people who have been clean

> *"$1 billion of retail food demand by food stamp participants generates 3,300 farm jobs."*
>
> *– USDA*

for years from receiving food stamps. People with criminal records face many hurdles trying to reintegrate into society. The federal government should assist in this process rather than continue to punish people after their formal sentences end.

Set Reasonable Asset Limits

The Food Stamp Program also limits the amount of assets that people can have and still be eligible for food stamps. The asset limit is $3,000 for seniors or disabled people and $2,000 for all other households. These limits were set so that government would not have to provide benefits to people capable of taking care of themselves. On the surface, this sounds quite reasonable. But the limits cause many problems. They have not been adjusted, even for inflation, in more than 20 years,[16] and they often lead to situations that do not make sense. Should seniors be forced to spend all their retirement savings in order to qualify for food stamps during what may be a short-term problem such as an illness? Does it make sense to discourage low-income households from saving money that might carry them through a job loss or car breakdown?

A closer look reveals still more problems with asset limits. The policy does not consider liabilities along with assets. A household with $3,000 in assets and $4,000 in debts would not be eligible for food stamps, while a household with $1,000 in the bank and no debt would be eligible. Other anti-poverty programs use asset limits that are different from those of the

Food Stamp Program. For example, some people are eligible for Medicaid but not for food stamps, because food stamps have a lower asset limit. In some programs, such as TANF, individual states set their own limits on assets. Standardization of the asset limits policies would make sense but could prove complicated and costly among so many programs, agencies and states.

Data compiled in 2003 yields some compelling insights about how eliminating asset limits could affect participation in the Food Stamp Program. Based on program data for 1999, "about 26 percent of households without elderly members and eligible by income were not fully eligible, but would become so if asset tests were eliminated. If 25 percent of this newly eligible group actually participated, the food stamp caseload would rise about 16 percent."[17]

Eliminating the asset limit does not guarantee a 16 percent increase in Food Stamp Program participation. For that matter, neither does simply expanding eligibility for childless adults or legal immigrants. But a good place to start addressing hunger in the United States is to expand food stamp eligibility to ensure that more hungry people are supported by this crucial safety net.

Increase Participation

As just discussed, expanding eligibility to low-income individuals not currently allowed to apply for food stamps is one way of improving the coverage of the Food Stamp Program. But many households which are eligible for food stamps are not participating in the program. Currently, the Food Stamp Program participation rate is 60 percent.[18] USDA's latest Strategic Plan intends to raise participation to 63 percent by 2007.[19]

Some people are wary of applying for food stamps because they feel the application process is degrading and

Enrollment in the Food Stamp Program remains low among immigrant groups. USDA has made it a priority to increase outreach efforts.

time-consuming, they associate food stamps with "welfare" or "handouts," or they fear that they will be embarrassed in the supermarket check-out line. Creating a positive image of the Food Stamp Program and improving service delivery are critical to addressing some of the barriers that keep many eligible individuals from participating.

Helping Seniors in Massachusetts Get Access to Food Stamps

– David Pope, Bill Emerson National Hunger Fellow

From 2001-2004, Massachusetts had the worst food stamp participation rate in the nation. Many of the eligible people not participating were senior citizens, and one reason for this was lack of assistance from the Massachusetts Department of Transitional Assistance (DTA).

Federal law requires that all state Social Security Administration offices accept food stamp applications from people who receive Supplemental Security Income (SSI), a federal income support program for people who are over 65, blind, or disabled. For years, Massachusetts DTA offices had disregarded federal law, and eligible SSI recipients had missed out on nutritional assistance from food stamps.

In August 2005, I arrived in Boston to work with Mass Law Reform as an Emerson National Hunger Fellow, a fellowship program supported by the Congressional Hunger Center. Massachusetts had recently begun a USDA demonstration project, called the Bay State Combined Application Project (Bay State CAP), that combined food stamp and SSI applications. Earlier in the year, the Massachusetts food stamp and DTA offices decided to jump-start Bay State CAP by automatically mailing food stamps to SSI recipients. Nearly 30,000 SSI recipients were mailed electronic benefit transfer (EBT) cards that work like debit cards for food stamp benefits. As long as the recipients used the food stamp EBT cards to buy food within a certain period of time, they were enrolled in the Food Stamp Program for 36 months. By the time I began work in August, more than 22,000 of the 30,000 people targeted by the mailing had used their EBT cards to buy food.

I was there to support the work Bay State CAP was already doing. This included participating in another

Celia Escudero Espadas

outreach effort targeting 33,000 SSI recipients in shared living arrangements such as senior centers. I had the opportunity to visit area senior centers and talk with elderly residents about the project. I explained that Bay State CAP required no extra verifications and no lengthy interview, and it granted a longer food stamp certification period than applying at the food stamp office.

Following my talk at one of the centers, there was an elderly gentleman who grabbed me by the shoulder. Aiming for my ear, he whispered, "Thank you." I tried to explain that I was only the messenger, that advocates and state officials had done all the hard work. He looked confused and started gazing at his friends around the room. He motioned for me to sit at one of the white plastic tables that framed the dining hall. For almost an hour, we sipped tea, talked about his childhood, and discussed his frustration with the food stamp application process at the government office.

Our table of two soon became a group of 20, all seniors who conveyed similar stories of hardship. One woman struggled to pay her rent and utility bills. Others said they often had to choose between paying for heat and paying for food. These people were grateful for the contribution Bay State CAP was going to make to their lives, health, and future. The gentleman who had grabbed me by the shoulder to say thank you even described the project as a "blessing in the mail."

By and large, Bay State CAP has been a success, extending food stamp benefits in the mail to almost 60,000 people and then to many others in person. After the successful outreach phases, SSI recipients no longer receive targeted outreach mailings. Instead, Bay State CAP's person-to-person component has begun. At the Social Security Office (or on the phone or by mail) during application for SSI or re-determination for continuing eligibility for SSI, office workers are required to ask clients a series of questions that, if answered affirmatively, enroll the client in Bay State CAP.

Today, Massachusetts probably no longer enjoys the dubious distinction of having the worst food stamp participation rate in the nation. In fact, in 2005, only one other state registered a higher percentage of new food-stamp eligible residents. Thanks to the hard work of Massachusetts advocates and state officials,

the combined application program that began as a "blessing in the mail" continues to provide thousands of SSI recipients with much-needed and much-appreciated nutritional assistance.

David Pope worked with advocates at the Mass Law Reform Institute in Boston, Massachusetts from August 2005 through January 2006 as a Congressional Hunger Center Bill Emerson National Hunger Fellow. He spent the remaining months of his one-year fellowship at the National Coalition for the Homeless in Washington, DC.

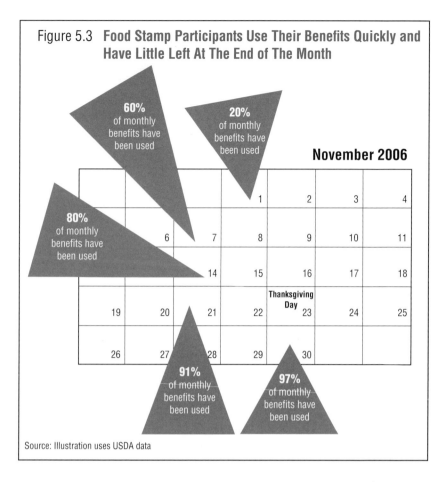

Figure 5.3 Food Stamp Participants Use Their Benefits Quickly and Have Little Left At The End of The Month

60% of monthly benefits have been used

20% of monthly benefits have been used

November 2006

80% of monthly benefits have been used

91% of monthly benefits have been used

97% of monthly benefits have been used

Source: Illustration uses USDA data

Another way to increase participation is to raise the minimum food stamp benefit, which is now $10 per month. Only 17.8 percent of people who are eligible for the minimum benefit are actually enrolled in the Food Stamp Program.[20] If the minimum benefit had been indexed to inflation, it would now be worth three times the amount set when it was first established in 1977. Increasing the minimum benefit might encourage more people to participate in the Food Stamp Program.

Food stamp participation rates vary widely across states. In 2003, the percentage of eligible people who received food stamps ranged from less than 45 percent in some states to more than 80 percent in others. Outreach is an important factor in increasing participation, and it is primarily the role of the states to fashion their own outreach programs. But it would be a mistake to blame states for the wide variance in participation rates. Many cannot afford to invest enough money in food stamp outreach, especially because in other areas, such as administrative cost sharing, the federal government is now doing less than it has in the past.

The Food Stamp Program requires more application information, more verification, and more frequent updates than most other assistance programs. The same quality control standards that have virtually eliminated waste, fraud, and abuse in the Food Stamp Program also increase the cost of administering the program. While the federal government used to shoulder an equal share of the cost of administering the program, states are now responsible for covering much of the administration cost. Following rule changes in 1998, states now receive a reimbursement from the government equivalent to 46 percent of the cost of administering the Food Stamp Program. Some states recover even less. The American Public Human Services Association (APHSA) reported that since these rule changes took effect, states have lost a total of $1.2 billion in administration reimbursements that they would have received under earlier policies.[21]

Despite resource constraints, some states are doing remarkable work to make people aware of the Food Stamp Program and ensure that the application process is clear and transparent. Several states have begun offering Internet-based food stamp services in an effort to boost participation rates, reduce demands on applicants and food stamp offices, and collect better data. Other states are working to better coordinate among different social service offices. Massachusetts and New York, for example, have developed systems to make follow-up calls to people who were referred to the Food Stamp Program, asking how many had submitted an application, how many were approved, how many were denied, and what if any obstacles were encountered.

Not all state efforts to improve services have been successful. Texas passed legislation in 2003 to outsource the administration of a number of human services. The state awarded an $899 million contract to a Bermuda-based company called Accenture and laid off thousands of state employees. State leaders believed that by privatizing human services, Texas taxpayers would save money. Accenture promised that its call centers would provide better service than clients were used to during in-person interviews at state offices. What clients got instead was an average of 20 minutes on hold, opera-

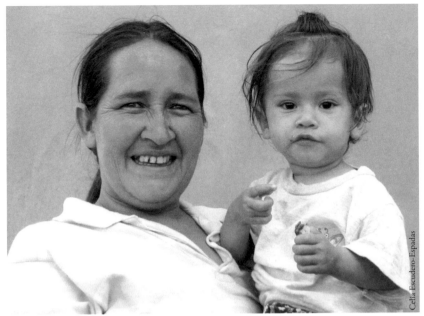

Whether in the developing world or here in the United States, the people most vulnerable to hunger are mothers and children.

Celia Escudero-Espadas

tors with little or no knowledge of the programs they were administering, lost paperwork and an ever-increasing backlog of people waiting to receive benefits.[22]

Food stamp outreach efforts would be more successful if administrators had a better understanding of not only how people make the decision to apply or not to apply for food stamps, but also how they make the decision to leave the Food Stamp Program. In order to design more effective programs, states need good data on how many people leave because they are earning more money and have become food secure without food stamp benefits, versus how many people are leaving, even though they are not food secure, because of particular obstacles within the program or other factors.[23] Because most states are cash strapped, they usually don't have the capacity to collect and analyze data that could lead to more effective delivery of services.

Thus, states need to be able to learn from each other. The federal government, specifically the Food and Nutrition Service (FNS) within USDA, can help facilitate the transfer of lessons learned and best practices across state borders. Greater cooperation between federal and state administrators benefits everyone, especially the millions of people who depend on the Food Stamp Program and whose view of the program is largely shaped by the service they receive at their local food stamp office.

Guarantee Access to Healthy Food

The main purpose of the Food Stamp Program is to help low-income households obtain a more nutritious diet by increasing their purchasing power.[24] So it is worth asking, are food stamps achieving this objective? In the 2006 Hunger Report, *Frontline Issues in Nutrition Assistance*, Bread for the World Institute reported that most families cannot afford a healthy diet using food stamps. Instead, they may be forced to purchase the cheapest foods available, which can stave off hunger but generally contain few nutrients and too many calories.

The difficulty that families face in affording enough healthy food is exacerbated by the difficulty of finding stores in their neighborhood that sell healthy foods. In urban and rural areas alike, poor communities often lack large grocery stores that offer the greatest range of brands, package sizes and quality choices. Moreover, studies show that compared to suburban neighborhoods, groceries are generally more expensive in poor communities.[25]

Food stamp benefits average $92.70 per person per month, a sum that is very likely inadequate to ensure that families can purchase healthy, nutritious foods. The food stamp benefit size is calculated using USDA's Thrifty Food Plan (TFP), a food basket model first developed for emergency use during the Great Depression and never intended to be followed for indefinite periods. Since it was introduced, the TFP has been updated several times, most recently in 2003.[26] Since the last update, the government has issued new dietary guidelines as well as a revised food pyramid.[27] As yet, the TFP has not been reviewed to assess whether it can meet the latest government recommendations for healthy eating.

What would it cost to create a

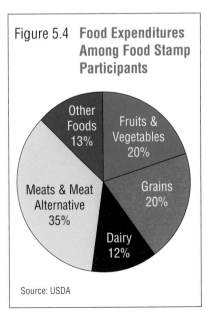

Figure 5.4 Food Expenditures Among Food Stamp Participants

- Other Foods 13%
- Fruits & Vegetables 20%
- Grains 20%
- Dairy 12%
- Meats & Meat Alternative 35%

Source: USDA

Oregon: A Food Stamp Success Story

– Nancy Weed, Oregon Hunger Relief Task Force

In 2000, Oregon had the highest hunger rate in the nation. By 2005, it had dropped down to number 17. Oregon was the only state with a statistically significant reduction in hunger. Over the same period, Oregon also increased food stamp participation to 80 percent of all those eligible—among the highest participation rates in the nation. One reason for the strong enrollment figures is a successful collaborative outreach project.

As a former food stamp consumer, I know firsthand the positive impact of the program. In the early and mid-1990s, I was a single mother of two boys, putting myself through college on loans and part-time work and relying on state-funded housing and welfare to scrape by. Food stamps were a welcome relief from the poverty that my children faced every day. Having extra money to buy food meant that not only was I able to feed my boys, but I also had the rare opportunity to give them a treat. The monthly arrival of the food stamps was an exciting occasion, marked by a trip down to the local grocery store where each boy was allowed to choose his own box of cereal. Seeing the delight they took in this ritual was part of what kept me going.

Using food stamps helped me make the best of an often stressful situation, but the process of obtaining them had a decidedly opposite effect. The procedure for applying for and using food stamps was time-consuming, involving a confusing 24-page application form, monthly report forms, repeated requirements for proof of verification, numerous trips to crowded branch offices, and long waits for service. Many offices

required applicants to arrive early in the morning to take an assigned number and wait their turn for an interview. For a working student-mother like me, this schedule was inconvenient at best. Given these sorts of hurdles, it was no surprise that participation in the Food Stamp Program was low.

Elizabeth Whelan

When I began work as the Outreach Coordinator of the Oregon Hunger Relief Task Force in January of 2000, improving the food stamp application procedure was one of the first issues that we addressed. Oregon's current simplified multi-service application for all services has 8 pages for clients to complete, with food stamp applicants only completing through page 5. The application is available online for applicants to download and print out.

We also worked with government branch offices to develop and adopt customer-friendly application procedures, such as scheduling appointments with applicants in advance to cut down on repeat visits and time spent waiting. The state has done its part to increase participation in the program by using a categorical eligibility policy which expands the eligibility of Oregon residents. Rather than following the federal rules, which limit eligibility to people living at or below 130 percent of the poverty line, people in Oregon can qualify for food stamps if they earn up to 185 percent of the poverty line. The eligibility policy also eliminated asset-limit rules that would prevent people who own a car or have some savings in the bank from benefiting from food stamps. Applicants are no longer forced to choose between keeping precious resources that might help them get back on their feet and accepting the help they need to stave off hunger.

Oregon has become a national model for developing strategies to increase the use of food stamps among working families.

Advocacy organizations around the state have done their best to make the most of this increased eligibility by actively promoting enrollment in the program. At the Hunger Relief Task Force, we have created a range of more than a dozen different materials aimed at populations—such as working families, students, immigrants and seniors—who are often unaware of their eligibility. Materials are available in multi-language translations and include a toll-free information line where live operators answer questions about applying. Distributed through elementary school packets, direct mailings and emergency food boxes, and handed out by partners in places ranging from local grocery stores to government offices, the materials have helped bring food stamps to populations that used to be the faces of Oregon's high hunger rate.

Community partners have also experimented with new kinds of outreach. One particularly effective program uses volunteers in food banks and other community partner sites to help people fill out the application for food stamps. Partner sites also help expedite the process by faxing applications to food stamp offices and scheduling appointments for clients. By reminding people which verification documents to bring to their appointments, partner sites can help people avoid the stigma and transportation costs associated with repeat visits.

Initiatives like these demonstrate how improving participation in food stamps has been above all a collaborative effort between the state government and non-governmental advocacy groups. Improving food stamp participation and fighting hunger is often a simple matter of addressing basic, practical problems that people in need often face. Oregon's success story was born of determination, focus, and cooperation by concerned citizens. Though there is still much we can do to fight hunger in Oregon, the actions we have taken so far are important steps toward making life a little easier for people living in poverty.

Nancy Weed is the Food Stamp Outreach Coordinator for the Oregon Hunger Relief Task Force.

The average monthly food stamp benefit is spent in local grocery stores. Every $5 in new food stamp benefits generates $9.20 in total community spending.

tivity. A study by the Children's Sentinel Nutrition Assessment Program has shown that babies and toddlers from food insecure households are more likely to be hospitalized than other young children. Prevention is better than cure, financially as well as medically: the cost of a single hospital stay for one young patient would pay for an entire family to receive the average food stamp benefit for five years.[31]

Commodity Distribution Programs

In addition to the Food Stamp Program, the USDA portfolio of nutrition programs includes several commodity distribution programs. Three of these are discussed in the following sections of this chapter: The Emergency Food Assistance Program (TEFAP), the Commodity Supplemental Food Program (CSFP) and the Food Distribution Program on Indian Reservations (FDPIR). All three come up for reauthorization in the farm bill, and each serves groups of people who face significant barriers to using food stamps. Fortunately, TEFAP, CSFP and FDPIR are effective alternatives. Their budgets are small compared to the Food Stamp Program budget, reflecting the targeted nature of the programs.

The following sections explain the relationship of these programs to the Food Stamp Program.

The Emergency Food Assistance Program (TEFAP)

The Emergency Food Assistance Program (TEFAP) supports hungry people in a very direct way: by supplying food. Each year, the government distributes $140 million worth of TEFAP commodities and allocates another $50 million for program administration. All TEFAP

food basket that in fact meets the latest health and nutrition guidelines? This question was posed by Dr. John Cook, associate professor at the Boston University School of Medicine.[28] In a survey of food costs at nine grocery stores in three neighborhoods in Boston, Dr. Cook found that a food basket comprised of items that meet the dietary recommendations of the American Heart Association would cost about 30 percent more than the typical TFP benefit.[29]

The maximum food stamp benefit is based on the cost of the TFP, but a household's benefit amount is also determined on the assumption that a family can spend one-third of its income on food. This assumption, which dates back to the 1960s, is unrealistic in the 21st century. As Dr. Cook observes, "The government has dramatically underestimated the amount of food stamp benefits participants need, not to mention the extent of poverty in the United States, by using the cost of the Thrifty Food Plan and the anachronistic multiplier of 'three times the Thrifty Food

Plan' as the basis for determining maximum food stamp allotments and poverty thresholds."[30] It is important that the size of Food Stamp Program benefits accurately reflect not only the cost of healthy and nutritious food, but also the cost of other basic necessities.

When the Food Stamp Program is reauthorized as part of the farm bill, raising benefit levels should be a priority. Such an increase would strengthen the program in three very important ways: First, it could help increase participation among eligible people. Second, it would help participants purchase the foods needed for a healthy diet. Finally, it would help the United States meet its pledge of cutting food insecurity in half by 2010.

Some fiscal conservatives might argue that raising food stamp benefits is simply too expensive to even contemplate. The cost must be weighed against the substantial benefits to the country as a whole: improved food security, lower health care costs, better educational outcomes, and higher work produc-

commodities must meet USDA nutrition standards. They include canned and dried fruits, canned vegetables, pasta, soups, meat, poultry and fish.[32]

America's Second Harvest: The Nation's Food Bank Network is the largest not-for-profit domestic hunger relief organization in the United States and the largest recipient of TEFAP funding. There are several hundred food banks in the network; together they supply USDA commodities to more than 40,000 charitable agencies.[33] TEFAP accounts for 15 percent of the total food received each year by food banks.[34]

Most of the food distributed through the emergency food network comes from private donations, which are not required to meet USDA standards. Anyone who has visited a food bank knows that it would be difficult to create a food basket that meets dietary requirements from donated foods. Of course food banks should not be faulted for accepting donations, because the struggle to put food on the table is a serious problem for tens of millions of people, and emergency providers must use all available resources to help solve that problem. But TEFAP is the backbone of efforts to make sure that even emergency food is nutritious.

In 2005, America's Second Harvest conducted one of the most intensive studies ever of hunger in the United States. *Hunger in America 2006* presented some alarming data. More than 25 million Americans, including nearly 9 million children and 3 million seniors, receive emergency food assistance each year through the America's Second Harvest network of charitable agencies—an 8 percent increase since the last large-scale study in 2001.[35]

Food banks have been the main

catalyst for the expansion of U.S. emergency food programs over the past 25 years. Food banking itself did not begin until the 1960s; in 1979, there were just 13 food banks in the entire country. But a decade later, every major U.S. city had at least one food bank. In 2004, America's Second Harvest reported

Assistance Program. The program was reauthorized in the 1990 farm bill and renamed The Emergency Food Assistance Program, TEFAP.

Hunger in America 2006 documents the growing numbers of people turning to food banks. A December 2005 report by the U.S. Conference of Mayors also

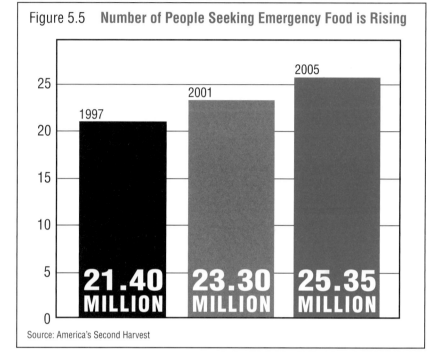

Figure 5.5 **Number of People Seeking Emergency Food is Rising**

1997 — **21.40 MILLION**
2001 — **23.30 MILLION**
2005 — **25.35 MILLION**

Source: America's Second Harvest

that more than 80 percent of the pantries and soup kitchens operating in the United States had opened their doors between 1980 and 2001.[36]

The rise of food banking in the early 1980s coincided with a disastrous confluence of events for hungry and poor people: the worst recession since the Great Depression and substantial cuts to federal spending on nutrition programs. In reaction to public outcry over these nutrition cuts, President Reagan issued an executive order to release government-held farm-support commodities, and this led to the establishment of the Temporary Emergency Food

underscores the importance of a strong TEFAP program. According to the Conference of Mayors report, emergency food resources cannot meet the rising demand for nutrition services in many parts of the country. In 43 percent of the cities included in the report, hunger-relief organizations reported that they had to turn away people in need due to lack of resources.[37]

Thus, one of the greatest challenges facing food banks and their partner agencies is meeting the increasing demand for emergency food. Yet TEFAP is not expanding. The TEFAP administrative budget has been frozen since 2002. At a USDA farm bill listening session in

Food Banks Play a Vital Role During National Emergencies

– Bread for the World Institute

America's Second Harvest and its network of food banks and food-rescue organizations are equipped to quickly respond to an emergency anywhere in the country. A perfect example is when Hurricane Katrina struck the Gulf Coast on August 29, 2005.

The day before the storm, the central office of America's Second Harvest in Chicago had already begun dispatching truckloads of extra food, water and supplies to the region. When the levees broke the next day, the water flooding the city prevented access to the Second Harvest Food Bank of Greater New Orleans and Acadiana, cutting off an important distribution site. None of the partner agencies to whom America's Second Harvest normally distributed food in the city were running—all had been wiped out by the flooding. To make things even more complicated, most of the local Second Harvest staff members were facing their own emergencies, having fled their homes in and around New Orleans.

Dealing with this situation took a concentrated effort by Second Harvest to reorganize and make use of the resources that were still available. Although the local network of distributors had been disrupted, America's Second Harvest was able to call up help from all around the country, redirecting food, water, and hygiene products from its warehouses to affected areas. A nationwide call center was set up in Second Harvest's Chicago headquarters to handle incoming calls for assistance. In the Gulf region, staff began to organize themselves, initially working from the Greater Baton Rouge Food Bank before obtaining access to an empty Wal-Mart building in Baker, just a few miles away. From there, they began directing loads of food to all areas of the city, sending out volunteers to locate the areas most in need. Staff members and volunteers worked round the clock with brief snatches of sleep on the floor.

More than 250 people from 30 food banks around the country eventually made their way to the warehouse to offer their assistance. By the Friday after the storm hit, 650,000 pounds of food had been moved to people who needed it.

In addition to mobilizing resources offered by private citizens, Second Harvest was an important partner for governmental officials. One week after the storm hit, USDA released an estimated 66 truckloads of emergency commodities. Without the Second Harvest network of staff, volunteers, and warehouses, the distribution of this food would have been much more difficult. "[The National Guard] was quite happy because we represented this logical structure, or what was left of one, to distribute food," said Brian Greene, the executive director of the America's Second Harvest Food Bank of Greater New Orleans and Acadiana. The Federal Emergency Management Agency helped find trucks and drivers, and Second Harvest coordinated the continuing effort to make sure Katrina victims had the basic necessities to survive.

In the following weeks, America's Second Harvest expanded its relief efforts by deploying additional truckloads of food and more than 5,000 volunteers to the Houston area in anticipation of people fleeing New Orleans. When Hurricane Rita hit almost a month later, more provisions were readied for the new wave of evacuees.

The success of America's Second Harvest in responding to Hurricane Katrina demonstrates the importance of food banks in maintaining homeland security during times of crisis. Food banks work with the government all year round to dispense extra commodities, but during disasters like Hurricane Katrina, it becomes clear that they are an indispensable government partner.

2006, Beverly Barrons, the administrator of TEFAP in Idaho for the Department of Health and Welfare, echoed the sentiments of other administrators who testified around the country: "The overall cost of running our program has increased significantly while our administrative funding has not."[38] Rising fuel prices, for example, have taken a huge bite out of food bank shipping budgets. Other operating expenses have also increased significantly.

In 2005, Bread for the World and a number of partners, including America's Second Harvest, asked Congress to pass the Hunger-Free Communities Act (HFCA). The legislation won broad bipartisan support with 165 cosponsors in the House and 44 in the Senate, although it had not been passed at the time of this report's release. Included in the bill is a provision to authorize up to $20 million for emergency feeding organizations to improve their infrastructure. This is not enough to make all the needed upgrades and repairs, but it will help at a time when food banks are under increasing pressure to do more with fewer resources. The HFCA, like TEFAP, deserves Congress's full consideration when the farm bill is reauthorized.

TEFAP complements the Food Stamp Program. The more people served by the Food Stamp Program, the less pressure on food banks to supply their network of partners with emergency food to distribute. Most food banks do some form of Food Stamp Program outreach. They help people learn about the program, pre-screen applications and advocate on behalf of clients. TEFAP helps make Food Stamp Program outreach possible by ensuring that a regular supply of food is on the shelves at food pantries, soup kitchens and cupboards. America's Second Harvest strongly supports the Food Stamp

Volunteers are crucial to the success of the emergency food network. As many as 90 percent of the food pantries in the America's Second Harvest network rely on volunteers.

Program. In 2001, for example, the network joined with the Food Research and Action Center and the American Public Human Services Association in calling for substantial enhancements to the Food Stamp Program in the 2002 farm bill.[39]

Commodity Supplemental Food Program (CSFP)

Each month, participants in the federal Commodity Supplemental Food Program (CSFP) receive a 45-pound package of nutritionally balanced foods. More than 85 percent of all CSFP participants are aged 60 or older. More than a third of the half-million seniors in the program are older than 75.[40] Along with seniors, other participants include pregnant, postpartum and nursing mothers and their children up to age six.

CSFP was established in 1968—six years before the start of

the WIC program—with the goal of improving the health and nutritional status of women and their young children. It was not until the 1980s that the focus shifted to seniors. WIC was established in 1974 and was soon viewed as a program that better met the needs of the mothers and children in CSFP. CSFP enrollment rates for women and children declined as their numbers in WIC increased. But seniors often preferred CSFP to the Food Stamp Program, and their participation began to soar.

Many seniors know about the Food Stamp Program but choose not to participate. Despite significant outreach efforts, less than a third of eligible seniors are enrolled. The stigma associated with food stamps is reported to be an important factor. While this is no doubt true, it is hard to say whether seniors consider stigma more of a problem than other people do. Physical and cognitive

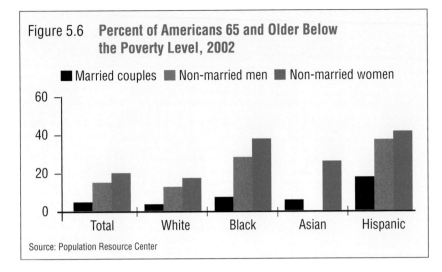

Figure 5.6 **Percent of Americans 65 and Older Below the Poverty Level, 2002**

■ Married couples ■ Non-married men ■ Non-married women

Source: Population Resource Center

impairments impede the ability of some elderly people to participate in the Food Stamp Program. This is especially true of those in their 80s and 90s, the fastest-growing segment of the U.S. population.

USDA deserves credit for its efforts to help seniors participate in the Food Stamp Program. Between 2002 and 2004, for example, the agency conducted a set of three demonstration projects using various models to look at ways of increasing senior participation. One model entailed a fundamental restructuring of how the program operates. Seniors were given the option of receiving a commodity package each month instead of accessing benefits through the EBT card. This model was tried in two areas: Hartford, Connecticut, and Alamance County, North Carolina. In Hartford, senior participation increased modestly, by 4 percent, but in Alamance County it jumped by nearly 36 percent.[41]

Researchers had assumed that seniors would prefer the commodity packages because they eliminated the stigma associated with using the EBT card in stores. In focus groups following the demonstrations, the researchers found that although avoiding stigma was one reason seniors chose the commodity pack-

ages, it was not the most important reason. Elderly people preferred the commodity packages mainly because they were getting more food. The commodity packages USDA put together for them were worth more than the retail value of their food stamp benefits. CSFP food packages cost USDA less than $20 but have a retail value of $55.[42]

In its evaluation of the demonstration project, USDA found strengths and weakness with all three models. (The other two demonstration models encouraged seniors to participate in the Food Stamp Program by removing some of the most onerous administrative requirements.) Interestingly, the major weakness of the commodity-alternative model was the "significant start-up costs" associated with procuring equipment for distribution and storage.[43] This would seem to make a strong case for allo-

cating more resources to the CSFP, which takes advantage of the existing volunteer networks provided by food banks and other charitable agencies to store and distribute its food.

In 1960, approximately one-third of all senior citizens were living in poverty. Today, the number is closer to one in ten—a remarkable achievement. The greatest reductions occurred between 1960 and 1975, largely due to the establishment of key safety net programs, such as Medicare, Medicaid, and the Food Stamp Program. It is important to note that senior poverty rates have remained mostly flat over the last two decades.[44]

In the coming decades, one of the monumental challenges facing U.S. policymakers will be how to address the needs of the growing population of seniors, especially those who will need federally subsidized healthcare, nutrition assistance and other services. Government reports predict that the number of people over 65

Because of its popularity with seniors, CSFP supporters have suggested expanding the program to cover all 50 states (32 are covered presently) and renaming it the Senior Nutrition Program.

will double by 2030,[45] and by 2050 the number of people 85 and older could make up 5 percent of the entire U.S. population.[46]

Significant demographic shifts often signal major social changes. Even if the percentage of low-income seniors remains constant, their actual numbers will continue to rise in the coming decades. The ramifications extend well beyond nutrition programming, but challenges in this area will be enormous and require attention from policymakers. What can be done now to address the special needs of seniors?

Perhaps the greatest weakness in the current array of federal nutrition programs is the lack of sufficient services for homebound seniors. Not all seniors on CSFP are homebound, but it is ideal for those who are. Consider the following: the most recent U.S. Census data indicates that more than 20 percent of people over 65 suffer some functional impairment that makes it difficult for them to leave their homes.[47] Addie Elbert, a 98-year-old CSFP participant in Kansas City, is a perfect example. Addie's box of food is delivered to her door every month. For someone in her 90s, traveling back and forth to the grocery store may be more than a little inconvenient.

In addition to the CSFP, other nutrition programs are available to seniors, including the Seniors Farmers Market, the Nutrition Services Incentive Program, the Elderly Nutrition Program, the Child and Adult Care Food Program, and of course the Food Stamp Program. All of these programs work for some seniors, but none is right for all.

Some of the reforms proposed earlier in this report will make it easier for many seniors to participate in the Food Stamp Program. The

problem remains of how to help seniors who are homebound or whose ability to participate in the Food Stamp Program is impeded by physical and cognitive difficulties. This is a group for whom food stamps may always be impractical. For these seniors, the CSFP may be the best alternative.

Many more seniors would participate in the program if they could. CSFP, like the Meals on Wheels program, maintains long waiting lists. CSFP operates on two Indian reservations and in 32 states and the District of Columbia. The remaining states are interested in operating CSFP programs, and it makes little sense for them to be excluded, since every state has seniors who qualify.

Food Distribution Program on Indian Reservations (FDPIR)

In July 2005, representatives from a number of Native American tribes that receive USDA commodities through the Food Distribution Program on Indian Reservations (FDPIR) met to discuss the program with Eric Bost, then the USDA Undersecretary of Food, Nutrition, and Consumer Services. "This is a program I care very much about," Bost told the tribal leaders.[48] It was an encouraging message to hear from a high-ranking official at USDA, because FDPIR is the only federal nutrition program specifically designed for Native Americans. Like CSFP, FDPIR provides a monthly package of nutritious foods. The program serves

low-income Native Americans living on or near reservations; more than 240 Native American tribes participate.

Back in 1993, tribal officials testified before Congress about the barriers to participating in the Food Stamp Program and the fact that many reservations relied on FDPIR commodities as their primary source of food.[49] Today, FDPIR is still a popular alternative to the Food Stamp Program. Anthony Nertoli, FDPIR administrator for the Sault tribe in Michigan's upper peninsula, explained why. "The remoteness of the reservation is the big reason. You add to this the transportation problems. There is no public transportation in many cases, and lots of people don't have a car. Then once you get to the grocery store, they don't carry a lot of goods and the prices are high."

The reservations administer

Native Americans living on a reservation are more likely to need food assistance than those living off the reservation.

FDPIR but are not allowed to administer the Food Stamp Program. "For a tribal member, it's a whole different experience going to the Food Stamp office than it is dealing with me on the reservation to get his

FDPIR package," explained Nertoli. "Why deal with the government if he can work with me?"

Nertoli has been involved with the program since its inception in 1977 and is one of the most experienced FDPIR administrators in the country. He distributes the food packages from the tailgate of his truck in eight locations around the reservation. He covers 1,600 square

All USDA commodities used in food distribution programs are required to meet government-mandated nutrition standards.

miles of territory and provides food to more than 1,000 people per month. The food packages vary from 50 to 75 pounds, depending on the size of a household. He also drops food packages off at homes whose residents are unable to travel to a distribution site.

In an average month in 2005, approximately 100,000 people participated in the FDPIR. Program participation peaked in 1987 with a rate of 146,000 people per month.

As participation declined in the early 1990s, USDA assumed that this was due to increasing participation in the Food Stamp Program, but in fact, "little is known about patterns of participation and nonparticipation in reservation food programs," concluded a USDA study in 2006.[50]

Until recently, the FDPIR food packages were not known for their high nutritional content. The food packages were updated in 1998 to add several new products and cut the overall fat content. Research to determine the health impacts of the updated packages has still not been conducted.

Poor nutrition is a well-documented problem on reservations. Native Americans suffer diabetes at three times the rate of the rest of the U.S. population; in fact, they have the highest rates of Type 2 diabetes in the world.[51] Genetics may have something to do with this, but diabetes is clearly a diet-related condition as well. Alaskan Indians with diets rich in salmon and seal oil—both foods linked with reduced rates of diabetes— experience significantly lower rates of the disease than other Native Americans.[52]

In studies of the Pima Indians of the Southwest between 1976 and 1996, researchers determined that the onset of diabetes in the children started even before birth.[53] Lacking access to healthy foods as they grow up, these children are essentially fated to become diabetics. The problem is not unique to the Pima. High rates of diabetes are common among all Native American children.

Type 2 diabetes among Native Americans is highest in the southern United States and the Southwest. It is especially common in areas known as "food deserts," which have a sparse number of grocery stores separated by long distances. These conditions are found on many Indian reservations. In food deserts, healthy foods, especially fresh fruits and vegetables, are the hardest foods of all to find. FDPIR food packages, because they meet strict nutrition standards, address hunger and the diabetes epidemic at the same time.

In their meeting with Secretary Bost, tribal leaders thanked him for his leadership but urged him to look closely at their own suggestions for strengthening the program. They focused on the need for greater cooperation between USDA and tribal organizations. As an example, they cited the abrupt termination of a program popular with Native American tribes, the Prime Vendor Pilot. The program established an Internet-based system for managing procurement and delivery of commodities. USDA terminated the pilot because it did not produce the anticipated cost savings, and it did so without consulting the tribes.

Ending Hunger and Food Insecurity

U.S. government leaders have pledged on several occasions to cut domestic food insecurity in half. In the *Healthy People 2010 Initiative*, the government has said it will "[increase] food security among U.S. households and in so doing reduce hunger."[54] This followed not long after the 1996 World Food Summit (WFS) in Rome, where the United States and 185 other countries said they would reduce the number of hungry people in the world in half by 2015. The WFS pledge was renewed in 2000 at the United

Nations as part of the Millennium Development Goals. At other events, presidents, secretaries of agriculture and other policymakers have restated their commitment to the goal.

In 1996, the food insecurity rate in the United States stood at 12 percent, making 6 percent the target for 2010.[55] Currently, the food insecurity rate in the United States is 11.0 percent.[56] It doesn't look like the number has moved much, and it may seem like time is running out, but reaching the goal—and even ending hunger entirely—is never actually out of reach. The United States is the wealthiest country in the world, it has well-designed safety net programs already in place to build on, and the public has said it supports programs to end hunger.[57] All that seems to be lacking is the political will.

Solving the problem of hunger and food insecurity once and for all requires a two-track approach. One is to develop long-term solutions that build sustainable livelihoods so that people can escape poverty. Fundamentally, it is poverty that affects people's ability to obtain sufficient amounts of food. The other track is to improve nutritional intake so that low-income people can participate as more effective agents in helping themselves out of poverty. The fastest, most direct way to reduce hunger is to improve nutrition assistance programs, and this is why the goal of ending hunger in the United States is still very much within reach.

Nutrition programs like food stamps and the commodity distribution programs discussed in this chapter are crucial to getting where we need to go. The Nutrition Title in the farm bill gives U.S. policymakers an opportunity to improve these programs and fulfill a pledge that all would agree makes the United States a stronger country.

Mainline Recommendation

The Food Stamp Program

- Raise the Food Stamp Program benefit to ensure that families have access to healthy foods. Food stamp benefits are calculated using USDA's Thrifty Food Plan, a plan originally developed for emergency use during the Great Depression. The plan does not meet the needs of families on food stamps in the 21st century.

- Expand eligibility for the Food Stamp Program to include all people who are food insecure. Some vulnerable groups are excluded because of asset limits or other program rules. The United States should not let any resident go hungry.

- Increase participation by providing states with greater financial support to administer the Food Stamp Program. States carry the burden of administering the program, and federal support has decreased while hunger has gone up. The federal government needs to be a more reliable partner.

- Reduce stigma by renaming the Food Stamp Program. 'Food Stamps' is an outdated label. The program now uses a debit card to process benefits instead of paper coupons. A change would accurately reflect a modernized program and would also reduce the stigma associated with the old name.

Commodity Distribution Programs:

- The Emergency Food Assistance Program, Commodity Supplemental Food Program and Food Distribution Program on Indian Reservations (TEFAP, CSFP and FDPIR) should be able to serve all people who are eligible for these programs. Many of the people who benefit from these programs choose them because they cannot effectively take advantage of the Food Stamp Program. Strengthening TEFAP, CSFP and FDPIR to provide for everyone who qualifies would therefore also strengthen the Food Stamp Program.

- The administrative budgets for these programs must keep pace with rapidly rising operating expenses. The increasing costs of operating these programs severely limit the number of people they can serve. The cost of fuel alone has dramatically increased since the programs were last reauthorized in the 2002 farm bill. Maintenance costs for equipment and repairs to other infrastructure soak up funding that is needed elsewhere.

Milestones in Food Stamps

1939-43

Between 1939 and 1943, the first Food Stamp Program operated by permitting people on relief to buy orange stamps equal to their normal food expenditures; for every $1 worth of orange stamps purchased, 50 cents worth of blue stamps were received. Orange stamps could be used to buy any food; blue stamps could only be used to buy food determined by the Department to be surplus.

1961

In 1961, President John F. Kennedy, having seen the debilitating effects of hunger while campaigning in Appalachia, directed the USDA to start a pilot Food Stamp program. The pilot programs retained the requirement that the food stamps be purchased, but eliminated the concept of special stamps for surplus foods.

1974

The Food Stamp Program began operating nationwide on July 1, 1974. Participation for July 1974 was almost 14 million.

1940   **1950**   **1960**   **1970**

1964-71

In 1964, President Johnson requested Congress to pass legislation making the Food Stamp Program permanent and Congress responded by enacting the Food Stamp Act of 1964.

Between 1965 and 1971, rapid increases in participation occurred, primarily due to geographic expansion. Participation topped 1 million in March 1966, 2 million in October 1967, 3 million in February 1969, 4 million in February 1970, 5 million one month later in March 1970, 6 million two months later in May 1970, and 10 million in February 1971.

Source: USDA Food & Nutrition Service

2002
2006

In May 2002, the Food Security and Rural Investment Act of 2002 was enacted, including reauthorization of the Food Stamp Program. Major changes include restoration of eligibility for qualified immigrants who have been in the United States at least five years and for their children regardless of how long they have been in the country.

November 2005: The number of people receiving food stamps reached 29.6 million, a jump of nearly 4 million in just three months. The dramatic increase occurred in the aftermath of hurricanes Katrina and Wilma. Also in November 2005, Congress rejected the administration's proposal to cut 300,000 people from the Food Stamp Program.

1977

In 1977, Congress voted to eliminate purchase requirements on food stamps. The change opened the program to the poorest people, those with the greatest need, who had previously only been allowed to purchase food stamps with cash of which many had desperately little of to spend.

1994

In March 1994, participation hit a new high of 28 million.

1980   **1990**   **2000**   **2006**

1981-87

In 1981 and 1982, major legislation was enacted cutting back on the Food Stamp Program.

Recognition of the severe domestic hunger problem in the latter half of the 1980s led to incremental improvements in 1985 and 1987, such as elimination of sales tax on food stamp purchases.

1996

In 1996, food stamp use dropped by 38 percent following passage of the Personal Responsibility and Work Opportunity Reconciliation Act, or "welfare reform." Between 1996 and 1997, the number of children living in extreme poverty increased by 425,000.

2004

In July 2004, all 50 states, the District of Columbia, Puerto Rico, the Virgin Islands and Guam were operating state-wide, city-wide and territory-wide Electronic Benefits Transfer systems to issue food stamp benefits, permanently replacing the paper coupons for which the Food Stamp Program is named.

Dakota EBT

508132 000 000000 0

Putting Food Into Farming:
How to Fix the Farm Bill

– Susan Sechler and Joe Guinan

Conclusion

Designpics

> "It should be the aim of every young farmer to do not only as well as his father, but to do his best; "to make two blades of grass grow where but one grew before."
>
> *— Isaac Newton,*
> *first Commissioner of the newly-formed*
> *U.S. Department of Agriculture, in 1864*

Farm-state legislators and commodity groups are gearing up for the 2007 farm bill. Rather than propose new legislation to replace the 2002 bill, which is set to expire, they are pushing for a "simple" two-year extension of current programs. "If it ain't broke, don't fix it," they say. "Our farmers think the 2002 farm bill was the biggest success ever."

The 2002 farm bill has succeeded in keeping a few wealthy U.S. farmers happy. The campaign contributions of those cheery farmers, the commodity PACs and corporations keep key lawmakers happy. That success aside, in every other way U.S. farm policies are wasteful, unfair, and destructive of other national aims.

Those are tough words, but an understatement. The damage done by U.S. farm policy increases with each passing farm bill. While the world and its needs change rapidly—and the needs of agriculture change just as dramatically—we merely tinker with reforming our farm programs. Thus they remain, in essence, what they were when they debuted in 1933 in the depths of the Great Depression. Secretary of Agriculture Henry Wallace apologetically introduced them as "a temporary solution to deal with an emergency."

That emergency bill's most enduring provisions, the so-called commodity programs (actually covering only a handful of crops), remain unchanged despite dramatic changes in consumer tastes, needs, and markets. At their heart is the federal government's assumed responsibility to protect the growing abundance of farm production from the vagaries of nature and from world markets through a complex system of production-related subsidies. The noise of coins pouring from the federal purse muffles the signals of market demand and other changing realities.

Imagine a Food Policy

Today, when three out of every five Americans are overweight, farm-state legislators have continued to "serve the public" by producing farm policies that support more production of those commodities. In the 15 farm bills to date, beginning with the Agricultural Adjustment Act of 1933, the word food has been in the bill's title only five times, most recently in 1990.

Imagine having a food policy instead of a farm production policy. Then our government would be promoting nutritional health rather than promoting more production and then using taxpayer dollars to find new ways to get people to consume that production. Commodity policies would become a subset of food policies, rather than today's situation, whereby the cart of commodities leads the horse of nutritional needs.

Earl Butz, that most colorful and most vilified of Agriculture Secretaries, is famous for linking agriculture's future to the conventions of industrial efficiency. More than three decades ago, his advice to farmers was that they should "plant fencerow-to-fencerow," and "get big or get out." These dictums not only sum up the vision of industrial efficiency in farming, they are in the very DNA of current farm programs. But Thomas Jefferson's yeomen farmers are all dead and gone, and they are not coming back.

Many of us cherish the values of family, community and individual initiative represented by the family farm. Many of us believe that we are better off with an agricultural system—indeed, an economy—where economic power is widely shared. So we mourn the passing of the traditional family farm. But if we fail to accept it as a reality, we could lose our chance to influence the future of rural America, the health of our population, the well-being of farm families, our food system, and our role in the world. Let us then strive to put rural areas, a healthy population, an improved food system, and

responsible global leadership toward the top rather than the bottom of farm policy concerns. And while we cannot legislate the family farm back into existence, we can at least remove the bias of current programs toward ever more concentration.

The Closed World of the Farm Bill

The roots of the farm bill go 80 years deep. Despite a mounting list of problems, farm-state legislators have been amazingly successful at resisting changes to the farm bill's basic premises and core purpose. Whenever they are pressured to expand the farm bill to accommodate a new constituency or target group, their reaction has been to paste on additional titles—be it food stamps, conservation, research, or agricultural trade.

New constituencies may get into the farm bill, but then they immediately get steamrollered by the commodity interests. Historically, the advocates for food stamps or conservation have always had to strike deals with the commodity interests to get through even a sliver of their agendas. Half a loaf has, understandably, been better than none. But this process has left the commodity title not only intact, but growing.

Reform is resisted by protecting commodity interests from competition, from broader policy development, and from public opinion. Efforts to inject a little transparency into the legislative process to ensure a balance of interests are swiftly vanquished. However, there was at least one moment when things might have turned out differently. It can help us understand what might happen with an open process in which all the constituents—including farmers—participate and are heard.

The People Speak—Once

When Jimmy Carter was elected president in 1976, he appointed three-term Minnesota congressman Bob Bergland as Secretary of Agriculture. Bergland's agricultural experience in Congress—reeling from one crisis to the next, patching and plugging without a clear sense of who would and should benefit from farm programs—caused him to question some of the fundamental assumptions of farm policy. These included the basic focus on "unit price" and the recourse to emergency bailouts that had long dominated federal thinking, even though there was no longer one single price level that would be good for everyone and the "emergencies" had become an annual event.

Bergland became convinced that good farm policy—particularly good family farm policy—should no longer be primarily about propping up the price of agricultural commodities. Additionally, although they would remain important, farmers should no longer claim central space in a progressive food and agriculture policy. Instead, the focus should be on a system leading to good nutrition and health for the whole population.

As a deeply religious man, Secretary Bergland also believed that the dominant role of the United States in international grain markets, and the special responsibility this role conferred, meant that there was a moral imperative to look at solutions to world hunger. He believed that U.S. agriculture policy could play an important role in world peace.

Bergland was determined that the 1981 farm bill would move toward a more coherent agriculture policy with a clear, honest purpose and direction. In 1979, speaking at the annual convention of the National Farmers Union in Kansas City, he stunned his audience by calling for a national dialogue on the future of agriculture. How had American agriculture developed in the way it had? Had it really promoted family farmers, or contributed to their demise? Was it what people wanted? If not, what was the role of the federal government in effecting change?

He told the staff at USDA that

no subject should be considered off-limits. If the federal tax code affected the structure of agriculture, then he wanted it explored. The "Structure Project" was born. That fall, Bergland conducted all-day public hearings in 10 regions, during which—unlike in traditional "listening sessions"—he reached out not only to farmers but to other rural residents. He wanted to hear directly from environmentalists, consumers, businesspeople, clergy and others who were affected.

Thousands of people attended and thousands more wrote in. This was to be the first farm bill with such a broad constituent base: lots of people figuring out how to build common ground around new goals based on longstanding values and to pursue these goals with more efficient and fairer programs. The 1981 farm bill process was to move away from the endless testimony and negotiations on support price, exports, and budget constraints, embracing instead a new way of thinking that would bring new constituencies and wider interests to the table.

Then, of course, things fell apart. In 1979, the Soviets invaded Afghanistan. Bergland agreed to an embargo on trade in grain with the Soviet Union. The Iranian hostage crisis continued to unfold. In the 1980 presidential election, Ronald Reagan defeated Carter. Bergland's team at USDA issued their report anyway, in January 1981, on their way out the door.[1]

Fight to the Finish

Today, more than ever, we need a food policy that recognizes the legitimate interests of all—farmers, consumers, nutrition, health, the country, and the growing food challenge facing the world—within economically and politically acceptable bounds. Our investments in the food system should promote our public policy goals, not frustrate them.

So, what should we do?

First, we must work to free agriculture from a sterile and meaningless attachment to conventional notions of industrial efficiency, and place the consumer and the environment in which we live at the center of food policy. We can

The 2007 farm bill debate is expected to focus much greater attention on rural development than it received in the 2002 bill. Small business development for depressed rural communities should be a priority.

no longer tolerate food policies that are derivatives of bad farm policies—that reduce the role of the public to surplus consumers of last resort, while putting farmers on a production treadmill that makes it impossible for them to adequately consider quality and safety and condemning the world's hungry people to a hungry future.

Second, we must replace the myth of the family farm with the reality of farm businesses that are good for families. The large farms that produce most of our food should not be afforded special treatment through nostalgia for a "way of life," but rather should be expected to perform efficiently and reliably with far less government intervention than today. The interventions that government does undertake must be aimed at supporting farmers to run businesses that respond to market signals, stay in tune with the safety and health concerns of their customers, reduce damage to the environment, and produce a product people want to buy.

Third, we should fight the farm subsidy structure. No compromise.

No buying off. We should work with members of Congress who are not beholden to the special interests of big agriculture. We should reach out to state officials, particularly governors, who can be persuaded that rural development block grants would be better overall for their states—and for their political future—than just supporting the status quo. Organizing at the state level will be critical. The Structure Project was correct: agriculture varies dramatically from place to place, and from crop to crop. The Washington lobby for commodity interests is far more single-minded in its defense of subsidies than are most farmers.

The Farm and Food Policy Project: Restoring Balance to the U.S. Agricultural and Food System

– Allen Hance

A diverse coalition of family farm, rural, public health, anti-hunger, conservation, faith-based, and other groups is forming to shape the 2007 farm bill—on a scale unprecedented in the history of farm policy debate. The cross-sector approach of the Farm and Food Policy Project (FFPP) reflects a commitment to advocate for policies that address the full spectrum of public needs addressed by this critical piece of legislation. This broad and growing coalition believes that by working together, we can make real progress toward supporting family farms and local communities, improving health and nutrition, ending hunger, increasing biodiversity, and improving the quality of our soil, water and air.

Underlying the project's dialogue is a shared set of beliefs and values:

- A widespread and diverse family farm system benefits rural communities and society as a whole;
- Extensive hunger and food insecurity in the United States are unacceptable;
- Strong stewardship commitments are key to maintaining farm and food systems that will promote environmental and public health for our children's generation;
- Stimulating new markets and restoring competition in the marketplace are vital to a fair, sustainable food system;
- Rectifying historic patterns of discrimination and making farm and food policies more responsive to an increasingly diverse society are critically important;
- Rural and urban communities can work together to create a healthier food system.

All communities deserve access to healthy food, including support to grow it themselves through grants for community-supported agriculture.

The FFPP believes that all the major sections of the farm bill—commodity, nutrition, rural development, credit, conservation, research, and energy—hold significant opportunities for crafting more cost-effective and higher-impact policies that can increase farm profitability and improve the health of individuals, communities, and the environment.

Coalition participants have identified core priorities and opportunities for innovation in four areas:

1) Advancing a new generation in farming and fostering market-based solutions through a comprehensive new and beginning farmer program; increased outreach and assistance to minority and socially disadvantaged farmers and ranchers; business planning and transition assistance; grants and loans for value-added (including bio-energy) enterprises; and marketing tools and infrastructure to support local and regional market development.

2) Reducing food insecurity and enhancing public health through strengthened federal food assistance and community food security programs; expanded and improved nutrition education, including school nutrition programs to implement wellness policies; support to promote innovative retail markets in urban and rural food deserts; and increased access to healthier foods through government food assistance programs—from food stamps and WIC to school lunch and breakfast programs to innovative farmers' markets and urban agriculture enterprises.

3) Capitalizing on rural community strength to enhance economic viability through rural entrepreneurship and micro-enterprise business development programs; a community entrepreneurial development program for local leadership, wealth, and asset creation; and individual homestead accounts to create savings incentives for families in rural communities.

4) Rewarding stewardship and improving environmental quality through strengthening working lands conservation programs and core land retirement programs; strengthening environmental standards linked to commodity and crop insurance programs; building the technical infrastructure to assist farmers and ranchers; encouraging locally-led collaborations to solve environmental problems; and creating incentives designed to reward innovation and performance.

For more information about the Farm and Food Policy Project, see www.farmandfoodproject.org.

Allen Hance is the Project Coordinator for the Farm and Food Policy Project and a Senior Analyst with the Northeast-Midwest Institute.

Fourth, we need to educate the broader public about the increasingly destructive role played by current farm policy and convince people that the commodity interests can be defeated. Surveys of public opinion—including the German Marshall Fund's annual Perspectives on Trade and Poverty Reduction[2]—show strong support for farmers. So we need to expose the emptiness of arguments that current farm programs function as a rural safety net, or help poor farmers, or preserve the family farm.

Fifth, consumers, the food industry, and advocates for the global poor have a strong common interest in shaping a food policy that responds to the needs of the 99 percent of Americans who are not farmers, and to the millions of people around the world who would eat more—or more nutritiously—if they were given a chance. The food industry must do its part, both as a group of powerful advocates for better public policy and as consumer-driven businesses, to help put good nutrition at the center of our farm policy and food system.

Finally, while too many people still cannot afford to buy healthy food, a lot of the people reading this article can. Until more consumers insist on environmentally-sound production methods, healthier and lower-fat products, and more ways to get locally-grown fruits and vegetables when in season, they will remain too expensive to be shared by all.

Susan Sechler is a former Deputy Assistant Secretary for Economics, Policy Analysis and Budget at the US Department of Agriculture, and is currently a Senior Fellow at the German Marshall Fund of the United States (GMF). Joe Guinan is a Program Officer with GMF's Economic Policy Program.

Appendix

Effects of Economic Growth in Developing Countries on U.S. Agriculture: Preliminary Evidence from a Global Computable General Equilibrium (CGE) Model

Report Prepared for Bread for the World Institute
Marcelle Thomas and Antoine Bouët[1]

Introduction

In an environment of slow advances in the multilateral agricultural trade negotiations, and with the current suspension of the WTO Doha Round negotiations, a continuous issue for U.S. agriculture is building export market opportunities for its products. While the largest share of U.S. trade is with other industrial countries, growth in developing countries may open new agricultural export opportunities. At the same time, growth among large agricultural producers, such as Brazil (a major exporter) or India (largely self-sufficient but with a huge rural population and increasing trade), may create competition for U.S. agriculture.

The argument that income growth abroad among low-income countries benefits U.S. agriculture has a long tradition. This argument has underlain support within large segments of agriculture for more open trade, as well as support for food aid and other foreign assistance programs aimed at generating foreign growth. The increased U.S. agricultural exports to several developed Asian countries, such as Japan, South Korea and Taiwan as they emerged from relative poverty in the 1950s-1960s to high-incomes by the 1980s-1990s, is often cited to demonstrate the positive growth effects. Driven by rising incomes, U.S. agricultural exports have increased to these countries simultaneously with substantial increases in their own domestic agricultural production and despite significant trade barriers.[2]

On the more cautious side, U.S. agricultural producers recognize that they face stiff competition in international markets. Growth in soybean production in Brazil as new technologies were developed is cited to illustrate the dynamic character of "comparative advantage" of countries as international sources of the world food supply. Agricultural interest group concerns over promoting production abroad have led to some restrictions on U.S. foreign aid programs.

This report presents estimates of the effects that increased GDP growth in selected developing countries would have on U.S. agricultural production and trade. The results are obtained from simulations using the MIRAGE (Modeling International Relationships in Applied General Equilibrium) global model.[3] There are substantial increases in export to the affected countries when GDP growth rates from 2007 to 2020 are simulated to increase to 7% per year. This level of GDP growth is within the range achieved by such fast-growth economies as China and recently India, but is a sharp increase from past growth rates among most poor countries. It also exceeds the future GDP growth rates projected by the World Bank (2006) for the countries considered.

With the simulated higher growth, our results suggest there is also a small positive effect at the aggregate level of U.S. production and trade.[4] The aggregate effects are smaller than the effects on exports to the regions assumed to experience higher growth because the countries for which we simulate increased growth represent only about 13 % of the U.S. agricultural trade volume. Gains are larger when we manipulate the model to partially mimic the shift toward lower shares of GDP in agriculture that has occurred historically in fast-growing countries.[5] Gains to U.S. agriculture depend also on the composition of countries where GDP growth occurs. Faster growth among net agricultural importers generates positive gains, while growth in developing countries that are large net agricultural exporters impact negatively on U.S. agriculture.

The model and results are discussed below. We note at the outset the preliminary nature of our analysis to date. This modeling exercise has opened many interesting research questions that merit further exploration before definitive conclusions are drawn.

Model Specification for the Growth Simulations

MIRAGE is a multi-region, multi-sector global computable general equilibrium (CGE) model. For the purposes of evaluating the effects of higher GDP growth rates, two important features are:

- The model has a sequential dynamic set-up from 2002 to 2020. In our analysis, exogenous changes to GDP growth rates are introduced and model simulation outcomes are compared with the results obtained from the "baseline" projections before the changes. Elements of MIRAGE that reflect its dynamic modeling capacity include investment, land supply, share of skilled and unskilled labor, economies of scale, and the emergence or closure of firms in certain sectors.[6] In our analysis, the model adjusts to the higher simulated growth rates by finding corresponding rates of total factor productivity (TFP), an endogenous variable that given other model outcomes is determined so that the economy replicates the assumed growth rate levels.

- CGE models require a "macroeconomic closure" rule. In MIRAGE, the macroeconomic closure assumes that the current account of each country/region is constant and equal to its initial value. To accomplish this, the real exchange rate is allowed to adjust to balance the current-account equation. Consequently, when forces stimulating exports arise, such as increased income growth abroad, they are partly offset by appreciation of the currency to retain current-account balance.

Growth Simulations

For the purpose of this analysis, the MIRAGE model is structured around 10 country/regional groups of various income levels, as shown in Table 1. The model includes 20 productive sectors, of which 11 are in agriculture (agro-food), as shown in Table 2.

In the baseline we generate with the MIRAGE model over the period 2002-2020, the GDP growth rates for the countries and regions are those forecasted by the World Bank (2006).[7] In the main simulation presented, the GDP growth rates in four selected regions are raised to 7% during the period 2007-2020. The selected regions include four developing-country groups that are net importers of agricultural products:

1. the low income African country-group (ldcf),
2. the middle income African country-group (micf)
3. the low income Asian country-group (ldcs)
4. the rest of the world (rotw), which is a mixture of low and middle income countries.

The simulated GDP growth rates represent a sizeable increase from the baseline. The World Bank (2006) forecasts over the period 2007-2020 are for GDP growth rates averaging 3.53% for low income Africa (ldcf); 3.76% for middle income Africa (micf), 3.66% for our rest of world (rotw); and 5.07% for low income Asia (ldcs).

In the baseline, TFP rises equally in all sectors to replicate the projected growth rates. For this reason, the shares of GDP from different sectors remain largely unchanged. In contrast, as noted above, the historical experience of fast-growing economies has been a shift toward relatively less GDP from agriculture and more from industry and services.

To introduce an effect along lines of the shifting shares of GDP from agriculture versus other sectors as rapid growth occurs, our main simulation makes the assumption that TFP growth in agriculture occurs at a declining rate compared to non-agriculture. After the basic results are presented, several other scenarios are briefly evaluated for comparative purposes.

Results

The four selected regions account for 7.7% of world GDP and 17% of world agricultural production in 2005.[8] Aggregate effects of faster GDP growth on U.S. agricultural production, exports and imports are shown in Table 3 as percentage changes from the baseline in 2020, the last year of the simulation period. In aggregate, the volume of U.S. production among the agro-food sectors is higher by 0.32%, while export and import volumes are 2.88% and 1.74% higher, respectively. Growth of total U.S. agricultural production, exports and imports from 2007 to 2020 are projected in the benchmark to be 54.40%, 89.35% and 33.99%, respectively, without the simulated faster growth of GDP among the selected developing-country regions.

In terms of specific agricultural products and subsectors, production of wheat, other cereals and rice register the highest gains (3.06%, 2.43% and 1.92%, respectively). Exports of other cereals increase by 8.05%, followed by rice (7.12%) and wheat (4.59%). Oilseeds, meat and meat products, fruits and vegetables, food products, and other agriculture are other sectors that show gains in export volumes, although this last sector's production declines. Sugar and plant based fibers show lower production and export volumes, while milk production increases slightly but exports decline.

Faster growth among the four regions also increases U.S. agricultural imports. In part this arises due to increased foreign supplies, and in part it reflects the real appreciation caused by expanded demand for U.S. exports and the constraint that the current account remains constant. Agricultural imports increase less in aggregate than exports, but imports increase in all sub-sectors, with the highest gains in plant-based fibers, rice, sugar and other agriculture.

The effects of higher GDP growth on the agricultural exports from the United States are shown by region and product in Table 4. For each product, the first row shows the percentage increase of U.S. exports in 2020 under the fast-growth simulation compared to the baseline. The second row shows the percentage of total U.S. exports of each product going to each region.

For the specified regions, the gains for U.S. exports from increased growth are significant. In 30 of 44 cases, they exceed 20% and are as high as 46.61% (other cereals exports to rotw). Overall, the largest percentage gains are for exports to middle income Africa and the rest of world regions (micf and rotw). The percentage gains are lower for the low-income regions, particularly for Asia (ldcs). Among products, percentage gains in exports to the regions are greatest for cereals (rice, wheat and other cereals), oilseeds, and fruits and vegetables. A few illustrative results are:

- Exports of rice to low income Africa (ldcf) represent 7.94% of U.S. rice exports and rise 26.43%. Rice exports to rotw represent another 16.95% of the total and increase by 27.76%.
- Wheat exports to middle income Africa (micf) represent 18.04% of total U.S. exports and increase by 17.73%. Wheat exports to rotw represent 10.1% of the total and increase by 25.96%.
- Other cereal exports to middle income Africa (micf) represent 11.86% of the total and increase 40.7%.
- Exports of oilseeds and fruits and vegetables increase by more than 19% to both the Africa and Asia low income regions (ldcf and ldcs) and by more than 30% to middle income Africa (micf), but the proportion of total U.S. exports of these products to each of these regions is less than 2%. Exports of oilseeds and fruits and vegetables to rotw represent 3-4% of the total and also increase by more than 30%.
- Exports of the remaining products to the low income Africa and Asia regions (ldcf and ldcs) and

middle income Africa (micf) each represent less than 4% (and often less than 1%) of the total U.S. exports. Percentage increases are often large, but from the very small baseline levels.

Alternative scenarios

To provide some context around these preliminary results about the effect of faster GDP growth among low-income and middle-income net food importing countries, we evaluated several alternative scenarios. The aggregate result for U.S. agricultural production, exports and imports are shown in Table 5 for five cases.

In the first and second alternative cases, simulating less increase in GDP growth rates in developing regions leads to smaller effects. Setting GDP growth rates to a minimum of 4% in ldcf and micf has almost no effects, while there are gains to production, exports and imports of 0.12%, 1.03% and 0.66%, respectively, when the minimum growth rate is 5% in ldcf, micf and rotw. In the third alternative, the growth in agricultural TFP is made equal that of non-agriculture sectors resulting in lower gains to U.S. agricultural production and exports, and increased U.S. agricultural imports, relative to the main simulation. U.S. agricultural production increases by only 0.19%, while U.S. agricultural exports increase by only 1.75%.

In the fourth alternative, we also simulate a 7% GDP growth in the Latin American region (amla) that includes large agricultural producers and exporters, as well as in the four initial regions (an increase from growth rates forecast to average 3.54%). The net results, even with slower TFP growth in agriculture than non-agriculture, are small losses to the U.S. agricultural production and exports, with an increase of agricultural imports.

Finally, we consider a "slower growth" rather than "faster growth" scenario. Specifically, we reduce the growth rate for the middle income Asia region (mics), which includes China, India and other high-growth performers. The GDP growth rates for the middle income Asia region is reduced from World Bank (2006) projected levels averaging 5.68% to just 3%. This change in isolation (no change from baseline growth rates for any other region and with equal TFP growth declines for agriculture and other sectors), results in a decline of U.S. agricultural production by -0.29%, a decline of agricultural exports by -4.12% and a decline of agricultural imports by -2.01%. As with our main simulation results, these alternative effects for a simulated growth slow-down for the recently fast-growing regions of Asia demonstrate that GDP growth abroad can have a beneficial effect on U.S. agriculture.

Conclusion

GDP growth in developing countries may generate gains for U.S. agriculture. We have examined these effects by simulating increased GDP growth in selected developing regions using the MIRAGE model. In our analysis, U.S. agriculture benefits from increased demand generated by higher income when these regions are net agricultural importers. We find that an ambitious growth rate of 7% in the selected developing countries with lower productivity growth in agriculture than in non-agriculture to reflect changes in sectoral composition as growth occurs generates gains to U.S. agricultural production and exports, as well as leading to increased U.S. agricultural imports. Gains also arise from the rapid recent growth among middle income Asian countries. A slow down of this rapid growth is shown to have deleterious effects. U.S. agriculture can also face increased competition from growth abroad among strong agricultural exporters, such as in Latin America.

The results we have presented are suggestive but preliminary. The research has raised interesting questions about growth and its effects and about adopting global CGE models such as MIRAGE to evaluate these effects. These questions merit further investigation before definitive conclusions are drawn about the effects of increased growth rates among low and middle income countries on U.S. agriculture.

References

Bouët, Antoine. 2006. "What can the poor expect from trade liberalization? Opening the "black box" of trade modeling." MTID Discussion Paper No. 93. Washington, DC: IFPRI.

Bouët, Antoine, Simon Mevel and David Orden. 2006. "Two Opportunities to Deliver on the Doha Development Pledge." Research Brief No. 6, IFPRI, July.

Gehlhar, Mark, and Erik Dohlman. 2006. "Macroeconomic and Global Influence on U.S. Agricultural Trade." Selected paper presented at the annual meeting of the American Agricultural Economics Association, Long Beach, California, July 23-26.

Mattson, Jeremy W., and Won W. Koo. 2005. "Characteristics of the Declining U.S. Agricultural Trade Surplus." Agribusiness and Applied Economics Report No. 572. Fargo, N.D.: North Dakota State University.

Thompson. Robert L. 2006. "Agricultural Policy Implications." Discussion of Modernizing America's Food and Farm Policy: Vision for a New Direction, Chicago Council on Global Affairs Report of the Agricultural Task Force. Presented at the Institute for International Economics, Washington D.C., September 27.

World Bank. 2006. World Development Indicators. CD-ROM. Washington, DC.

Table 1. Geographical Structure of the MIRAGE Model for the Growth Simulations

Regions	Model designation	Description
United States	usam	
European Union	euro	EU-25 (as of May 2004) except Poland
Australia/New Zealand	aunz	
Rest of OECD	oecd	Hong Kong, Japan, Korea, Canada, Mexico, Switzerland, rest of EFTA
Latin America	amla	Bolivia, Colombia, Ecuador, Peru, Venezuela, Argentina, Brazil, Chile, Uruguay, rest of South America,[1] Central America, rest of Free Trade Area of the Americas, rest of the Caribbean
Middle income countries-Asia	mics	China, Taiwan, rest of East Asia, Indonesia, Malaysia, Philippines, Singapore, Thailand, Viet Nam, India, Pakistan, Sri Lanka, rest of South Asia
Low income countries-Asia	ldcs	Bangladesh, rest of South-East Asia
Middle income countries-Africa	micf	Morocco, Tunisia, rest of North Africa, Bostwana, South Africa, Mauritius, Zimbabwe, Tanzania, rest of Southern Africa Development Community, Nigeria
Low income countries-Africa	ldcf	Rest of South African Custom Union, Malawi, Mozambique, Zambia, Madagascar, Uganda, rest of Sub-Saharan Africa.
Rest of the World	rotw	Albania, Bulgaria, Croatia, Poland, Romania, Russian Federation, rest of Former Soviet Union, Turkey, Iran, rest of Europe, rest of the Middle East, rest of Oceania, rest of North America

[1] "Rest of...." refers to countries in the specified region not listed separately in any of the country groupings.

Table 2. Sectoral Structure of the MIRAGE Model for the Growth Simulations

Group Sectors	Commodity sectors	Description
Agro-food		
	Rice	Paddy rice and processed rice
	Wheat	Wheat
	Other cereals	Cereal grains nec[1]
	Fruits and vegetables	Vegetables, fruits, nuts
	Oilseeds	Oilseeds
	Sugar	Sugar cane, sugar beets, sugar
	Plant based fibers	Plant based fibers
	Other agricultural products	Crops nec, wool, silk-worm cocoons
	Meat and meat products	Cattle, sheep, goats, horses, animal products nec, meat (cattle, sheep, goats, horses), meat products nec, vegetable oils and fats
	Milk	Raw milk, dairy products
	Food products	Food products nec, beverage and tobacco products
Industry		
	Forestry	Forestry
	Fish	Fish
	Other primary	Coal, oil, gas, mineral nec
	Textile and apparel	Textiles, wearing apparel, leather products
	Other manufactures	Wood products, paper products, publishing, electronic equipment, machinery and equipment nec, manufactures nec, electricity, gas manufacture, distribution
	Petroleum chemicals	Petroleum, coal products, chemicals, rubber, plastic products, mineral products nec, ferrous metals, metals nec, metal products
	Motor vehicles and equipment	Motor vehicles and parts, transport equipment nec
Services		
	Other services	Water, construction, communication, financial services nec
	Transport and trade	Trade, transport nec, sea transport, air transport

[1] "nec" indicates not elsewhere classified.

Table 3. Effects on U.S. Agricultural Production and Trade from Higher Growth Rates among Selected Regions (percent change from baseline)

	Production	Export (in percent)	Import
Agriculture	0.32	2.88	1.74
Rice	1.92	7.12	5.29
Wheat	3.06	4.59	2.29
Other cereals	2.43	8.05	0.80
Fruits and vegetables	0.30	1.35	1.10
Oilseeds	0.38	0.51	2.47
Sugar	-0.05	-1.47	3.99
Plant based fibers	-0.46	-0.14	8.30
Other agriculture	-0.13	1.54	4.00
Meat and meat products	0.30	2.51	1.47
Milk	0.13	-0.26	0.55
Food products	0.27	3.45	1.43

Source: MIRAGE simulation results.

Table 4. Effects on U.S. Agricultural Export Volume to Selected Regions with Higher Growth Rates
(percent change from baseline and percentage of total U.S. exports)

	Low income Africa (ldcf)	Middle income Africa (micf)	Importers Low income Asia (ldcs)	Rest of the World (rotw)	World
			(in percent)[1]		
U.S. agriculture exports					
Rice	26.43	35.43	3.17	27.76	
	7.94	*2.55*	*0.75*	*16.95*	*100*
Wheat	32.08	17.73	15.73	25.96	
	2.19	*18.04*	*0.70*	*10.10*	*100*
Other cereals	31.27	40.70	24.00	46.61	
	0.45	*11.86*	*0.09*	*6.74*	*100*
Fruits and vegetables	25.65	33.45	19.27	38.60	
	0.33	*0.61*	*0.08*	*3.57*	*100*
Oilseeds	20.92	33.62	22.43	38.34	
	0.05	*1.14*	*0.00*	*4.03*	*100*
Sugar	14.01	23.94	13.74	26.74	
	0.34	*0.76*	*0.02*	*2.15*	*100*
Plant based fibers	20.72	21.02	12.18	28.18	
	0.00	*0.13*	*3.44*	*9.32*	*100*
Other agriculture	5.62	20.86	16.41	32.57	
	0.55	*1.14*	*0.17*	*7.10*	*100*
Meat and meat products	9.67	19.34	7.69	25.43	
	0.53	*1.34*	*0.09*	*11.37*	*100*
Milk	24.61	24.28	9.68	21.22	
	0.42	*1.30*	*0.15*	*5.94*	*100*
Food products	22.65	31.21	13.89	35.24	
	0.69	*1.65*	*0.10*	*8.82*	*100*

[1] For each commodity top line is increase in exports to the region; second line is region's share of total U.S. exports.

Source: MIRAGE simulation results.

Table 5. Effects on U.S. Agricultural Production and Trade from Alternative Scenarios (percent change from baseline)

	Production	Export	Import
Alternative scenarios		(in percent)	
A1: 4% minimum growth	0.00	0.00	0.08
A2: 5% minimum growth	0.12	1.03	0.66
A3: The main simulation with TFP growth for agriculture equal to non-agriculture	0.19	1.75	2.17
A4: 7% growth in amla and four initial regions	-0.29	-0.10	8.93
A5: Reduced growth rate for mics to 3%	-0.29	-4.12	-2.01

Source: MIRAGE simulations.

Brief description of the MIRAGE model

MIRAGE is a multi-region, multi-sector CGE model that incorporates a sequential dynamic set-up. There is full employment of labor and other resources within each country/region and these factor endowments can not be moved internationally. Either perfect or imperfect competition can be assumed for industrial sectors. Goods produced by different countries/regions are imperfect substitutes. As in other CGE models, a set of assumed "trade elasticities" influence the extent to which consumer choices among domestic and foreign goods are affected by changes in their relative prices. In MIRAGE, substitutability between intermediate goods used in the production process is also modeled, and again depends on relative prices. The only factor of production for which supply is constant, is natural resources. Labor grows with projected population growth, the capital stock can increase with investment, and land can be brought into or removed from production in response to higher or lower returns. Skilled labor is the only factor perfectly mobile within each country/region. Capital is sector-specific and unskilled labor has somewhat limited mobility between agriculture and non-agriculture.

The macroeconomic closure assumes that the current account is constant and equal to its initial value leaving the real exchange rate to adjust to balance the current-account equation.

Margaret W. Nea

Endnotes

Introduction

[1] Becker, G. (7 June 2002). *The 2002 Farm Law At A Glance,* CRS Report for Congress RS21233. Washington, D.C.: Congressional Research Service, 5.

[2] Thomisee, J. (Fall 2005). "The Cotton Debate: A Global Industry Argues Over Government Subsidies," *Worldview* 18(3):21.

[3] Bruckner, T. (2006). *Conservation and the 2007 Farm Bill,* Policy Paper. Lyons, NE: Center for Rural Affairs, 3.

[4] Oxfam International (18 June 2004). "WTO Cotton Ruling Could Reform US Farm Subsidies, Global Trade," Press Release. Oxford: Oxfam International.

[5] Bread for the World Institute (July 2005). "The Cotton Case," *Trade Matters: A Bread for the World Institute Newsletter.* Washington, D.C: BFWI.

[6] Dietz, W. (1998). "Health Consequences of Obesity in Youth: Childhood Predictors of Adult Disease," *Pediatrics* 101:518-525

[7] Yee S., et al. (2005). "The Nutrition and Physical Activity Program to Prevent Obesity and Other Chronic Diseases: Monitoring Progress in Funded States," *Preventing Chronic Disease* 3(1).

[8] Center for Disease Control and Prevention National Center for Health Statistics. *Prevalence of Overweight Among Children and Adolescents: 1999-2002.* Retrieved October 9, 2006, http://www.cdc.gov/nchs/products/pubs/pubd/hestats/overwght99.htm

Chapter 1

[1] Becker, G., & J. Womach (May 2002). *Farm Counter-Cyclical Assistance,* CRS Report for Congress. Washington, D.C.: CRS, 3.

[2] United States Department of Agriculture Economic Research Service (2006). *Farm Family Income Background Paper.* Washington, D.C.: USDA ERS.

[3] Offutt, S., & C. Gunderson (September 2005). "Farm Poverty Lowest in US History," *Amber Waves* 3(4).

[4] Babcock, B. (Spring 2005). "Judging the Performance of the 2002 Farm Bill," *Iowa Ag Review* 11(2).

[5] Pasour & Rucker (2005). *Plowshares and Pork Barrels: The Political Economy of Agriculture.* USA: Independent Institute, 88.

[6] Ibid., 92.

[7] *The Agricultural Adjustment Act of 1933* (12 May 1933). Public Law 73-10, 73rd Congress, 1st Session.

[8] Dimitri, C., & A. Effland (June 2005). "Milestones in US Farming and Farm Policy," *Amber Waves* 3(3).

[9] Jolliffe, D. (July 2004). "Rural Poverty at a Glance," *Rural Development Research Report* 100.

[10] Drabenstott, M. (March 2005). "Do Farm Payments Promote Rural Economic Growth?" *The Main Street Economist.*

[11] McGranahan D., & P. Sullivan (February 2005). "Farm Programs, Natural Amenities and Rural Development," *Amber Waves* 3(1).

[12] Kind, R. "Agriculture, the Backbone of Wisconsin." Retrieved September 8, 2006, http://www.house.gov/kind/issues_ag.shtml.

[13] Becker, G., & J. Womach (May 2002). *Farm Counter-Cyclical Assistance,* CRS Report for Congress. Washington, D.C.: CRS, 3.

[14] O'Donoghue, E., & R. Hoppe (March 2005). "Large and Small Farms: Trends and Characteristics," in *Structural and Financial Characteristics of US Farms: 2004 Family Farm Report.* Banker, D. & J. MacDonald, eds. Washington, D.C.: USDA ERS, 23.

[15] Ryan J., Barnard, C., & R. Collender (June-July 2001). "Government Payments to Farmers Contribute to Rising Land Values," *Agricultural Outlook.*

[16] Hoppe, R., & P. Korbe (March 2005). "Large and Small Farms: Trends and Characteristics," in *Structural and Financial Characteristics of US Farms: 2004 Family Farm Report.* Banker, D. & J. MacDonald, eds. Washington, D.C.: USDA ERS, 7.

[17] O'Donoghue, E., & R. Hoppe (March 2005). "Farm Household Income, Farm Structure, and Off-Farm Work," in *Structural and Financial Characteristics of US Farms: 2004 Family Farm Report.* Banker, D. and J. MacDonald, eds. Washington, D.C.: USDA ERS, 23.

[18] Environmental Working Group (2006). *Farm Subsidy Database.* Retrieved September 8, 2006, www.ewg.org/farm.

[19] Environmental Working Group (2006). "After Hong Kong, Redraw America's Farm Subsidy Map," *Farm Subsidy Database.* Retrieved September 12, 2006, www.ewg.org:16080/farm/redraw.

[20] Environmental Working Group (2006). "What's the Plan? US Farm Subsides, 1995 Through 2003," *Farm Subsidy Database.* Retrieved August 29, 2006, www.ewg.org/farm/whatstheplan.php.

[21] MacDonald, et al. (March 2006). *Growing Farm Size and the Distribution of Farm Payments,* USDA ERS Economic Brief 6. Washington, D.C.: USDA ERS 2.

[22] National Beef Association (16 August 2004). Press Release. Hexham, UK: NBA.

[23] Babcock, B. (Spring 2006). "Cheap Food and Farm Subsides: Policy Impacts of a Mystical Connection," *Iowa Ag Review* 12(2).

[24] Thaemert, J. (23 March 2006). "Against the Alternatives, Food Policy is a Bargain," *Wall Street Journal,* A17.

25 Jerado, A. (February 2004). "The U.S. Ag Trade Balance…More Than Just a Number," *Amber Waves* 2(1):41.

26 Leopold Center for Sustainable Agriculture (14 October 2004). "New Leopold Center Report Explores Iowa's Geography of Taste," Press Release. Ames, IA: LCSA.

27 Gale, F. (December 2002). *Rural America* 173. Washington, D.C.: USDA ERS.

28 Orden, D. (24 February 2005). *Key Issues for the Next Farm Bill: Is a Farm Program Buyout Possible?* Washington, D.C.: USDA Agriculture Outlook Forum.

29 Environmental Working Group (2006). *Dead in the Water: Reforming Wasteful Farm Subsidies Can Restore Gulf Fisheries.* Retrieved August 30, 2006, http://www.ewg.org/reports/deadzone/execsumm.php.

30 American Farmland Trust (2006). *Rewarding Farmers and Ranchers for Environmental Stewardship: Green Payments.* Washington, D.C.: AFT.

31 Ibid.

32 Dismukes, R., & R. Durst (June 2006). "Whole-Farm Approaches to a Safety Net," *Economic Information Bulletin* 15. Washington, D.C.: USDA ERS, 4.

Chapter 2

1 Combs-Lay, C. (2006). "We Are a Community and These Are Our Neighbors," *Hunger Report 2006: Frontline Issues in Nutrition Assistance*. Washington, D.C.: BFWI, 5.

2 Carsey Institute (Fall 2005). *Rural America Depends on the Food Stamp Program to Make Ends Meet*, Policy Brief 1. Durham, NH: University of New Hampshire, 1.

3 Nord, M., Andrews, M., & S. Carlson (2006). *Household Food Security in the United States 2005*, Economic Research Report 11. Washington, D.C.: USDA Economic Research Service, 11.

4 Johnson, K. (2006). *Demographic Trends in Rural and Small Town America*. Durham, NH: University of New Hampshire, 29.

5 Nord, M., Andrews, M., & S. Carlson (2004). *Household Food Security in the United States 2004*, Economic Research Report 11. Washington, D.C.: USDA Economic Research Service, 17.

6 United States Department of Agriculture Economic Research Service (January 2005). *Rural Transportation at a Glance*, Agricultural Information Bulletin 795. Washington, D.C.: USDA ERS.

7 Ibid.

8 United States Department of Agriculture Economic Research Service (July 2004). *Rural Poverty at a Glance*, Rural Development Research Report 100. Washington, D.C.: USDA ERS, 1.

9 Matthews, L., & W. Woodwell, Jr. (November 2005). *A Portrait of Rural America – Challenges and Opportunities: Research Brief on America's Cities 2005*. Washington, D.C.: National League of Cities, 3.

10 Cowan, T. (26 August 2004). *An Overview of USDA Rural Development Programs*, CRS Report for Congress. Washington, D.C.: CRS, 6.

11 Ibid., 7.

12 Rural Poverty Research Center (2006). *What Are Persistent Poverty Counties?* Retrieved March 13, 2006, http://www.rprconline.org/.

13 United States Census Bureau (2006). *State and County Quick Facts*. Retrieved March 13, 2006, http://quickfacts.census.gov/qfd/states/01/01105.html.

14 United States Department of Agriculture Economic Research Service (21 August 2003). *Measuring Rurality: What is Rural?* Retrieved September 20, 2006, http://www.ers.usda.gov/Briefing/Rurality/WhatisRural/.

15 United States Department of Agriculture Economic Research Service (12 September 2006). *Rural Population and Migration*. Retrieved September 20, 2006, http://www.ers.usda.gov/Briefing/Population/.

16 Clinton, J., et. al. (2005). *The New Architecture of Rural Prosperity: The 2005 Report on the Future of the South*. Research Triangle Park, NC: Southern Growth Policies Board, 3.

17 Carsey Institute (Fall 2005). *Rural America Depends on the Food Stamp Program to Make Ends Meet*, Policy Brief 1. Durham, NH: University of New Hampshire, 4.

18 Dimitri, C., Effland, A., & N. Conklin (June 2005). The 20th Century Transformation of the U.S. Agriculture and Farm Policy, Economic Information Bulletin 3. Washington, D.C.: USDA ERS, 2.

19 Ibid.

20 Ibid.

21 Ibid.

22 Whitener, L., & D. McGranham (February 2003). "Rural America: Opportunities and Challenges," *Amber Waves* 1(1).

23 Environmental Working Group (2006). *Farm Subsidy Database*. Retrieved September 21, 2006, http://www.ewg.org/farm/progdetail.php?fips=00000&progcode=totalfarm&page=conc.

24 Dimitri, C., Effland, A., & N. Conklin (June 2005). *The 20th Century Transformation of the U.S. Agriculture and Farm Policy*, Economic Information Bulletin 3. Washington, D.C.: USDA ERS.

25 Dorr, T. (13 September 2005). Speech before the National Rural Economic Developers in Washington, DC.

26 Gibbs, R, Kusmin, L., & J. Cromartie (November 2004). "Low-Skill Jobs: A Shrinking Share of the Rural Economy," *Amber Waves* 2(5):40.

27 Hamrick, K., ed. (September 2005). *Rural America at a Glance*, Economic Information Bulletin 4. Washington, D.C.: USDA ERS.

28 Ibid.

29 Florida Fish and Wildlife Conservation Commission (2004). *Economics of Fish and Wildlife Recreation*. Tallahassee, FL: FFWCC.

30 Washington Department of Fish and Wildlife (2000). *Wildlife Watching: Untapped Economic Boost for Rural Communities*. Retrieved September 21, 2006, http://wdfw.wa.gov/viewing/watchwld/watchwld.htm.

31 Hassebrook, C. (Winter 2005). "A Better Future for Rural Communities," Catholic Rural Life. Des Moines, IA: The National Catholic Rural Life Conference.

32 Drabenstott, M. (March 2005). "Do Farm Payments Promote Rural Economic Growth?" *The Main Street Economist*.

33 McGranahan, D., & P. Sullivan (February 2005). "Farm Programs, Natural Amenities, and Rural Development," *Amber Waves* 3(1):3.

34 Bread for the World Institute (2005). *Hunger Report 2005: Strengthening Rural Communities*. Washington, D.C.: BFWI, 46.

35 Environmental Working Group (2006). *Farm Subsidy Database*. Retrieved September 21, 2006, http://www.ewg.org:16080/farm/top_recips.php?fips=00000&progcode=totalfarm.

36 Barton, P. (2 January 2006). "Experts See the Decline of Rural U.S. Quickening," *Arkansas Democrat Gazette*.

37 Henderson, J. (August 2002). "Are High-Growth Entrepreneurs Building the Rural Economy?" *The Main Street Economist*.

38 *The Agriculture, Conservation and Rural Enhancement Act of 2001* (November 2001). S. 1731, 107th Congress.

39 Bailey, J. (2006). *Rural Development and the 2007 Farm Bill: A Center for Rural Affairs Policy White Paper*. Lyons, NE: CRA.

40 Appalachian Regional Commission (2006). *About ARC: History*. Retrieved September 22, 2006, http://www.arc.gov/index.do?nodeId=7.

41 Ibid.

42 Breed, A. (16 June 2002). "Appalachia Boundaries Blur into Delta," Associated Press.

43 Rosmann, M. (2004). "Agricultural Mental Health," *ASH-NET* 2001.

44 Ibid.

45 Ibid, 24.

46 Lyson, T. (January 2005). "The Importance of Schools to Rural Community Vitality," in *The Role of Education: Promoting the Economic and Social Vitality of Rural America*. Beaulieu, L., & R. Givvs, eds. Washington, D.C.: USDA ERS, 23.

47 United States Department of Agriculture (2006). *DLT Grant Program Features*. Retrieved September 22, 2006, http://www.usda.gov/rus/telecom/dlt/dlthighlights.htm.

48 United States Department of Agriculture (18 October 2005). *Transcript of Georgia Farm Bill Forum with Agriculture Secretary Mike Johanns and Moderator Randall Weisman of Southeast Ag Net*. Washington, D.C.: USDA.

49 Bruckner, T. (2006). *Conservation and the 2007 Farm Bill: A Center for Rural Affairs Policy White Paper*. Lyons, NE: CRA, 3.

50 Looker, D. (2006). "Q&A: Other Sources of Loans for Beginning Farmers," *Agriculture Online*.

51 Bailey, J., & K. Preston (August 2005). *Building Wealth in Rural Communities and Individual Homestead Accounts*. Lyons, NE: CRA.

52 American Farmland Trust (8 May 2006). *Agenda 2007: A New Framework and Direction for U.S. Farm Policy*. Washington, D.C.: AFT, 21.

Chapter 3

1 Whitten, C. (February 2004). *Processed Agricultural Exports Led the Gains in U.S. Agricultural Exports Between 1976 and 2002*, Outlook Report FAU8501. Washington, D.C.: USDA, 8.

2 Thompson, R. (September 2005). *The US Farm Bill and the Doha Negotiations: On Parallel Tracks or a Collision Course?* IPC Issue Brief. Washington, D.C.: IPC.

3 Bread for the World Institute (2003). *Hunger Report 2003: Agriculture in the Global Economy*. Washington, D.C.: BFWI, 20.

4 Diao, X., Diaz-Bonilla, E., & S. Robinson (2003). *How Much Does it Hurt? The Impact of Agricultural Trade Policies on Developing Countries*, IFPRI Issue Brief. Washington, D.C.: IFPRI.

5 Organization of Economic Cooperation and Development (2005). *Agricultural Policies in OECD Countries*. Paris: OECD, 36.

6 Bread for the World Institute calculation based on World Bank, *World Development Indicators* (2005).

7 Environmental Working Group (2006). *Farm Subsidy Database*. Retrieved October 11, 2006, http://ewg.org/farm/.

8 Baffes, J. (2003). *Cotton in Developing Countries: A Case Study in Policy Coherence*. Washington, DC: World Bank Group.

9 Coulibaly, S. (2006). *Global Trade: US Farm Policies Hurt Many*, Press Release. Boston: Oxfam America.

10 Institute for Agriculture and Trade Policy (2005). *WTO Agreement on Agriculture: A Decade of Dumping*. Minneapolis, MN: IATP, 2.

11 Babcock, B. (Winter 2006). "FAPRI Analyzes the U.S. Proposal to the WTO," *Iowa Ag. Review* 12(1):6-8.

12 International Trade Administration (2006). *Employment Changes in U.S. Manufacturing: The Impact of Sugar Prices*. Washington, D.C.: US DOC, 2.

13 Food and Agriculture Organization of the United Nations (2003). *Commodity Market Review 2003-2004*. Rome: FAO, 115 Tariff levels as reported in 1999 for the United States and 2000 for the European Union.

14 Anderson, K., de Gorter, H., & W. Martin (2006). "Market Access Barriers in Agriculture and Options for Reform," in *Trade, Doha, and Development: A Window into the Issues*. Newfarmer, R., ed. Washington, DC: World Bank, 88.

15 Mugambwa, P. Interview with Bread for the World Institute on June 6, 2006.

16 World Trade Organization (20 November 2001). WTO Minsterial Declaration. Retrieved October 11, 2006, http://www.wto.org/english/thewto_e/minist_e/min01_e/mindecl_e.htm.

17 Polaski, S. (2006). *Winners and Losers: Impact of the Doha Round on Developing Countries*. DC: Carnegie Endowment for International Peace.

18 Ibid, 33.

19 Ibid, 35.

20 Ibid, 38.

21 Bouet, A., Mervel, S., & D. Orden (2006). *More or Less Ambition? Modeling the Development Impact of US-EU Agricultural Proposals in the Doha Round*, Policy Brief. Washington, D.C.: IFPRI.

22 Ibid.

23 Ibid, 3.

24 Bread for the World Institute (July 2005). "The Cotton Case," *Trade Matters: A Bread for the World Institute Newsletter*. Washington, D.C.: BFWI.

25 In the case brought by Brazil before the WTO, the Dispute Settlement Body (DSB) found that several programs administered by the U.S. Department of Agriculture were not compliant with WTO rules. Specifically, the DSB found that the Step 2 program, the export credit guarantee program and the Supplier Credit Guarantee were subsidies. Additionally, the dispute settlement panel found that subsidies provided to cotton producers under Title I of the farm bill cause serious economic prejudice to the interests of Brazil. To date, the U.S. has eliminated the Step 2 program. Additionally, the USDA has offered proposals to change or eliminate offending export credit programs. To date, those proposals have not been enacted into law. No changes have been made to subsidies provided to cotton producers under title I of the farm bill. More information about the U.S. response to the WTO cotton decision can be found at http://www.nationalaglawcenter.org/assets/crs/RS22187.pdf#search=%22cotton%20WTO%20USDA%22.

26 Thompson, R. (August 2006). "The Doha Round Suspension: The Role of US Politics," *Bridges* 10 (5): 17.

27 World Trade Organization (2006). *Net Food-Importing Developing Countries*. Retrieved October 11, 2006, http://www.wto.org/English/tratop_e/agric_e/ag_intro06_netfood_e.htm.

28 Stiglitz, J., & A. Charlton (March 2006). *Aid for Trade: A Report for the Commonwealth Secretariat*. Paris: OFCE, 14.

29 World Trade Organisation (22 December 2005). Doha Work Programme Ministerial Declaration adopted on December 18, 2005, Hong Kong.

30 Bembatoum-Young, S. Interview with Bread for the World Institute on June 6, 2006.

31 Federal Democratic Government of Ethiopia, Ministry of Finance and Economic Development (July 2002). *Ethiopia: Sustainable Development and Poverty Reduction Program*. Addis Ababa, Ethiopia.

32 International Lawyers and Economists Against Poverty (April 2006). *An African Perspective on Aid for Trade*. Douala, Cameroon: ILEAP, 21.

33 International Lawyers and Economists Against Poverty (April 2006). *An African Perspective on Aid for Trade*. Douala, Cameroon: ILEAP, 6.

34 Bread for the World Institute (2003). *Hunger Report 2003: Agriculture in the Global Economy*. Washington, D.C.: BFWI, 65.

35 Stiglitz, J., & A. Charlton (March 2006). *Aid for Trade: A Report for the Commonwealth Secretariat*. Paris: OFCE, 19.

36 Minot, N., & Ngigi, M. (2004). *Are Horticultural Exports a Replicable Success Story? Evidence from Kenya and Côite d'Ivoire*. Washington, DC: IFPRI, 38.

37 Ibid., 42.

38 Diao, X, et al. (2006). *The Role of Agriculture in Development: Implications for Sub-Saharan Africa*. Washington, D.C.: IFPRI, 39.

39 Ibid., 10.

40 The World Bank (2006). *Repositioning Nutrition as Central Development: A Strategy for Large-Scale Action*. Washington, D.C.: The World Bank, 24.

41 Diao, X, et al. (2006). *The Role of Agriculture in Development: Implications for sub-Saharan Africa*. Washington, D.C.: IFPRI, 7.

Chapter 4

1 Mills, N. (Spring 2006). "Hurricane Katrina and Robert Kennedy," *Dissent*. New York: Foundation for the Study of Independent Social Ideas.

2 Norris, M. (22 June 2006). *Still Hungry in America: A Return to Mississippi*. National Public Radio. Audio Recording. Retrieved October 4, 2006, http://www.

npr.org/templates/story/story. php?storyId=5495641.

3   Organisation for Economic Co-operation and Development (2006). *OECD Health Data 2006: Statistics and Indicators for 30 Countries.* Paris, France: OECD.

4   Haskins, R., Paxson, C. & E. Donahue (Spring 2006). "Fighting Obesity in the Public Schools," *The Future of Children,* Policy Brief. Washington, D.C.: Brookings Institute, 1.

5   Townsend, M. (January 2006). "Obesity in Low-Income Communities: Prevalence, Effects, a Place to Begin," *Journal of the American Dietetic Association* 106(1). Chicago: American Dietetic Association, 34.

6   Center for Disease Control and Prevention National Center for Health Statistics (2006). *Prevalence of Overweight and Obesity Among Adults: United States, 2003-2004.* Retrieved October 5, 2006, http:// www.cdc.gov/nchs/products/pubs/ pubd/hestats/obese03_04/over-wght_adult_03.htm#Table%201.

7   Center for Disease Control and Prevention National Center for Health Statistics (2006). *Prevalence of Overweight Among Children and Adolescents: 1999-2002.* Retrieved October 5, 2006, http://www.cdc. gov/nchs/products/pubs/pubd/ hestats/overwght99.htm.

8   Institute of Medicine Food and Nutrition Board, Committee on Progress in Preventing Childhood Obesity (16 September 2006). "Progress Is Slow in Reversing Childhood Obesity Trend," Press Release. Washington, D.C.: The National Academics.

9   Center for Disease Control and Prevention (2004). *Data and Trends: National Diabetes Surveillance System.* Retrieved October 5, 2006, http://www.cdc.gov/diabetes/statis-tics/prev/national/tnumage.htm.

10 Bhattacharya, J., et al. (2004). "Poverty, Food Insecurity, and Nutritional Outcomes in Children and Adults," *Journal of Health Economics* 23:856-862.

11 Javitt, J., & Y. Chiang (1995). Economic Impact of Diabetes," *Diabetes in America, 2nd Edition.* Bethesda, MD: National Institutes of Health, 601.

12 Finklestein, A., Fiebelkorn, I., & G. Wang (14 May 2003). "National Medical Spending Attributable to Overweight and Obesity: How Much, and Who's Paying?" *Health Affairs* W3:219-226.

13 Bowman, S.A., Lino, M., Gerrior, & S.A., Basiotis, (1998). *The Healthy Eating Index: 1994-96.* Washington, D.C.: USDA Center for Nutrition Policy and Promotion.

14 Townsend, M.S. (2006). "Obesity in Low-Income Communities: Prevalence, Effects, a Place to Begin," *Journal of the American Dietetic Association* 106 (1):34-37.

15 Sen, A. (1981). *Poverty and Famines: An Essay on Entitlement and Deprivation.* USA: Oxford University Press.

16 Nord, M., Andrews, M., & S. Carlson (2006). *Household Food Security in the United States, 2005,* Economic Research Report 11. Washington, D.C.: USDA ERS, 5.

17 World Hunger Year (2006). *Rural Poverty.* Retrieved October 5, 2006, http://www.worldhun-geryear.org/fslc/faqs/ria_074. asp?section=14&click=9.

18 Townsend, M.S., et al (2001). "Food Insecurity is Positively Related to Overweight in Women," *Journal of Nutrition* 131:1738-1745.

19 Fields, S. (October 2004). "The Fat of the Land: Do Agricultural Subsidies Foster Poor Health?" *Environmental Health Perspectives* 112(14):A820-3.

20 Drewnowski, A. (2004). "Fat and Sugar: An Economic Analysis," *Journal of Nutrition*, Supplement 838-840.

21 Data obtained from USDA Economic Research Service (January 2003). *Weighing in on Obesity – Food Review* 25(3). Converted to real dollars.

22 Kaufman, P. (1997). "Do the Poor Pay More for Food?" *Agricultural Economics Report* 759.

23 Information Please Database (2006). *Federal Minimum Wage Rates, 1955 – 2006.* Retrieved October 5, 2006, http://www.info-please.com/ipa/A0774473.html.

24 Valentine, V. (2006). "Q&A: The Causes Behind Hunger in America," NPR Series *Hunger in America.* Retrieved October 5, 2006, http:// www.npr.org/templates/story/story. php?storyId=5021812.

25 Kaufman, P. (1999). "Rural Poor Have Less Access to Supermarkets, Large Grocery Stores," *Rural Development Perspectives* 13(3):19-26.

26 Schlosser, E. (2001). *Fast Food Nation: The Dark Side of the All-American Meal.* Boston: Houghton.

27 Stewart, H. (September 2004). "Let's All Eat Out: Full Service or Fast Food?" *Amber Waves* 2(4).

28 Haskins, R. (20 August 2006). "Welfare Reform, 10 Years Later." *The Baltimore Sun.*

29 Bray, G., Nielsen, S., & B. Popkin (April 2004). "Consumption of High-Fructose Corn Syrup in Beverages May Play a Role in the Epidemic of Obesity," *American Journal of Clinical Nutrition* 79(4).

30 Putnam, J., Allshouse, J., & L. Kantor (2002). "US Per Capita Food Supply Trends: More Calories, Refined Carbohydrates, and Fats," *FoodReview* 25(3):2-15.

31 Ploeg, M., Mancino, L., & B. Lin (February 2006). "Food Stamps and Obesity: Ironic Twist or Complex Puzzle?" *Amber Waves* (4)1:32-37.

32 Dietz, W. (1998). "Health Consequences of Obesity in Youth: Childhood Predictors of Adult Disease," *Pediatrics* 101:518-525.

33 Olshansky, et. al. (17 March 2005) "A Potential Decline in Life Expectancy in the United States in the 21st Century," *New England Journal of Medicine* 352(11):1138-45.

34 Center for Science in the Public Interest (May 2004). *Dispensing Junk: How School Vending Undermines Efforts to Feed Children Well.* Washington, D.C.: CSPI, 3-4.

35 Busby, J., Guthrie, J., & L. Kantor (May 2005). *Evaluation of the USDA Fruit and Vegetable Pilot Porgram.* Report to Congress. Washington, D.C.: USDA Economic Research Service, vi.

36 Waters, A. (2006). *A Delicious Revolution.* Center for Ecoliteracy. Retrieved October 5, 2006, http://www.ecoliteracy.org/publications/rsl/alice-waters.html.

37 Poppendieck, J. (1986). *Breadlines Knee-Deep in Wheat: Food Assistance in the Great Depression.* New Brunswick: Rutgers University Press, 122.

38 Becker, G. (26 August 2005). *Farm and Food Support Under USDA's Section 32 Program*, CRS Report RS20235. Washington, D.C: CRS, 2.

39 United States Department of Agriculture Agricultural Marketing Service (2006). *Farmers Market Facts.* Retrieved October 6, 2006, http://www.ams.usda.gov/farmers-markets/facts.htm.

40 United States Department of Agriculture Agricultural Marketing Service (14 March 2006). *USDA to Offer New Farmers Market Promotion Grants.* Retrieved October 6, 2006, http://www.usda.gov/wps/portal/!ut/p/_s.7_0_A/7_0_1OB?contentidonly=true&contentid=2006/03/0087.xml.

41 United States Department of Agriculture Food and Nutrition Service (June 2006). *An Analysis of Food Stamp Program Redemption Patterns.* Washington, D.C.: USDA FNS. Retrieved October 6, 2006, http://www.fns.usda.gov/oane/MENU/Published/FSP/FILES/ProgramOperations/EBTTransaction.pdf.

42 Jetter, K., & D. Cassady (2005). *The Availability and Cost of Healthier Food Items,* AIC Issues Brief 29. Davis, CA: University of California Agricultural Issues Center.

43 Schoonover, H., & M. Muller (2006). *Food Without Thought: How U.S. Farm Policy Contributes to Obesity.* Minneapolis, MN: IATP, 4.

44 Miner, J. (2006). "Market Incentives Could Bring U.S. Agriculture and Nutrition Policies into Accord," *California Agriculture* 60(1).

45 Masser, K. (1 May 2006). *Testimony of Keith Masser before the House Agriculture Committee, United Fresh Fruits and Vegetable Association: Specialty Crop Industry Priorities for the 2007 Farm Bill*,109th Congress.

46 Bertini, C., Schumacher, Jr., A., & R. Thompson (2006). *Modernizing America's Food and Farm Policy: Vision for a New Direction.* Chicago: The Chicago Council on Global Affairs, 46.

Chapter 5

1 Kotz, N. (1979). *Hunger in America: The Federal Response.* New York: Field Foundation.

2 Monke, J. (27 January 2006). *Agriculture and Related Agencies: FY 2006 Appropriations*, CRS Report for Congress. Washington, D.C.: CRS.

3 Rank, M., & T. Hirschl (2003). *Estimating the Probabilities and Patterns of Food Stamp Use Across the Life Course*, Center for Poverty Research Working Paper 327. Chicago: Joint Center for Poverty Research, Northwestern University/University of Chicago.

4 American Association of Retired Persons (September 2005). *Georgia: A State Fact Sheet for Grandparents and Other Relatives Raising Children.* Washington, D.C.: AARP.

5 Witt, H. (13 November 2005). "Still Adrift After the Storm," *Chicago Tribune.*

6 Cauthen, N., & H. Lu (August 2003). *Living at the Edge*, Research Brief 1. New York: National Center for Children in Poverty.

7 United States Government Accountability Office (May 2005). *Food Stamp Program: States Have Made Progress Reducing Payment Errors, and Further Challenges Remain.* Washington, D.C.: GAO, 3.

8 McCarrick, Cardinal (11 February 2003). Letter to U.S. House of Representatives, reprinted on U.S. Conference of Catholic Bishops website. Retrieved August 4, 2006, http://www.usccb.org/sdwp/national/hr4ltr.htm.

9 Fremstad, S., & S. Parrott (2004). *'Superwaiver' Provision in House TANF Reauthorization Bill Could Significantly Weaken Public Housing, Food Stamps, and Other Low-Income Programs.* Washington, D.C.: CBPP.

10 Rosenbaum, D. (12 July 2006). *The Food Stamp Program is Growing to Meet Need,* CBPP Report.. Washington, D.C.: CBPP, 5.

11 Vollinger, E., & J. Weill (29 December 2005). Letter to Secretary of USDA Mike Johanns. Retrieved August 4, 2006, http://www.frac.org/news/usda_letter05.html.

12 Food Research and action Center, et al. (20 September 2005). Letter to Congress. Retrieved August 4, 2006, http://www.frac.org/html/news/09_20_05.html

13 Kellogg, S. (10 September 2005). "Hurricane May Help Advocates Protect Medicaid, Food Stamps From Planned Cuts," Press Release.

Washington, D.C.: Washington Bureau.

14 Ibid.

15 Available from Current Population Surveys 2002-2005, published by the U.S. Census Bureau.

16 The value of a house a person owns and lives in is not counted.

17 Chen, H., & R. Lerman (2005). *Do Asset Limits in Social Programs Affect the Accumulation of Wealth?* Opportunity and Owenership Project Policy Brief 4. Washington, D.C.: The Urban Institute, 5.

18 Barrett, A., & A. Poikolainen (June 2006). *Food Stamp Program Participation Rates: 2004.* Washington, D.C.: USDA Food and Nutrition Service, xi.

19 Castner, N., & A. Schirm (February 2004). *Reaching Those in Need: State Food Stamp Participation Rates in 2001.* Washington, D.C.: USDA FNS.

20 Barret, A., & A. Poikolainen (June 2006). *Food Stamp Program Participation Rates: 2004.* Washington, D.C.: USDA FNS, xi.

21 American Public Human Services Association (2005). *Crossroads II: New Directions in Social Policy.* Washington, D.C.: APHSA, 102.

22 Garcia, G. (25 May 2006). "Congressmen Attack Privatization Plan," *San Antonio Express-News.*

23 Oliveira, V. (March 2006). *The Food Assistance Landscape.* Washington, D.C.: USDA ERS.

24 *The Food Stamp Act of 1977.* PL 102-351.

25 Nord, M., & Leibtag, E. (2005). "Is the "Cost of Enough Food" Lower in Rural Areas?" *Review of Regional Studies* 35(3):291-310.

26 United States Department of Agriculture Center for Nutrition Policy and Promotion (2003). *The Low-Cost, Moderate-Cost and Liberal Food Programs,* Administrative Report. Washington, D.C.: USDA CNPP.

27 United States Department of Health and Human Services &

United States Department of Agriculture (January 2005). *Dietary Guidelines for Americans 2005.* Washington, D.C.: USDHHS & USDA.

28 Oliveira, V. (March 2006). *The Food Assistance Landscape.* Washington, D.C.: USDA ERS.

29 Bread for the World Institute (2006). *Hunger Report 2006: Frontline Issues in Nutrition Assistance.* Washington, D.C.: BFWI, 38-39.

30 Ibid.

31 Children's Sentinel Nutrition Assessment Program (July 2004). *The Safety Net in Action: Protecting the Health and Nutrition of Young American Children.* Boston: C-SNAP, 3.

32 The Emergency Food Assistance Program (March 2005). *Food Distribution Fact Sheet.* Washington, D.C.: USDA FNS.

33 O'Brien, D., & H. Torres Aldeen (2006). *Hunger in America 2006: Executive Summary.* Chicago: America's Second Harvest.

34 Tiehen, L. (August 2002). *The Private Provision of Food Aid: The Emergency Food Assistance System, Food Assistance and Nutrition Research* Report. Washington, D.C.: USDA ERS, 26-5.

35 Cohen, R., Kim, M., & J. Ohls (March 2006). *Hunger in America 2006.* Princeton: Mathematica Policy Research, Inc.

36 O'Brien, D., et. al. (31 March 2004). "The Charitable Food Assistance System: The Sector's Role in Ending Hunger in America," Discussion paper presented by America's Second Harvest at the National Hunger Forum at the Congressional Hunger Center. Chicago: A2H.

37 United States Conference of Mayors (December 2005). *Hunger and Homelessness Survey: A Status Report on Hunger and Homelessness in America's Cities.* Washington, D.C.: U.S. Conference of Mayors, 4.

38 Bost, E. (6 October 2005). Farm Bill Healthier US Forum Before USDA Under Secretary Eric Bost, Oakland, California.

39 Food Research and Action Center (24 July 2001). Press Release. Washington, D.C.: FRAC.

40 Center on Budget and Policy Priorities (6 February 2006). "President's Budget Would Cut Food for Over 400,000 Low-Income Seniors," Press release. Washington, D.C.: CBPP.

41 Cody, S., & J. Ohls (June 2005). *Reaching Out: Nutrition Assistance for the Elderly: Evaluation of the USDA Elderly Nutrition Demonstrations.* Princeton: Mathematica Policy Research, Inc., 4.

42 Center on Budget and Policy Priorities (6 February 2006). "President's Budget Would Cut Food for Over 400,000 Low-Income Seniors," Press release. Washington, D.C.: CBPP.

43 Cody, S., & J. Ohls (June 2005). *Reaching Out: Nutrition Assistance for the Elderly: Evaluation of the USDA Elderly Nutrition Demonstrations.* Princeton: Mathematica Policy Research, Inc., 13.

44 Friedland, R., & L. Summer (March 2005). *Demography is Not Destiny, Revisited.* Washington, D.C.: Georgetown University Center on an Aging Society, 43.

45 United States Department of Health and Human Services Administration on Aging (2001). *A Profile of Older Americans: 2001.* Washington, D.C.: USDHHS AOA.

46 Friedland, R., & L. Summer (March 2005). *Demography is Not Destiny, Revisited.* Washington, D.C.: Georgetown University Center on an Aging Society, 8.

47 Waldrop, J., & S. Stern (2003). *Disability Status: 2000,* U.S. Census Brief C2KBR-17.

Washington, D.C.: Government Printing Office.

48 Steen, J. (29 July 2005). "Tribes, USDA Talk About Food Distribution Programs," *Rapid City Journal*.

49 U.S. Senate Committee on Indian Affairs and Senate Committee on Nutrition and Forestry (1993). *Barriers to Participation in the Food Stamp Program and Other Programs of the Department of Agriculture by People Residing on Indian Lands: Joint Hearing Before the Committee on Indian Affairs*, 103rd Cong., 1st Session.

50 Finegold, K., et al. (January 2005). *Background Report on the Use and Impact of Food Assistance Programs on Indian Reservations,* USDA Economic Research Service Report. Washington, D.C.: USDA ERS, iii.

51 United Sates Department of Health and Human Services, Indian Health Services (2006). *Fact Sheet on Diabetes.* Retrieved August 7, 2006, http://info.ihs.gov/Files/Diabetes-Jan2006.pdf.

52 Naylor, J., et al. (2003). "Diabetes Among Alaska Natives: A Review," *International Journal of Circumpolar Health* 62(4):363-87.

53 Dabelea, D., et al. (1998). "Increasing Prevalence of Type II Diabetes in American Indian Children," *Diabetologia* 41:904-910.

54 United States Department of Health and Human Services (November 2000). *Healthy People 2010.* Washington, D.C.: USDHHS.

55 Interagency Working Group on Food Security & Food Security Advisory Council (March 1999). *US Action Plan on Food Security: Solutions to Hunger.* Washington, D.C.: USDA, 41.

56 Nord, M., Andrews, M., & S. Carlson (2006). *Household Food Security in the United States, 2005*, USDA Economic Research Report 11. Washington, D.C.: USDA ERS, 5.

57 Alliance to End Hunger (July 20, 2005). *Americans Care Deeply About Hungry People and for Many, it is a Powerful Moral Issue.* Retrieved October 10, 2006, http://www.alliancetoendhunger.org/pressroom/july_20_2005.htm.

Conclusion

1 United States Department of Agriculture (January 1981). *A Time to Choose: Summary Report of the Structure of Agriculture.* Washington, D.C.: USDA.

2 German Marshall Fund of the United Sates (2005). *Perspectives on Trade and Poverty Reduction: A Survey of Public Opinion.* Washington, D.C.: GMF.

Appendix

1 Marcelle Thomas is Research Analyst and Antoine Bouet is Senior Research Fellow, International Food Policy Research Institute (IFPRI), Washington D.C. 20006. The authors thank David Orden for helpful suggestions and review comments.

2 The positive growth effect has been highlighted recently by analysts such as Robert Thompson (2006). He makes a common-sense argument for the benefits for U.S. agriculture that would occur if the incomes of the hundreds of millions of poor people in low-income countries living on $1-$2 per day were to rise to $5-$10 per day. In this range, demand for food rises relatively sharply with higher incomes as consumption quantities increase and diet quality improves.

3 The MIRAGE model was developed at the Centre d'Etudes Prospectives et d'Informations Internationales (CEPII) in Paris. A full description of the model is available at the CEPII's web site (www.cepii.fr). For a technical description of the model, see Bouet (2006). A brief description is given in the Appendix to this report.

4 See Mattson and Koo (2005) and Gehlhar and Dohlman (2006) for different approaches to evaluating the effects of foreign income growth on U.S. agricultural exports.

5 To illustrate the historical transformations, in China, for example, where total GDP growth averaged more than 9% during the 1980s and 1990s, growth in agricultural GDP was only around 5%, while industry and services GDP grew more than 10% annually. By 2000, agriculture's share of GDP was 16% of the total, compared to 30% before the rapid-growth decades. Similar shift occur in other high-growth countries. With more rapid growth in industry and services than agriculture, a given overall GDP growth raises demand for imported agricultural products by more than if agriculture grows at the same pace as non-agriculture.

6 The dynamic feature is also important to simulate changes such as trade policy reforms that are almost always implemented over a number of years. MIRAGE and similar models have been designed and used primarily to evaluate changes in trade policy, such as scenarios of reforms that might emerge from WTO negotiations (see for example, Bouet, Mevel and Orden, 2006).

7 The rates for the geographical regions are weighted averages of individual countries that compose them.

8 These shares are estimated from MIRAGE baseline results.

Acronyms

AAA	Agricultural Adjustment Act	**FRAC**	Food Research and Action Center
AFT	American Farmland Trust	**FSA**	Farm Savings Accounts
AGRA	Alliance for a Green Revolution in Africa	**GDP**	Gross Domestic Product
APHSA	American Public Human Services Association	**HFCA**	Hunger-Free Communities Act
ARC	Appalachian Regional Commission	**IATP**	Institute for Agriculture and Trade Policy
BFRDP	Beginning Farmer and Rancher Development Program	**IFPRI**	International Food Policy Research Institute
BMI	Body Mass Index	**LDCs**	Least Developed Countries
CAP	Combined Application Project	**LDP**	Loan Deficiency Payment
CARD	Center for Agricultural Research and Development	**LSP**	Land Stewardship Project
CBF	Cooperative Baptist Fellowship	**MDGs**	Millennium Development Goals
CCA	Counter-Cyclical Account	**NGO**	Nongovernmental Organization
CDC	Centers for Disease Control and Prevention	**NFIDCs**	Net Food-Importing Developing Countries
CRP	Conservation Reserve Program	**NPR**	National Public Radio
CSFP	Commodity Supplemental Food Program	**OECD**	Organization for Economic Cooperation and Development
CSP	Conservation Security Program	**SACI**	Strengthening America's Communities Initiative
CSPI	Center for Science in the Public Interest	**SARE**	Sustainable Agriculture Research and Education
DoD	Department of Defense	**SSI**	Supplemental Security Income
DRA	Delta Regional Authority	**TANF**	Temporary Aid to Needy Families
DTA	Department of Transitional Assistance	**TEFAP**	The Emergency Food Assistance Program
EBT	Electronic Benefits Transfer	**TFP**	Thrifty Food Plan
EDA	Economic Development Administration	**UFFVA**	United Fresh Fruits and Vegetable Association
EPA	Environmental Protection Agency	**USDA**	U.S. Department of Agriculture
EQIP	Environmental Quality Incentive Program	**VAPG**	Value-Added Producer-Grant
EU	European Union	**WFS**	World Food Summit
FARP	Farm and Ranch Profitability Grant program	**WIC**	Special Supplemental Nutrition Program for Women, Infants and Children
FARRM	Farm and Ranch Risk Management	**WRP**	Wetlands Reserve Program
FDPIR	Food Distribution Program on Indian Reservations	**WTO**	World Trade Organization
FFPP	Farm and Food Policy Project		
FNS	Food and Nutrition Service		

Glossary

Agribusiness—Agriculturally related businesses that supply farm inputs (such as fertilizer or equipment) or are involved in the marketing of farm products (such as warehouses, processors, wholesalers, transporters, and retailers). Farms are not usually included when the term agribusiness is used.

Aid for Trade—Defined in the Doha Development Round as assistance to build supply-side capacity and trade-related infrastructure so that developing countries can improve their ability to trade.

Beginning farmer or rancher—An eligibility term used in some farm programs, usually to identify a subgroup who may benefit from additional assistance.

Biofuels—Fuels made from biomass, i.e. any organic matter that is available on a renewable or recurring basis, including agricultural crops.

Block grants—Federal government lump-sum payments to the states, which then have wide discretion over the use of these funds.

Body mass index (BMI)—A measure of body weight relative to height. BMI can be used to determine if people are at a healthy weight, overweight, or obese.

Box—In agriculture, a category of domestic support. Green box: supports considered not to distort trade and therefore permitted with no limits. Blue box: permitted supports linked to production, but subject to production limits, and therefore minimally trade-distorting. Amber box: supports considered to distort trade and therefore subject to reduction commitments.

Buyout—In the context of commodity and farm support policy, the term buyout relates to compensation for the loss or decline in value of assets due to a change in policy or program design.

Codex Alimentarius Commission— A joint commission of the Food and Agriculture Organization (FAO) and the World Health Organization created in 1962 to ensure consumer food safety, establish fair practices in food trade, and promote the development of international food standards. The Commission, often referred to simply as Codex, drafts nonbinding standards for sanitary and phytosanitary standards governing food additives, veterinary drugs, pesticide residues, and other substances that affect consumer food safety.

Commodities—Six agricultural crops (corn, cotton, peanuts, rice, tobacco, and wheat) declared by permanent law (in the Agricultural Adjustment Act of 1938) as requiring federal price support. Since first defined in 1938, other farm products have been added to the list of commodities that qualify for price support.

Conservation—The management of natural resources to provide maximum benefits over a sustained period of time. Conservation practices focus on conserving soil, water, energy, and biological resources.

Consolidation—In agriculture and other economic sectors, consolidation usually is a reference to the trend from numerous smaller-sized operations toward fewer and larger ones. Consolidation can lead to higher concentration.

Developed countries—A term to differentiate the more highly industrialized nations, including most of those that are members of the Organization for Economic Cooperation and Development, from developing countries or less developed countries.

Developing countries—Countries with a low per capita income. Terms such as less developed country, least developed country, underdeveloped country, poor, southern or third world have been used to describe developing countries.

Dietary Guidelines for Americans—Recommendations for nutritional health published by the U.S. Department of Agriculture (USDA) and U.S Department of Health and Human Services, reflecting the most current scientific knowledge in nutrition for preventing chronic illnesses.

Doha Development Round—The name given to the current round of multilateral trade negotiations under the auspices of the WTO. The name derives from the launch of a new round of multilateral trade negotiations at a WTO ministerial conference held in Doha, Qatar, in November 2001.

Domestic support—In agriculture, any domestic subsidy or other measure which acts to maintain producer prices at levels above those prevailing in international trade.

Dumping —Under World Trade Organization rules, dumping occurs when the price to the importer is less than the normal price of the product charged to the buyer in the country of origin or other third country markets.

Emergency food assistance—The distribution of donated food items to hungry people. Such programs typically are run by private, nonprofit community organizations.

Entitlement—A legal obligation on the federal government to make payments to a person, business, or unit of government that meets the criteria set in law. Entitlement spending is a subset of mandatory spending.

Farm bill—A phrase that refers to a multi-year, omnibus law that contains federal commodity and farm support policies, as well as other farm-related provisions. Beginning in 1973, farm bills have included titles on commodity programs, trade, rural development, farm credit, conservation, agricultural research, food and nutrition programs, marketing, etc.

Farm size—The most common way to measure farm size is by the value of gross farm sales. Acreage is not used for comparisons across differing kinds of farms because in some cases a farm need not have land (i.e., bee hives may be in constant rotation among parcels not belonging to the beekeeper).

Farm—For statistical purposes, a farm is defined as any place from which $1,000 or more of agricultural products were produced or sold or would have been sold during the agriculture census year. There are about 2.1 million farms in the United States.

Farmer Savings Accounts—Designed to encourage farmers to manage risk by making deposits to special accounts in high income years and making withdrawals, when needed, in low-income years; the government would provide incentives, such as tax deferrals and/or matching contributions, to encourage farmer participation and to help farmers accumulate reserves.

Farming-dependent county—ERS classified a county as farming dependent if 15 percent or more of earnings (in 1998-2000) or employment (in 2000) came from farming.

Food aid—The distribution of food commodities to support development projects and emergency food assistance in situations of natural and man-made disasters.

Food bank—A charitable organization that solicits, receives, inventories, stores and distributes food and grocery products from various sources to charitable organizations.

Food insecurity—A condition of uncertain availability of or ability to acquire safe, nutritious food in socially acceptable ways.

Food security—Assured access to enough nutritious food to sustain an active and healthy life with dignity.

Green payments—Payments made to producers as compensation for environmental benefits that accrue as a result of or in conjunction with their farming activities.

Gross domestic product (GDP)—The value of all goods and services produced within a nation during a specified period, usually a year.

Hunger—A condition in which people do not get enough food to provide the nutrients (carbohydrate, fat, protein, vitamins, minerals and water) for fully productive, active and healthy lives.

Industrialized countries—See Developed Countries.

Infrastructure—The basic facilities, services and installations needed for the functioning of a community or society such as transportation, communications, financial, educational and health care systems.

Least developed countries (LDCs)—Low-income countries that suffer from long-term handicaps to economic growth, in particular low levels of human resource development and/or severe structural weakness.

Malnutrition—A condition resulting from inadequate consumption (undernutrition) or excessive consumption (overnutrition) of a nutrient, which can impair physical and mental health, and can be the cause or result of infectious diseases.

Market access—The extent to which a country allows imports.

Microenterprises—A business with five or fewer employees and little working capital.

Millennium Development Goals (MDGs)—A set of objectives for the betterment of quality of life for all people first laid out in a series of international conferences in the 1990s, then officially adopted by the United Nations in 2000 with the Millennium Declaration. The goals serve as a road map for development to be achieved by the year 2015.

Multilateral agreement—A trade agreement involving many countries (as with the World Trade Organization).

Nongovernmental organizations (NGOs)—Groups and institutions that are entirely or largely independent of government and that have primarily humanitarian or cooperative rather than commercial objectives. Citizen groups that raise awareness and influence policy also are NGOs.

Persistent Poverty Counties—Persistent poverty counties are those where 20 percent or more of the county population in each of four Census years (1960, 1970,1980, 1990) had household incomes below poverty.

Poverty—The lack of sufficient money or resources to provide the basic needs of survival for oneself and one's family.

Poverty line—An official measure of poverty defined by national governments. In the United States, it is calculated as three times the cost of the USDA's Thrifty Food Plan, which provides a less-than-adequate diet. Poverty also can be measured internationally, by determining the percentage of per capita income levels under $1 or $2 per day for a population. Income levels are adjusted for purchasing power parity so that they are comparable from country to country.

Price support—Programs operated by USDA that are intended to raise farm prices when supply exceeds demand and prices are unacceptably low.

Producer—For purposes of commodity payments, the 2002 farm bill defines a producer as an owner-operator, landlord, tenant, or sharecropper that shares in the risk of producing a crop and is entitled to a share of the crop produced on the farm.

Productivity—A measure of technical efficiency, typically expressed as the added output for an additional unit of input or the average output per unit of input, i.e., labor, land, capital productivity.

Program crops—Refers to commodity crops currently eligible for price supports.

Revenue insurance—A generic term for any crop insurance program that provides coverage to producers against lost revenues (or incomes) caused by low prices, low yields, or a combination of low prices and low yields.

Rural—According to the U.S. Bureau of the Census, rural areas comprise open country and settlements with fewer than 2,500 residents. Territory outside of urbanized areas is designated rural and can have population densities as high as 999 per square mile or as low as 1 person per square mile.

Sanitary and phytosanitary (SPS) measures and agreements—See Codex Alimentarius Commission.

Social safety nets—Government policies and charitable programs designed to ensure basic needs are met among low-income, disabled and other vulnerable social groups.

Specialty crops—USDA classifies specialty crops as all farm commodities other than livestock and program crops. This definition includes fruits and vegetables and horticultural crops.

Subsidy—A direct or indirect benefit granted by a government for the production or distribution (including export) of a good or to supplement other services.

Surplus—The amount by which available supplies are greater than the quantity that will bring producers an adequate income. A surplus may be due to production outrunning demand, a decline in consumption, or a general decline in consumer income or buying power.

Sustainable agriculture—A systematic approach to farming intended to reduce agricultural pollution, enhance natural resource and financial sustainability, and improve efficiency.

Tariff—A tariff is a list or schedule of taxes, while a duty is the tax imposed on a specific item. However, the terms duty and tariff have come to be used interchangeably. In international trade, these taxes must be paid to a government on selected imported or sometimes exported goods.

Tariff escalation—Higher import duties on semi-processed products than on raw materials, and higher still on finished products. This practice protects domestic processing industries and discourages the development of processing activity in the countries where raw materials originate.

Thrifty Food Plan (TFP)—The USDA-calculated cost of a diet for persons of different ages, and the basis upon which Food Stamp allotments are determined.

Trade barriers—Laws, regulations, policies that protect domestic products from foreign competition or artificially stimulate exports of domestic products.

Trade Distortion—When prices and production are higher or lower than levels that would usually exist in a competitive market.

Trade liberalization—A term which describes the complete or partial elimination of trade distorting government policies.

Undernutrition—A condition resulting from inadequate consumption of calories, protein and/or nutrients to meet the basic physical requirements for an active and healthy life.

Uruguay Round—Multilateral trade negotiations launched in Punta del Este, Uruguay, in 1986 and concluded in December 1993. The final Uruguay Round agreement signed in Marrakech in April 1994 created the World Trade Organization, embracing 110 participating countries.

Value-added products—Products that have increased in value because of processing.

World Trade Organization (WTO)—The international organization established to oversee international trade agreements and settle disputes between member countries. Currently there are 149 member countries. See Uruguay Round.

TABLE 1: Global Hunger—Life and Death Indicators

| | Population | | | | | | Life expectancy at birth | | Under-1 mortality rate per 1,000 2004 | % of low birth weight infants 1998-2004[o] | % of 1-yr-old children immunized (measles) 2004 | Under-5 mortality rate per 1,000 live births | | Maternal mortality rate per 100,000 live births 1990-2004[o] reported[k] | Refugees as of December 31, 2005 | |
	Total (millions) mid-2006	Projected (millions) 2025	Projected population change (%) 2006-2050	Total fertility rate 2004	% below age 15 2005	% urban 2004	Male	Female				1960	2004		Country of origin[q]	Country of asylum
Developing Countries	**5,339**[m]	**6,685**[m]	**50**[m]	**2.9**	..	**43**	**64**[m]	**67**[m]	**59**	**17**	**74**	**216**	**87**	..	..	..
Africa (sub-Saharan)	**767.0**	**1,151.0**	**128**	**5.4**[e]	..	**36**[e]	**47**	**49**	**102**[e]	**14**[e]	**66**[e]	**261**[e]	**171**[e]	..	..	..
Angola	15.8	25.9	165	6.7	47	36	39	42	154	12	64	345	260	..	213,500	14,900
Benin	8.7	14.3	154	5.7	44	45	53	55	90	16	85	296	152	500	..	32,000
Botswana	1.8	1.7	-6	3.1	38	52	35	33	84	10	90	173	116	330	..	3,200
Burkina Faso	13.6	23.2	187	6.6	47	18	48	49	97	19	78	315	192	480	..	..
Burundi	7.8	14.0	229	6.8	45	10	44	45	114	16	75	250	190	..	438,000	40,600
Cameroon	17.3	24.3	87	4.5	41	52	50	52	87	11	64	255	149	430	3,900	58,900
Cape Verde	0.5	0.7	90	3.6	40	57	68	74	27	13	69	..	36	76	..	..
Central African Republic	4.3	5.5	51	4.9	43	43	43	44	115	14	35	327	193	1100	43,700	26,500
Chad	10.0	17.2	214	6.7	47	25	43	45	117	10	56	325	200	830	49,900	275,500
Comoros	0.7	1.0	118	4.7	42	36	62	66	52	25	73	265	70	520[x]	..	..
Congo, Dem. Rep. of	62.7	108.0	192	6.7	47	32	49	52	129	12	64	302	205	1300	450,800	204,500
Congo, Rep.	3.7	5.9	161	6.3	47	54	50	52	81	..	65	220	108	..	24,300	69,600
Côte d'Ivoire	19.7	27.1	84	4.9	42	45	49	53	117	17	49	290	194	600	25,300	44,100
Djibouti	0.8	1.1	92	4.9	42	84	52	54	101	..	60	289	126	74	..	10,500
Equatorial Guinea	0.5	0.8	127	5.9	44	49	43	44	122	13	51	316	204	..	..	..
Eritrea	4.6	7.4	146	5.4	45	20	53	57	52	21[x]	84	..	82	1000	215,300	6,000
Ethiopia	74.8	107.8	94	5.7	45	16	48	50	110	15	71	269	166	870	63,900	101,100
Gabon	1.4	1.8	62	3.9	40	85	53	55	60	14	55	..	91	520	..	13,400
Gambia	1.5	2.4	148	4.6	40	26	52	55	89	17	90	364	122	730	..	8,800
Ghana	22.6	32.7	110	4.2	39	46	57	58	68	16	83	215	112	210[x]	10,000	59,000
Guinea	9.8	15.2	139	5.8	44	36	54	54	101	16	73	380	155	530	2,600	67,300
Guinea-Bissau	1.4	2.4	225	7.1	48	35	44	46	126	22	80	..	203	910	..	7,800
Kenya	34.7	49.4	87	5.0	43	41	49	47	79	10	73	205	120	410	11,400	314,600
Lesotho	1.8	1.7	-11	3.5	39	18	35	36	61	14	70	203	82	..	..	..
Liberia	3.4	5.8	217	6.8	47	47	41	44	157	..	42	288	235	580[x]	219,800	16,100
Madagascar	17.8	28.2	135	5.3	44	27	53	57	76	17	59	186	123	470	..	..
Malawi	12.8	23.8	248	6.0	47	17	44	47	110	16	80	361	175	1100	..	9,600
Mali	13.9	24.0	202	6.8	48	33	48	49	121	23	75	500	219	580	..	13,100
Mauritania	3.2	5.0	137	5.7	43	63	53	55	78	..	64	310	125	750	..	30,600
Mauritius	1.3	1.4	20	2.0	25	44	69	76	14	14	98	92	15	22	..	..
Mozambique	19.9	27.6	89	5.4	44	37	41	42	104	15	77	313	152	410	..	6,000
Namibia	2.1	2.5	49	3.8	42	33	47	47	47	14	70	206	63	270	..	14,300
Niger	14.4	26.4	248	7.8	49	23	44	44	152	13	74	354	259	590	..	..
Nigeria	134.5	199.5	122	5.7	44	48	43	44	101	14	35	207	197	..	..	9,400
Rwanda	9.1	13.8	128	5.6	44	20	46	48	118	9	84	206	203	1100	102,500	49,500
Senegal	11.9	17.3	94	4.9	43	50	55	58	78	18	57	300	137	560	..	23,400
Sierra Leone	5.7	8.7	143	6.5	43	40	39	42	165	23	64	390	283	1800	..	60,100
Somalia	8.9	14.9	188	6.3	44	35	46	50	133	..	40	..	225	..	328,000	2,900
South Africa	47.3	48.0	2	2.8	33	57	45	49	54	15	81	..	67	150	..	169,800
Sudan	41.2	61.3	104	4.3	39	40	57	59	63	31	59	208	91	550	670,900	231,700
Swaziland	1.1	1.0	-34	3.8	41	24	33	35	108	9	70	225	156	230	..	..
Tanzania	37.9	53.6	92	4.9	43	36	44	45	78	13	94	241	126	580	5,400	549,100
Togo	6.3	9.6	115	5.2	44	36	53	57	78	18	70	267	140	480	..	9,700
Uganda	27.7	55.5	371	7.1	51	12	47	47	80	12	91	224	138	510	35,100	254,400
Zambia	11.9	16.4	92	5.5	46	36	38	37	102	12	84	213	182	730	..	155,900
Zimbabwe	13.1	14.4	21	3.4	40	35	38	37	79	11	80	159	129	700	..	14,000
South Asia	..	..	..	**3.2**	..	**28**	..	..	**67**	**31**	**61**	**239**	**92**	..	..	..
Afghanistan	31.1	50.3	164	7.4	47	24	41	42	165	..	61	360	257	1600	2,192,100	..
Bangladesh	146.6	190.0	58	3.2	36	25	61	62	56	36	77	247	77	380	45,300	150,100
Bhutan	0.9	1.3	99	4.2	38	9	62	64	67	15	87	300	80	260	122,300	..
India	1,121.8	1,363.0	45	3.0	32	28	62	63	62	30	56	236	85	540	11,700	515,100
Maldives	0.3	0.4	80	4.1	41	29	70	70	35	22	97	300	46	140	..	..
Nepal	26.0	36.2	85	3.6	39	15	62	63	59	21	73	297	76	540	201,800	130,600

	Total (millions) mid-2006	Projected (millions) 2025	Projected population change (%) 2006-2050	Total fertility rate 2004	% below age 15 2005	% urban 2004	Life expectancy at birth Male	Life expectancy at birth Female	Under-1 mortality rate per 1,000 2004	% of low birth weight infants 1998-2004°	% of 1-yr-old children immunized (measles) 2004	Under-5 mortality rate per 1,000 live births 1960	Under-5 mortality rate per 1,000 live births 2004	Maternal mortality rate per 100,000 live births 1990-2004° reported[k]	Refugees as of December 31, 2005 Country of origin[q]	Refugees as of December 31, 2005 Country of asylum
Pakistan	165.8	228.8	78	4.1	38	34	61	63	80	19[x]	67	226	101	530	16,500	1,088,100
Sri Lanka	19.9	22.2	13	1.9	24	21	71	77	12	22	96	133	14	92	79,100	..
East Asia and the Pacific	..	..	..	**1.9[f]**	..	**42[f]**	..	..	**29[f]**	**7[f]**	**83[f]**	**201[g]**	**36[f]**	..	..	..
Brunei	0.4	0.5	87	2.4	30	77	72	77	8	10	99	87	9	0	..	..
Cambodia	14.1	19.6	81	4.0	37	19	57	63	97	11	80	..	141	440	..	..
China	1,311.4	1,476.0	10	1.7	21[j]	40	70	74	26	4	84	225	31	51	156,300	352,700
Hong Kong[c]	7.0	8.1	24	..	14	..	79	84	..	..	..	..	..	..	..	..
Fiji	0.8	0.9	9	2.9	32	52	66	71	16	10	62	97	20	38	..	..
Indonesia	225.5	263.7	26	2.3	28	47	67	72	30	9	72	216	38	310	..	..
Korea, DPR (North)	23.1	25.8	14	2.0	25	61	68	73	42	7	95	120	55	110	51,400	..
Korea, Rep. of (South)	48.5	49.8	-13	1.2	19	81	74	81	5	4	99	127	6	20	..	2,100
Lao, PDR	6.1	8.7	91	4.7	41	21	53	56	65	14	36	235	83	530	..	..
Malaysia	26.9	34.6	51	2.8	32	64	72	76	10	9	95	105	12	30	..	152,700
Mongolia	2.6	3.1	35	2.4	31	57	64	68	41	7	96	..	52	99	..	..
Myanmar (Burma)	51.0	59.0	25	2.3	30	30	57	63	76	15	78	252	106	230	727,100	..
Papua New Guinea	6.0	8.2	77	3.9	40	13	55	56	68	11[x]	44	214	93	370[x]	..	10,000
Philippines	86.3	115.7	65	3.1	35	62	67	72	26	20	80	110	34	170	67,700	..
Singapore	4.5	5.2	19	1.3	20	100	78	82	3	8	94	40	3	6	..	..
Solomon Islands	0.5	0.7	120	4.2	41	17	62	63	34	13[x]	72	185	56	550[x]	..	..
Thailand	65.2	70.2	12	1.9	24	32	68	75	18	9	96	148	21	24	..	477,500
Vietnam	84.2	102.9	37	2.3	30	26	70	73	17	9	97	105	23	170	305,500	15,400
Latin America and the Caribbean	**566[d]**	**700[d]**	**41[d]**	**2.5**	..	**77**	**69[d]**	**75[d]**	**26**	**9**	**92**	**153[g]**	**31**	..	..	..
Argentina	39.0	46.4	38	2.3	26	90	71	78	16	8	95	72	18	44	..	3,900
Belize	0.3	0.4	61	3.1	37	48	67	74	32	6	95	104	39	140	..	..
Bolivia	9.1	12.1	59	3.8	38	64	62	66	54	7	64	255	69	230	..	..
Brazil	186.8	228.9	39	2.3	28	84	68	76	32	10[x]	99	177	34	64	..	3,700
Chile	16.4	19.1	23	2.0	25	87	75	81	8	5	95	155	8	17	..	..
Colombia	46.8	58.3	42	2.6	..	77	69	75	18	9	92	125	21	78	257,900	..
Costa Rica	4.3	5.6	48	2.2	28	61	77	81	11	7	88	123	13	33	..	12,200
Cuba	11.3	11.8	-2	1.6	19	76	75	79	6	6	99	54	7	34	..	..
Dominican Republic	9.0	11.6	57	2.7	33	60	66	69	27	11	79	149	32	180	..	..
Ecuador	13.3	17.5	54	2.7	32	62	71	77	23	16	99	178	26	80	..	47,400
El Salvador	7.0	9.1	55	2.8	34	60	67	73	24	7	93	191	28	170	..	..
Guatemala	13.0	20.0	115	4.5	43	47	63	71	33	12	75	202	45	150	..	..
Guyana	0.7	0.7	-35	2.2	29	38	72	80	48	12	88	126	64	190	..	..
Haiti	8.5	13.0	121	3.9	38	38	51	54	74	21	54	253	117	520	..	..
Honduras	7.4	10.7	100	3.6	39	46	67	74	31	14	92	204	41	110	..	..
Jamaica	2.7	3.0	27	2.4	31	52	69	73	17	10	80	74	20	110	..	..
Mexico	108.3	129.4	28	2.3	31	76	73	78	23	8	96	134	28	65	..	3,400
Nicaragua	5.6	7.7	67	3.2	39	58	66	70	31	12	84	193	38	83	..	..
Panama	3.3	4.2	52	2.7	30	57	73	78	19	10	99	88	24	70	..	..
Paraguay	6.3	8.6	63	3.8	38	58	69	73	21	9[x]	89	90	24	180	..	..
Peru	28.4	34.1	27	2.8	32	74	67	72	24	11[x]	89	234	29	190	..	..
Suriname	0.5	0.5	-5	2.6	30	77	66	73	30	13	86	..	39	150	..	..
Trinidad and Tobago	1.3	1.3	-6	1.6	22	76	67	73	18	23	95	73	20	45	..	..
Uruguay	3.3	3.5	12	2.3	24	93	71	79	15	8	95	56	17	26	..	..
Venezuela	27.0	35.2	54	2.7	31	88	70	76	16	9	80	75	19	68	3,400	180,100
Middle East and North Africa	..	..	..	**3.2[h]**	..	**58[h]**	..	..	**44[h]**	**15[h]**	**89[h]**	**250[h]**	**56[h]**	..	..	..
Algeria	33.5	43.1	48	2.5	30	59	74	76	35	7	81	280	40	120	1,000	94,500
Bahrain	0.7	1.0	56	2.4	27	90	73	75	9	8	99	160	11	46	..	..
Cyprus	1.0	1.1	4	1.6	20	69	75	80	5	..	86	36	5	0	..	..
Egypt	75.4	101.1	67	3.2	34	42	67	72	26	12	97	282	36	84	2,200	86,700

TABLE 1: Global Hunger—Life and Death Indicators

| | Population | | | | | | Life expectancy at birth | | Under-1 mortality rate per 1,000 2004 | % of low birth weight infants 1998-2004° | % of 1-yr-old children immunized (measles) 2004 | Under-5 mortality rate per 1,000 live births | | Maternal mortality rate per 100,000 live births 1990-2004° reported[k] | Refugees as of December 31, 2005 | |
	Total (millions) mid-2006	Projected (millions) 2025	Projected population change (%) 2006-2050	Total fertility rate 2004	% below age 15 2005	% urban 2004	Male	Female				1960	2004		Country of origin[q]	Country of asylum
Iran	70.3	89.0	45	2.1	29	67	69	72	32	7[x]	96	281	38	37	31,900	994,000
Iraq	29.6	44.7	116	4.7	41	67	57	60	102	15	90	171	125	290	888,700	63,400
Jordan	5.6	7.9	75	3.4	37	79	71	72	23	10[x]	99	139	27	41	..	609,500
Kuwait	2.7	3.9	91	2.3	24	96	77	79	10	7	97	128	12	5	..	14,300
Lebanon	3.9	4.6	30	2.3	29	88	70	74	27	6	96	85	31	100[x]	..	296,800
Libya	5.9	8.3	83	2.9	30	87	74	78	18	7[x]	99	270	20	77	..	12,000
Morocco	31.7	38.8	43	2.7	31	58	68	72	38	11[x]	95	211	43	230	117,400	2,300
Oman	2.6	3.1	50	3.6	35	78	73	75	10	8	98	280	13	23	..	..
Qatar	0.8	1.2	86	2.9	22	92	71	76	18	10	99	140	21	10	..	..
Saudi Arabia	24.1	35.6	96	3.9	37	88	70	74	21	11[x]	97	292	27	..	..	240,800
Syria	19.5	28.1	84	3.3	37	50	71	75	15	6	98	201	16	65	4,400	866,300
Tunisia	10.1	11.6	20	1.9	26	64	71	75	21	7	95	254	25	69	..	..
Turkey	73.7	86.0	23	2.4	29	67	69	74	28	16	81	219	32	130[x]	..	..
United Arab Emirates	4.9	7.1	94	2.5	22	85	75	80	7	15[x]	94	223	8	3	..	..
West Bank and Gaza[a]	3.9	7.1	188	5.4	46	72	71	74	22	9	96	..	24	..	2,971,600	1,685,000
Yemen	21.6	38.8	214	6.0	46	26	59	62	82	32[x]	76	340	111	370	..	82,700
Countries in Transition[b]	..	..	..	..	..	..	..	..	..	..	..	112[i]	..	..	..	..
Albania	3.2	3.5	12	2.2	27	44	72	79	17	3	96	151	19	23	..	..
Armenia	3.0	3.4	12	1.3	21	64	67	75	29	7	92	..	32	9	..	11,300
Azerbaijan	8.5	9.7	37	1.8	26	50	70	75	75	11	98	..	90	25	..	3,300
Belarus	9.7	9.4	-12	1.2	15	71	63	75	9	5	99	47	11	18	..	2,700
Bosnia and Herzegovina	3.9	3.7	-18	1.3	17	45	71	77	13	4	88	160	15	10	..	10,800
Bulgaria	7.7	6.6	-34	1.2	14	70	69	76	12	10	95	70	15	15	..	5,200
Croatia	4.4	4.3	-14	1.3	16	59	71	78	6	6	96	98	7	2	59,600	2,900
Czech Republic	10.3	10.2	-8	1.2	15	74	73	79	4	7	97	25	4	3	..	..
Estonia	1.3	1.2	-23	1.4	15	70	66	78	6	4	96	52	8	46	..	..
Georgia	4.4	3.9	-33	1.4	19	52	69	75	41	7	86	70	45	52	..	2,500
Hungary	10.1	9.6	-11	1.3	16	66	69	77	7	9	99	57	8	5	..	8,800
Kazakhstan	15.3	16.0	-1	1.9	23	56	61	72	63	8	99	..	73	50	..	..
Kyrgyzstan	5.2	6.6	58	2.6	32	34	64	72	58	7[x]	99	180	68	44	..	..
Latvia	2.3	2.2	-23	1.3	15	66	67	77	10	5	99	44	12	25	..	..
Lithuania	3.4	3.1	-15	1.3	17	67	66	78	8	4	98	70	8	13	..	..
Macedonia, Republic of	2.0	2.1	-7	1.5	20	60	71	76	13	6	96	177	14	7	..	2,200
Moldova	4.0	3.8	-21	1.2	18	46	65	72	23	5	96	88	28	44	..	..
Poland	38.1	36.7	-17	1.2	16	62	71	79	7	6	97	70	8	4	..	6,200
Romania	21.6	18.1	-29	1.3	15	55	68	75	17	9	97	82	20	31	..	2,300
Russian Federation	142.3	130.0	-22	1.3	15	73	59	72	17	6	98	64	21	32	34,000	149,200
Serbia and Montenegro[p]	10.1[n]	9.8[n]	-14[n]	1.6	18	52	69[n]	75[n]	13	4	96	..	15	7	24,700	78,600
Slovakia	5.4	5.2	-12	1.2	17	58	70	78	6	7	98	40	9	16	..	3,100
Slovenia	2.0	2.0	-5	1.2	14	51	74	81	4	6	94	45	4	17	..	..
Tajikistan	7.0	9.3	58	3.7	39	24	61	66	91	15	89	140	118	45	54,200	..
Turkmenistan	5.3	6.6	38	2.7	32	46	58	67	80	6	97	..	103	14	..	..
Ukraine	46.8	41.7	-28	1.1	15	67	63	74	14	5	99	53	18	13	..	4,000
Uzbekistan	26.2	33.0	43	2.7	33	36	63	70	57	7	98	..	69	34	1,900	44500
Industrial Countries	..	..	..	1.6	..	77	..	..	5	7	92	39	6	..	..	..
Australia	20.6	24.6	36	1.7	20	92	78	83	5	7	93	24	6	..	..	14,800
Austria	8.3	8.7	8	1.4	16	66	76	82	5	7	74	43	5	..	..	17,300
Belgium	10.5	10.8	4	1.7	17	97	76	82	4	8[x]	82	35	5	..	..	14,100
Canada	32.6	37.6	29	1.5	18	81	77	82	5	6	95	33	6	..	..	39,500
Denmark	5.4	5.6	1	1.8	19	85	76	80	4	5	96	25	5	10	..	2,000
Finland	5.3	5.4	0	1.7	17	61	75	82	3	4	97	28	4	6	..	2,400
France	61.2	63.4	5	1.9	18	76	77	84	4	7	86	34	5	10	..	25,500
Germany	82.4	82.0	-9	1.3	14	88	76	82	4	7	92	40	5	8	..	64,200
Greece	11.1	11.4	-4	1.2	14	61	77	81	4	8	88	64	5	1	..	11,300
Ireland	4.2	4.5	11	1.9	20	60	75	80	5	6	81	36	6	6	..	2,400

	Population						Life expectancy at birth		Under-1 mortality rate per 1,000 2004	% of low birth weight infants 1998-2004o	% of 1-yr-old children immunized (measles) 2004	Under-5 mortality rate per 1,000 live births		Maternal mortality rate per 100,000 live births 1990-2004o reportedk	Refugees as of December 31, 2005	
	Total (millions) mid-2006	Projected (millions) 2025	Projected population change (%) 2006-2050	Total fertility rate 2004	% below age 15 2005	% urban 2004	Male	Female				1960	2004		Country of originq	Country of asylum
Israel	7.2	9.3	52	2.8	28	92	78	82	5	8	96	39	6	5	..	..
Italy	59.0	58.7	-5	1.3	14	67	78	83	4	6	84	50	5	7	..	5,800
Japan	127.8	121.1	-21	1.3	14	66	79	86	3	8	99	40	4	8	..	..
Luxembourg	0.5	0.5	37	1.7	19	92	75	81	5	8	91	41	6	0	..	..
Netherlands	16.4	16.9	3	1.7	18	66	77	81	5	..	96	22	6	7	..	14,400
New Zealand	4.1	4.6	18	2.0	21	86	77	81	5	6	85	26	6	15	..	..
Norway	4.7	5.2	25	1.8	20	80	78	83	4	5	88	23	4	6	..	4,300
Portugal	10.6	10.4	-12	1.5	16	55	75	81	4	8	95	112	5	8	..	..
Spain	45.5	46.2	-4	1.3	14	77	77	84	3	6x	97	57	5	6	..	..
Sweden	9.1	9.9	16	1.7	18	83	78	83	3	4	94	20	4	5	..	19,400
Switzerland	7.5	7.4	-4	1.4	17	68	79	84	5	6	82	27	5	5	..	10,500
United Kingdom	60.5	65.8	14	1.7	18	89	76	81	5	8	81	27	6	7	..	14,600
United States	299.1	349.4	40	2.0	21	80	75	80	7	8	93	30	8	8	..	176,700
World	**6,555.0**	**7,940.0**	**41**	**2.6**	**..**	**49**	**65**	**69**	**54**	**16**	**76**	**196**	**79**	**..**	**..**	**..**

..   Data not available.
a   Palestinian Territory.
b   Central and Eastern Europe countries and the newly independent states of the former Soviet Union.
c   Special administrative region, data exclude China.
d   Data include Antigua and Barbuda, Bahamas, Barbados, Dominica, French Guiana, Grenada, Guadeloupe, Martinique, Netherland Antilles, Puerto Rico, St. Kitts-Nevis, Saint Lucia, and St.Vincent and the Grenadines.
e   Data include São Tomé and Principe and Seychelles. Data exclude Djibouti and Sudan.
f   Data include Cook Islands, Kiribati, Marshall Islands, Micronesia, Nauru, Niue, Palau, Samoa, Tonga, Tuvalu and Vanautu. Data exclude Hong Kong.
g   Data include Antigua and Barbuda, Bahamas, Barbados, Dominica, Grenada, St. Kitts and Nevis, St. Lucia, and St. Vincent and the Grenadines.
h   Data include Djibouti, West Bank and Gaza, and Sudan. Data exclude Turkey.
i   Data include Andorra, Holy See, Monaco and San Marino. Data exclude Slovenia.
j   For statistical purposes the data for China do not include Hong Kong and Macao Special Administrative Regions.
k   The maternal mortality data in this column are reported by national authorities.
m   Refers to "Less Developed" countries as defined by the World Population Data Sheet of the Population Reference Bureau.
n   As of a May 2006 referendum Serbia and Montenegro have been recognized as separate countries. However, data have been combined in this year's report for the sake of consistency with our sources.
o   Data refer to most recent year available.
p   Data from years 1992-2002 refer to the Federal Republic of Yugoslavia. Data from before 1992 refer to the Socialist Federal Republic of Yugoslavia.
q   Data for this column are comprised of statistics from both Country Reports and Table 8 of the 2006 World Refugee Survey. Figures of less than 1,000 were excluded.
x   Data refer to a period other than the one specified in the column heading, differ from standard deviation, or refer to only part of a country.

TABLE 2: Global Food, Nutrition and Education

| | Food Supply | | | Adult Literacy rate (% age 15 and above) 2004[c] | | | Educational enrollment (% of relevant age group) | | | |
| | Per Capita dietary energy supply (DES) (calories/day) 2001-2003 | Food production per capita 2005 | Vitamin A supplementation coverage rate (6 to 59 months) 2003 | | | | Primary school (net) 2000-2004[m] | | Primary secondary, tertiary (gross %) 2004 | |
				Total	Female	Male	Female	Male	Female	Male
Developing Countries	..	**107.26**	**61[i]**	..	..	..	**83**	**88**	..	..
Africa (sub-Saharan)	..	..	**64[p]**	..	..	..	**62[p]**	**70[p]**	..	..
Angola	2,070	124.39	68	67.4	54.2	82.9	57[x]	66[x]	24[x]	28[x]
Benin	2,530	106.08	98[k]	34.7	23.3	47.9	47	69	41	58
Botswana	2,180	102.07	..	81.2	81.8	80.4	83	79	72	69
Burkina Faso	2,460	102.75	95[k]	21.8	15.2	29.4	31	42	23	30
Burundi	1,640	87.61	95	59.3	52.2	67.3	52	62	32	40
Cameroon	2,270	98.96	86	67.9	59.8	77.0	..	..	56	69
Cape Verde	..	82.89	..	..	..	..	98	100	67	67
Central African Republic	1,940	100.82	84	48.6	33.5	64.8	..	..	23[x]	36[x]
Chad	2,160	95.62	..	25.7	12.8	40.8	51	75	25	44
Comoros	..	90.57	..	..	..	..	50	59	42	50
Congo, Dem. Rep.	1,610	83.91	80[k]	67.2	54.1	80.9	..	..	24[x]	30[x]
Congo, Rep.	2,150	96.98	89	..	..	..	53	55	49	55
Côte d'Ivoire	2,630	90.24	..	48.7	38.6	60.8	54	67	32[x]	47[x]
Djibouti	..	121.25	75	..	..	..	32	40	21	27
Equatorial Guinea	..	82.56	..	87.0	80.5	93.4	78	91	52[x]	64[x]
Eritrea	1,520	83.38	52	..	..	..	42	49	29	41
Ethiopia	1,860	100.80	65	..	..	..	47	55	30	42
Gabon	2,670	92.63	30	71.0	..	..	78	79	68[x]	72[x]
Gambia	2,280	91.17	91	..	..	..	78	79	50	51
Ghana	2,650	105.01	78[k]	57.9	49.8	66.4	53	65	44	50
Guinea	2,420	104.31	98[k]	29.5	18.1	42.6	58	73	35	49
Guinea-Bissau	..	95.62	..	..	..	..	37	53	29[x]	45[x]
Kenya	2,150	98.21	33	73.6	70.2	77.7	66	66	58	62
Lesotho	2,620	104.91	75[k]	82.2	90.3	73.7	89	83	66	65
Liberia	1,940	84.97	..	..	..	..	61	79	..	..
Madagascar	2,040	92.74	91[k]	70.7	65.3	76.5	79	78	55	58
Malawi	2,140	90.83	92	64.1[m]	54.0[m]	74.9[m]	..	..	64	65
Mali	2,220	103.43	61	19.0[m]	11.9[m]	26.7[m]	39	50	30	40
Mauritania	2,780	90.99	..	51.2	43.4	59.5	67	68	44	47
Mauritius	2,960	100.07	..	84.4	80.5	88.4	98	96	74	75
Mozambique	2,070	97.64	50	..	..	..	53	58	44	53
Namibia	2,260	127.22	93	85.0	83.5	86.8	81	76	69[x]	66[x]
Niger	2,160	84.92	95	28.7	15.1	42.9	31	45	18	25
Nigeria	3,700	93.41	27	..	..	..	60	74	50	60
Rwanda	2,070	107.41	86	64.9	59.8	71.4	88	85	52	52
Senegal	2,310	88.52	..	39.3	29.2	51.1	54	61	36	41
Sierra Leone	1,930	94.73	84[k]	35.1	24.4	46.9	..	..	55	75
Somalia	..	85.62	..	..	..	..	..	..	..	..
South Africa	..	107.63	..	82.4[m]	80.9[m]	84.1[m]	89	89	77[x]	76[x]
Sudan	2,260	104.75	34	60.9	51.8[x]	71.1[x]	42	50	34	39
Swaziland	2,360	99.31	80	79.6	78.3	80.9	75	75	57[x]	59[x]
Tanzania	1,960	99.95	91[k]	69.4	62.2	77.5	81	83	47	49
Togo	2,320	103.79	84[k]	53.2	38.5	68.7	83	99	46	64
Uganda	2,380	93.23	..	66.8	57.7	76.8	..	..	65	67
Zambia	1,930	92.12	73[k]	68[m]	59.8[m]	76.3[m]	68	69	52	56
Zimbabwe	2,010	72.36	46	..	86.3	93.8	80	79	51[x]	54[x]
South Asia	..	..	**58**	..	..	..	**80**	**86**	..	..
Afghanistan	..	92.38	86[k]	..	..	..	..	..	..	..
Bangladesh	2,200	99.72	87[k]	..	..	..	86	82	58[x]	56[x]
Bhutan	..	87.93	..	47.0	..	..	..	..	..	..
India	2,440	98.55	45[k]	61.0	47.8	73.4	85	90	58	66
Maldives	..	79.15	..	96.3	96.4	96.2	93	92	69	68

| | Food Supply | | | Adult Literacy rate (% age 15 and above) 2004[c] | | | Educational enrollment (% of relevant age group) | | | |
| | Per Capita dietary energy supply (DES) (calories/day) 2001-2003 | Food production per capita 2005 | Vitamin A supplementation coverage rate (6 to 59 months) 2003 | | | | Primary school (net) 2000-2004[m] | | Primary secondary, tertiary (gross %) 2004 | |
				Total	Female	Male	Female	Male	Female	Male
Nepal	2,450	101.41	96[k]	48.6	34.9	62.7	66	75	52[x]	62[x]
Pakistan	2,340	99.96	95[k]	49.9	36.0	63.0	50	68	32	44
Sri Lanka	2,390	102.10	..	90.7	89.1	92.3	..	..	64[x]	63[x]
East Asia and the Pacific	..	**107.77[o]**	**73[e,i]**	..	..	..	**96[e]**	**96[e]**	..	..
Brunei	..	127.74	..	92.7	90.2	95.2	..	..	78	76
Cambodia	2,060	97.65	47	73.6	64.1	84.7	91	96	55[x]	65[x]
China	2,940	117.24	..	90.9	86.5	95.1	99	99	70	71
Hong Kong[a]	..	117.24	..	..	..	..	..	..	74	79
Fiji	..	91.11	..	..	..	..	100	100	76	74
Indonesia	2,880	115.47	62	90.4	86.8	94.0	92	93	67	70
Korea, DPR (North)	2,150	109.70	95[k]	..	..	..	..	..	..	..
Korea, Rep. (South)	3,040	92.72	..	98.0	..	..	100	100	88	101
Lao, PDR	2,320	102.10	64	68.7	60.9	77.0	82	88	55	66
Malaysia	2,870	114.88	..	88.7	85.4	92.0	93	93	76[x]	70[x]
Mongolia	2,250	69.04	87[k]	97.8	97.5	98.0	80	78	83	72
Myanmar (Burma)	2,900	116.43	87[k]	89.9	86.4	93.9	85	84	50	48
Papua New Guinea	..	96.77	1	57.3	50.9	63.4	69	79	38[x]	43[x]
Philippines	2,450	104.32	76[k]	92.6	92.7	92.5	95	93	84	79
Singapore	..	113.09	..	92.5	88.6	96.6	..	..	..	..
Solomon Islands	..	102.91	..	76.6[x]	..	..	..	..	45[x]	49[x]
Thailand	2,410	100.19	..	92.6	90.5	94.9	84	87	74	73
Vietnam	2,580	118.35	99[k,j]	90.3[m]	86.9[m]	93.9[m]	92	98	61	65
Latin America and Caribbean	..	**109.81[n]**	..	..	..	..	**94[f]**	**95[f]**	..	..
Argentina	2,980	106.76	..	97.2	97.2	97.2	..	..	94[x]	85[x]
Belize	..	105.72	..	75.1	..	..	100	98	81	81
Bolivia	2,220	105.81	38	86.7	80.7	93.1	95	95	83	89
Brazil	3,060	119.01	..	88.6	88.8	88.4	91	98	88[x]	84[x]
Chile	2,860	112.94	..	95.7	95.6	95.8	84	85	80	82
Colombia	2,580	106.24	..	92.8	92.7	92.9	87	88	74	71
Costa Rica	2,850	97.71	..	94.9	95.1	94.7	91	90	69[x]	67[x]
Cuba	3,190	101.68	..	99.8	99.8	99.8	93	94	81[x]	79[x]
Dominican Republic	2,290	101.99	40	87.0	87.2	86.8	94	99	78	70
Ecuador	2,710	104.91	..	91.0	89.7	92.3	100	99	..	..
El Salvador	2,560	89.69	..	..	..	..	90	90	69	70
Guatemala	2,210	89.23	..	69.1	63.3	75.4	86	89	63	69
Guyana	2,730	104.37	..	96.5[x]	..	..	98	100	78[x]	78[x]
Haiti	2,090	94.09	25	..	..	..	..	..	..	..
Honduras	2,360	134.43	35	80.0	80.2	79.8	88	87	74	68
Jamaica	2,680	93.57	..	79.9[m]	85.9[m]	74.1[m]	95	94	79	75
Mexico	3,180	101.76	..	91.0	89.6	92.4	100	99	76	75
Nicaragua	2,290	111.39	91	76.7	76.6	76.8	85	86	71	69
Panama	2,260	94.90	..	91.9	91.2	92.5	99	100	83	76
Paraguay	2,530	95.68	..	..	..	..	89	89	70[x]	69[x]
Peru	2,570	106.74	..	87.7	82.1	93.5	100	100	88	85
Suriname	2,660	101.39	..	89.6	87.2	92.0	98	96	77[x]	68[x]
Trinidad and Tobago	2,760	106.44	..	..	..	..	90	91	68	66
Uruguay	2,850	115.18	..	..	..	..	91	90	95[x]	84[x]
Venezuela	2,350	85.94	..	93.0	92.7	93.3	91	90	76[x]	73[x]
Middle East and North Africa	..	..	..	..	..	..	**78[h]**	**84[h]**	..	..
Algeria	3,040	112.40	..	69.9	60.1	79.6	94	96	73	73
Bahrain	..	125.78	..	86.5	83.6	88.6	91	89	89	82
Cyprus	..	101.44	..	96.8	95.1	98.6	96	96	79	78

TABLE 2: Global Food, Nutrition and Education

| | Food Supply | | Vitamin A supplementation coverage rate (6 to 59 months) 2003 | Adult Literacy rate (% age 15 and above) 2004c | | | Educational enrollment (% of relevant age group) | | | |
	Per Capita dietary energy supply (DES) (calories/day) 2001-2003	Food production per capita 2005					Primary school (net) 2000-2004m		Primary secondary, tertiary (gross %) 2004	
				Total	Female	Male	Female	Male	Female	Male
Egypt	3,350	105.77	..	71.4	59.4	83.0	90	93	..	..
Iran	3,090	107.37	..	77.0	70.4	83.5	85	88	70	74
Iraq	..	103.02	..	..	..	..	83	98	..	..
Jordan	2,680	104.81	..	89.9	84.7	95.1	93	91	80	78
Kuwait	3,060	112.53	..	93.3	91.0	94.4	84	82	79	69
Lebanon	3,170	94.70	..	..	..	..	90	91	85	82
Libya	3,330	92.78	..	..	..	..	..	..	98x	91x
Morocco	3,070	109.65	..	52.3	39.6	65.7	87	92	54	62
Oman	..	82.46	..	81.4	73.5	86.8	72	72	68	69
Qatar	..	105.37	..	89.0	88.6	89.1	94	95	82	71
Saudi Arabia	2,820	98.77	..	79.4	69.3	87.1	54	55	58	59
Syria	3,060	104.43	..	79.6	73.6	86.0	96	100	60	65
Tunisia	3,250	104.02	..	74.3	65.3	83.4	97	97	77	74
Turkey	3,340	97.73	..	87.4	79.6	95.3	84	89	63	75
United Arab Emirates	3,220	55.64	..	..	..	..	82	84	68x	54x
West Bank and Gazag	..	94.99	36	92.4	88.0	96.7	91	91	83	80
Yemen	2,020	90.26	36	..	..	..	59	84	42	68
Countries in Transitionb	..	..	..	..	..	..	..	..	..	..
Albania	2,860	103.49	..	98.7	98.3	99.2	94	96	67x	69x
Armenia	2,260	133.80	..	99.4	99.2	99.7	93	95	77	71
Azerbaijan	2,620	123.87	..	98.8m	98.2m	99.5m	79	81	67	69
Belarus	2,960	122.59	..	99.6m	99.4m	99.8m	94	95	90	86
Bosnia and Herzegovina	2,710	103.75	..	96.7	94.4	99.0	..	..	..	..
Bulgaria	2,850	97.06	..	98.2	97.7	98.7	90	91	81	81
Croatia	2,770	94.35	..	98.1	97.1	99.3	89	90	75x	72x
Czech Republic	3,240	97.22	..	..	..	..	87	87	82	81
Estonia	3,160	112.30	..	99.8	99.8	99.8	94	95	98	86
Georgia	2,520	105.78	..	100.0x	..	..	88	89	76	75
Hungary	3,500	109.93	..	..	..	..	90	91	90	85
Kazakhstan	2,710	114.28	..	99.5m	99.3m	99.8m	91	92	93	89
Kyrgyzstan	3,050	94.08	..	98.7m	98.1m	99.3m	88	91	80	77
Latvia	3,020	130.28	..	99.7	99.7	99.8	85	86	97	84
Lithuania	3,370	111.59	..	99.6	99.6	99.6	91	91	96	87
Macedonia, Republic of	2,800	102.47	..	96.1	94.1	98.2	91	91	71	69
Moldova	2,730	113.00	..	98.4	97.7	99.1	79	79	73	68
Poland	3,370	102.00	..	..	..	..	98	98	90	82
Romania	3,520	108.30	..	97.3	96.3	98.4	88	89	77	73
Russian Federation	3,080	115.61	..	99.4	99.2	99.7	90	89	92	84
Serbia and Montengrod	2,670	109.04	..	..	..	..	96	96	..	..
Slovakia	2,830	109.16	..	100.0	..	..	86	85	78	75
Slovenia	2,970	104.89	..	..	..	..	93	94	100	91
Tajikistan	1,840	143.88	..	99.5	99.2	99.7	91x	97	65	77
Turkmenistan	2,750	110.57	..	98.8m	98.3m	99.3m	..	..	..	..
Ukraine	3,030	118.19	93k	99.4	99.2	99.7	84	84	87	83
Uzbekistan	2,270	106.52	93k	..	..	..	..	..	72	75
Industrial Countries	..	**93.33l**	..	..	..	..	**96**	**95**	..	..
Australia	..	91.42	..	..	..	..	97	96	114	112
Austria	..	100.22	..	..	..	..	91	89	92	90
Belgium	..	96.37	..	..	..	..	100	100	96	93
Canada	..	102.85	..	..	..	..	100	100	96x	90x
Denmark	..	99.87	..	..	..	..	100	100	106	97
Finland	..	108.38	..	..	..	..	100	100	104	97
France	..	95.38	..	..	..	..	99	99	95	91
Germany	..	97.64	..	..	..	..	84	82	88	89

	Food Supply		Vitamin A supplementation coverage rate (6 to 59 months) 2003	Adult Literacy rate (% age 15 and above) 2004c			Educational enrollment (% of relevant age group)			
	Per Capita dietary energy supply (DES) (calories/day) 2001-2003	Food production per capita 2005					Primary school (net) 2000-2004m		Primary secondary, tertiary (gross %) 2004	
				Total	Female	Male	Female	Male	Female	Male
Greece	..	93.37	..	96.0	94.2	97.8	99	99	96	91
Ireland	..	92.00	..	..	..	..	97	95	101	97
Israel	..	105.82	..	97.1	95.9	98.5	99	99	92	87
Italy	..	97.68	..	98.4	98	98.8	99	100	92	87
Japan	..	96.38	..	..	..	..	100	100	84	86
Luxembourg	..	90.86	..	..	..	..	91	90	89	88
Netherlands	..	91.02	..	..	..	..	99	100	98	99
New Zealand	..	110.65	..	..	..	..	99	100	105	95
Norway	..	100.80	..	..	..	..	100	100	105	96
Portugal	..	99.75	..	92.0	..	..	99	100	93	86
Spain	..	94.13	..	98.0	..	..	99	100	99	93
Sweden	..	99.43	..	..	..	..	99	100	102	91
Switzerland	..	100.03	..	..	..	..	99	99	83	88
United Kingdom	..	95.40	..	..	..	..	100	100	96	90
United States	..	101.27	..	..	..	..	93	92	97	89
World	..	**104.66**	**61i**	..	..	..	**85**	**88**	..	..

The number '0' (zero) means zero or less than half the unit shown.
..   Data not available.
a   Special Administrative Region, data exclude China.
b   Central and Eastern European countries and newly independent states of the former Soviet Union.
c   Data refer to national literacy estimates from censuses or surveys conducted between 2000 and 2004, unless otherwise noted. Due to differences in methodology and timeliness of underlying data, comparisons across countries and over time should be made with caution.
d   Data from the years 1992-2002 refer to the Federal Republic of Yugoslavia. Data from before 1992 refer to the Socialist Federal Republic of Yugoslavia.
e   Data include the Cook Islands, Kiribati, Marshall Islands, Micronesia, Nauru, Nieu, Palau, Samoa, Tonga, Tuvalu and Vanuatu.
f   Data include Antigua and Barbuda, Bahamas, Barbados, Dominica, St. Kitts and Nevis, St. Lucia, and St. Vincent and the Grenadines.
g   Palestinian Territory.
h   Data include Djibouti, West Bank and Gaza, and Sudan. Data exclude Turkey.
i   This regional figure for East Asia and Pacific does not include China.
j   Identifies countries with Vitamin A supplementation programs that do not target children up to 59 months of age.
k   Identifies countries that have achieved a second round of vitamin A coverage greater than or equal to 70%.
l   Data include Iceland, Malta, and South Africa.
m   Data refer to the most recent year available.
n   Data include Antigua and Barbuda, Bahamas, Barbados, Dominica, Falkland Island, French Guiana, Grenada, Guadeloupe, Martinique, Puerto Rico, St. Kitts and Nevis, St. Lucia, and St. Vincent/Gernadines.
o   Data exclude China, Hong Kong, Fiji, Papua New Guinea and Solomon Islands.
p   Data include Sao Tomé and Principe and Seychelles. Data exclude Djibuti and Sudan.
x   Data refer to a period other than specified in the column heading, differ from the standard definition or refer to only part of a country.

TABLE 3: Hunger, Malnutrition and Poverty

	Undernourished population		% under-5 (1996-2004†) suffering from:				% population using improved drinking water sources 2002			Population in poverty(%)			
			Underweight		Wasting	Stunting				Below national poverty line 1985-2004†			Below international poverty line $1 a day 1989-2004†,g
	Proportion of the population undernourished (%) 2001-2003	Number of undernourished people (millions) 2001-2003	Moderate & severe	Severe	Moderate & severe	Moderate & severe	Total	Urban	Rural	National	Urban	Rural	
Developing Countries	**17**	**820.2**	**27**	**10**	**10**	**31**	**79**	**92**	**70**	..	..	..	..
Africa (sub-Saharan)	**32i**	**206.2i**	**28c**	**8c**	**9c**	**38c**	**57c**	**82c**	**44c**	..	..	..	**44.0**
Angola	38	5.0	31	8	6	45	50	70	40	..	..	..	..
Benin	14	0.9	23	5	8	31	68	79	60	29.0	23.3	33.0	30.9
Botswana	30	0.5	13	2	5	23	95	100	90	..	..	..	23.5
Burkina Faso	17	2.1	38	14	19	39	51	82	44	46.4	19.2	52.4	27.2
Burundi	67	4.5	45	13	8	57	79	90	78	36.4	43.0	36.0	54.6
Cameroon	25	4.0	18	4	5	32	63	84	41	40.2	22.1	49.9	17.1
Cape Verde	..	..	14x	2x	6x	16x	80	86	73	..	..	..	..
Central African Republic	45	1.7	24	6	9	39	75	93	61	..	..	..	66.6
Chad	33	2.7	28	9	11	29	34	40	32	64.0	63.0	67.0	..
Comoros	..	..	25	9	12	42	94	90	96	..	..	..	..
Congo, Dem. Rep.	72	37.0	31	9	13	38	46	83	29	..	..	..	..
Congo, Rep.	34	1.2	14	3	4	19	46	72	17	..	..	..	..
Côte d'Ivoire	14	2.2	17	5	7	21	84	98	74	..	..	..	14.8
Djibouti	..	..	18	6	13	26	80	82	67	..	..	..	..
Equatorial Guinea	..	..	19	4	7	39	44	45	42	..	..	..	..
Eritrea	73	2.9	40	12	13	38	57	72	54	53.0	..	..	..
Ethiopia	46	31.5	47	16	11	52	22	81	11	44.2	37.0	45.0	23.0
Gabon	5	0.1	12	2	3	21	87	95	47	..	..	..	..
Gambia	27	0.4	17	4	9	19	82	95	77	57.6	48.0	61.0	59.3
Ghana	12	2.4	22	5	7	30	79	93	68	39.5	18.6	49.9	44.8
Guinea	24	2.0	21	..	11	33	51	78	38	40.0	..	..	..
Guinea-Bissau	..	..	25	7	10	30	59	79	49	..	..	..	..
Kenya	31	9.7	20	4	6	30	62	89	46	52.0	49.0	53.0	22.8
Lesotho	12	0.2	18	4	5	46	76	88	74	..	..	..	36.4
Liberia	49	1.6	26	8	6	39	62	72	52	..	..	..	..
Madagascar	38	6.5	42	11	13	48	45	75	34	71.3	52.1	76.7	61.0
Malawi	34	4.0	22	..	5	45	67	96	62	65.3	54.9	66.5	41.7
Mali	28	3.5	33	11	11	38	48	76	35	63.8	30.1	75.9	72.3
Mauritania	10	0.3	32	10	13	35	56	63	45	46.3	25.4	61.2	25.9
Mauritius	6	0.1	15x	2x	14x	10x	100	100	100	..	..	..	..
Mozambique	45	8.3	24	6	4	41	42	76	24	69.4	62.0	71.3	37.9
Namibia	23	0.4	24	5	9	24	80	98	72	..	..	..	34.9
Niger	32	3.7	40	14	14	40	46	80	36	63.0	52.0	66.0	60.6
Nigeria	9	11.5	29	9	9	38	60	72	49	34.1	30.4	36.4	70.8
Rwanda	36	3.0	27	7	6	41	73	92	69	60.3	14.3	65.7	51.7
Senegal	23	2.2	23	6	8	25	72	90	54	33.4	23.7	40.4	22.3
Sierra Leone	50	2.4	27	9	10	34	57	75	46	70.2	56.4	79.0	57.0
Somalia	..	..	26	7	17	23	29	32	27	..	..	..	..
South Africa	..	..	12	2	3	25	87	98	73	..	..	..	10.7
Sudan	27	8.8	17x	7x	..	..	69	78	64	..	..	..	..
Swaziland	19	0.2	10	2	1	30	52	87	42	..	..	..	..
Tanzania	44	16.1	22	4	3	38	73	92	62	35.7	29.5	38.7	57.8
Togo	25	1.2	25	7	12	22	51	80	36	32.3	..	..	..
Uganda	19	4.6	23	5	4	39	56	87	52	37.7	12.2	41.7	..
Zambia	47	5.1	23	..	5	49	55	90	36	72.9	56.0	83.1	75.8
Zimbabwe	45	5.7	13	2	6	27	83	100	74	34.9	7.9	48.0	56.1
South Asia	**22i**	**298.5i**	**46**	**16**	**14**	**44**	**84**	**94**	**80**	..	..	..	**31.2**
Afghanistan	..	..	39	12	7	54	13	19	11	..	..	..	..
Bangladesh	30	43.1	48	13	13	43	75	82	72	49.8	36.6	53.0	36.0
Bhutan	..	..	19	3	3	40	62	86	60	..	..	..	..
India	20	212.0	47	18	16	46	86	96	82	28.6	24.7	30.2	34.7
Maldives	..	..	30	7	13	25	84	99	78	..	..	..	..

	Undernourished population		% under-5 (1995-2004[f]) suffering from:				% population using improved drinking water sources 2002			Population in poverty(%)			
			Underweight		Wasting	Stunting				Below national poverty line 1985-2004[f]			Below international poverty line $1 a day
	Proportion of the population undernourished (%) 2001-2003	Number of undernourished people (millions) 2001-2003	Moderate & severe	Severe	Moderate & severe	Moderate & severe	Total	Urban	Rural	National	Urban	Rural	1989-2004[f,g]
Nepal	17	4.1	48	13	10	51	84	93	82	30.9	9.6	34.6	24.1
Pakistan	23	35.2	38	12	13	37	90	95	87	32.6	24.2	35.9	17.0
Sri Lanka	22	4.1	29	..	14	14	78	99	72	25.0	15.0	27.0	5.6
East Asia and the Pacific	..	..	**15[d]**	..	..	**19[d]**	**78[d]**	**92[d]**	**68[d]**	..	..	..	**11.6**
Brunei	..	..	..	..	..	..	..	..	..	..	..	..	..
Cambodia	33	4.6	45	13	15	45	34	58	29	35.9	13.9	40.1	34.1
China	12	150.0	8	..	..	14	77	92	68	4.6	<2.0	4.6	16.6
Hong Kong[a]	..	..	..	..	..	..	..	..	..	..	..	..	..
Fiji	..	..	8[x]	1[x]	8[x]	3[x]	..	..	..	..	..	..	..
Indonesia	6	13.8	28	9	..	..	78	89	69	27.1	16.1	34.4	7.5
Korea, DPR (North)	35	7.9	23	8	7	37	100	100	100	..	..	..	..
Korea, Rep. (South)	<2.5	0.8	..	..	..	..	92	97	71	..	..	..	<2.0
Lao, PDR	21	1.2	40	13	15	42	43	66	38	38.6	26.9	41.0	27.0
Malaysia	3	0.6	11	1	..	..	95	96	94	15.5	..	..	<2.0
Mongolia	28	0.7	13	3	6	25	62	87	30	35.6	39.4	32.6	27.0
Myanmar (Burma)	5	2.7	32	7	9	32	80	95	74	..	..	..	..
Papua New Guinea	..	..	35[x]	..	..	..	39	88	32	37.5	16.1	41.3	..
Philippines	19	15.2	28	..	6	30	85	90	77	36.8	21.5	50.7	15.5
Singapore	..	..	14[x]	..	4[x]	11[x]	..	100	..	..	..	..	..
Solomon Islands	..	..	21[x]	4[x]	7[x]	27[x]	70	94	65	..	..	..	..
Thailand	21	13.4	19[x]	..	6[x]	16[x]	85	95	80	13.1	10.2	15.5	<2.0
Vietnam	17	13.8	28	4	7	32	73	93	67	28.9	6.6	35.6	..
Latin America and the Caribbean	**10**	**52.4**	**7[h]**	**1[h]**	**2[h]**	**16[h]**	**89[h]**	**95[h]**	**69[h]**	..	..	..	**8.9**
Argentina	<2.5	0.9	5	1	3	12	..	97	..	..	29.9	..	7.0
Belize	..	..	6[x]	1[x]	..	..	91	100	82	..	..	..	..
Bolivia	23	2.0	8	1	1	27	85	95	68	62.7	50.6	81.7	23.2
Brazil	8	14.4	6	1	2	11	89	96	58	22.0	14.7	51.4	7.5
Chile	4	0.6	1	..	0	2	95	100	59	17.0	..	..	<2.0
Colombia	14	5.9	7	1	1	14	92	99	71	64.0	55.0	79.0	7.0
Costa Rica	4	0.2	5	0	2	6	97	100	92	22.0	19.2	25.5	2.2
Cuba	<2.5	0.2	4	0	2	5	91	95	78	..	..	..	..
Dominican Republic	27	2.3	5	1	2	9	93	98	85	28.6	20.5	42.1	2.5
Ecuador	5	0.6	12	..	..	26	86	92	77	46.0	30.0	69.0	15.8
El Salvador	11	0.7	10	1	1	19	82	91	68	48.3	43.1	55.7	19.0
Guatemala	23	2.8	23	4	2	49	95	99	92	56.2	27.1	74.5	13.5
Guyana	9	0.1	14	3	11	11	83	83	83	..	..	..	..
Haiti	47	3.8	17	4	5	23	71	91	59	65.0	..	66.0	53.9
Honduras	22	1.5	17	..	1	29	90	99	82	48.0	37.0	58.0	20.7
Jamaica	10	0.3	4	..	2	5	93	98	87	18.7	12.8	25.1	<2.0
Mexico	5	5.1	8	1	2	18	91	97	72	20.3	11.4	34.8	4.5
Nicaragua	27	1.5	10	2	2	20	81	93	65	47.9	30.5	68.5	45.1
Panama	25	0.8	7	..	1	14	91	99	79	37.3	15.3	64.9	6.5
Paraguay	15	0.8	5	..	1	14	83	100	62	21.8	19.7	28.5	16.4
Peru	12	3.3	7	1	1	25	81	87	66	49.0	40.4	64.7	12.5
Suriname	10	0.0	13	2	7	10	92	98	73	..	..	..	..
Trinidad and Tobago	11	0.1	7[x]	0[x]	4[x]	5[x]	91	92	88	21.0	24.0	20.0	12.4
Uruguay	3	0.1	5[x]	1[x]	1[x]	8[x]	98	98	93	..	24.7	..	<2.0
Venezuela	18	4.5	4	..	3	13	83	85	70	31.3	..	..	8.3
Middle East and North Africa	**9[j]**	**37.6[j]**	**14[e]**	**3[e]**	**6[e]**	**21[e]**	**87[e]**	**95[e]**	**77[e]**	..	..	..	**1.6**
Algeria	5	1.5	10	3	8	19	87	92	80	22.6	14.7	30.3	<2.0
Bahrain	..	..	9[x]	2[x]	5[x]	10[x]	..	100	..	..	..	..	..

TABLE 3: Hunger, Malnutrition and Poverty

| | Undernourished population | | % under-5 (1995-2004f) suffering from: | | | | % population using improved drinking water sources 2002 | | | Population in poverty(%) | | | |
	Proportion of the population undernourished (%) 2001-2003	Number of undernourished people (millions) 2001-2003	Underweight Moderate & severe	Underweight Severe	Wasting Moderate & severe	Stunting Moderate & severe	Total	Urban	Rural	Below national poverty line 1985-2004f National	Below national poverty line 1985-2004f Urban	Below national poverty line 1985-2004f Rural	Below international poverty line $1 a day 1989-2004f,g
Cyprus	..	..	..	..	..	..	100	100	100	..	..	..	..
Egypt	3	2.4	9	1	4	16	98	100	97	16.7	22.5	23.3	3.1
Iran	4	2.7	11	2	5	15	93	98	83	..	..	..	<2.0
Iraq	..	..	16	2	6	22	81	97	50	..	..	..	..
Jordan	7	0.4	4	1	2	9	91	91	91	11.7	..	..	<2.0
Kuwait	5	0.1	10	3	11	24	..	..	..	..	..	..	..
Lebanon	3	0.1	3	0	3	12	100	100	100	..	..	..	..
Libya	<2.5	0.0	5x	1x	3x	15x	72	72	68	..	..	..	..
Morocco	6	1.9	9	2	4	24	80	99	56	19.0	12.0	27.2	<2.0
Oman	..	..	24x	4x	13x	23x	79	81	72	..	..	..	..
Qatar	..	..	6x	..	2x	8x	100	100	100	..	..	..	..
Saudi Arabia	4	0.9	14	3	11	20	..	97	..	..	..	..	..
Syria	4	0.6	7	1	4	18	79	94	64	..	..	..	..
Tunisia	<2.5	0.1	4	1	2	12	82	94	60	7.6	3.6	13.9	<2.0
Turkey	3	2.0	4	1	1	12	93	96	87	27.0	22.0	34.5	3.4
United Arab Emirates	<2.5	0.1	14x	3x	15x	17x	..	..	..	..	..	..	..
West Bank and Gazam	..	..	4	1	3	9	94	97	86	..	..	..	..
Yemen	37	7.1	46	15	12	53	69	74	68	41.8	30.8	45.0	15.7
Countries in Transitionb	**6**	**24.7**	..	..	..	..	**91**	**98**	**79**	..	..	..	..
Albania	6	0.2	14	1	11	34	97	99	95	25.4	19.8	29.6	<2.0
Armenia	29	0.9	3	0	2	13	92	99	80	50.9	51.9	48.7	<2.0
Azerbaijan	10	0.8	7	1	2	13	77	95	59	49.0	55.0	42.0	<2.0
Belarus	3	0.3	..	..	..	..	100	100	100	41.9	..	..	<2.0
Bosnia and Herzegovina	9	0.4	4	1	6	10	98	100	96	19.5	13.8	19.9	..
Bulgaria	9	0.7	..	..	..	..	100	100	100	12.8	..	..	<2.0
Croatia	7	0.3	1	..	1	1	..	..	..	..	..	..	<2.0
Czech Republic	<2.5	0.1	1x	0x	2x	2x	..	..	..	..	..	..	<2.0
Estonia	3	0.0	..	..	..	..	..	..	..	8.9	6.8	14.7	<2.0
Georgia	13	0.7	3	0	2	12	76	90	61	54.5	56.2	52.7	6.5
Hungary	<2.5	0.0	2x	0x	2x	3x	99	100	98	17.3	..	..	<2.0
Kazakhstan	8	1.2	4	0	2	10	86	96	72	34.6	30.0	39.0	<2.0
Kyrgyzstan	4	0.2	11	2	3	25	76	98	66	47.6	41.2	51.0	<2.0
Latvia	3	0.1	..	..	..	..	..	..	..	..	..	..	<2.0
Lithuania	..	0.0	..	..	..	..	..	..	..	..	..	..	<2.0
Macedonia, Republic of	7	0.1	6	1	4	7	..	..	..	..	..	..	<2.0
Moldova	11	0.5	3	..	3	10	92	97	88	48.5	42.6	67.2	22.0
Poland	<2.5	0.3	..	..	..	..	..	100	..	23.8	..	..	<2.0
Romania	<2.5	0.1	6x	1x	3x	8x	57	91	16	21.5	20.4	27.9	<2.0
Russian Federation	3	4.1	3x	1x	4x	13x	96	99	88	30.9	..	..	<2.0
Serbia and Montenegrok	10	1.1	2	0	4	5	93	99	86	..	..	..	..
Slovakia	6	0.3	..	..	..	..	100	100	100	..	..	..	<2.0
Slovenia	3	0.1	..	..	..	..	..	..	..	..	..	..	<2.0
Tajikistan	61	3.8	..	..	5	36	58	93	47	..	..	..	7.4
Turkmenistan	8	0.4	12	2	6	22	71	93	54	..	..	..	12.1
Ukraine	3	1.2	1	0	0	3	98	100	94	19.5	..	28.4	<2.0
Uzbekistan	26	6.7	8	2	7	21	89	97	84	27.5	22.5	30.5	..
Industrial Countries	..	..	..	..	..	..	**100**	**100**	**100**	..	..	..	..
Australia	..	..	..	..	..	..	100	100	100	..	..	..	..
Austria	..	..	..	..	..	..	100	100	100	..	..	..	..
Belgium	..	..	..	..	..	..	..	100	..	..	..	..	..
Canada	..	..	..	..	..	..	100	100	99	..	..	..	..
Denmark	..	..	..	..	..	..	100	100	100	..	..	..	..
Finland	..	..	..	..	..	..	100	100	100	..	..	..	..
France	..	..	..	..	..	..	..	100	..	..	..	..	..

| | Undernourished population | | % under-5 (1995-2004[f]) suffering from: | | | | % population using improved drinking water sources 2002 | | | Population in poverty(%) | | | |
| | Proportion of the population undernourished (%) 2001-2003 | Number of undernourished people (millions) 2001-2003 | Underweight | | Wasting | Stunting | | | | Below national poverty line 1985-2004[f] | | | Below international poverty line $1 a day 1989-2004[f,g] |
			Moderate & severe	Severe	Moderate & severe	Moderate & severe	Total	Urban	Rural	National	Urban	Rural	
Germany	..	..	..	..	..	..	100	100	100	..	..	..	..
Greece	..	..	..	..	..	..	..	..	..	..	..	..	..
Ireland	..	..	..	..	..	..	..	100	..	..	..	..	..
Israel	..	..	..	..	..	..	100	100	100	..	..	..	..
Italy	..	..	..	..	..	..	..	100	..	..	..	..	..
Japan	..	..	..	..	..	..	100	100	100	..	..	..	..
Luxembourg	..	..	..	..	..	..	100	100	100	..	..	..	..
Netherlands	..	..	..	..	..	..	100	100	99	..	..	..	..
New Zealand	..	..	..	..	..	..	..	100	..	..	..	..	..
Norway	..	..	..	..	..	..	100	100	100	..	..	..	..
Portugal	..	..	..	..	..	..	..	..	..	..	..	..	<2.0
Spain	..	..	..	..	..	..	..	..	..	..	..	..	..
Sweden	..	..	..	..	..	..	100	100	100	..	..	..	..
Switzerland	..	..	..	..	..	..	100	100	100	..	..	..	..
United Kingdom	..	..	..	..	..	..	..	100	..	..	..	..	..
United States	..	..	1[x]	0[x]	1[x]	2[x]	100	100	100	..	..	..	..
World	..	..	**26**	**10**	**10**	**31**	**83**	**95**	**72**	..	..	..	**19.4**

The number '0' (zero) means zero or less than half the unit of measure.

.. Data not available.

a Special Administrative Region, data exclude China.

b Central and Eastern European countries and the newly independent states of the former Soviet Union.

c Data include São Tomé and Principe and Seychelles. Data exclude Djibouti and Sudan.

d Data include the Cook Islands, Kiribati, Marshall Islands, Micronesia, Nauru, Nieu, Palau, Samoa, Tonga, Tuvalu and Vanuatu. Data exclude Hong Kong.

e Data include Djibouti, West Bank and Gaza, and Sudan. Data exclude Turkey.

f Data refer to the most recent year available during the period specified in the column heading.

g Measured in 1985 international prices and adjusted to local currency using purchasing power parities. Poverty rates comparable across countries, but revisions in PPP exchange rates prevents comparing this data to previous rates reported.

h Data include Antigua and Barbuda, Bahamas, Barbados, Dominica, St. Kitts and Nevis, St. Lucia, and St. Vincent and the Grenadines.

i Data exclude Afghanistan.

j Although not listed separately, provisional estimates for Afghanistan, Iraq, Paupa New Guinea and Somalia have been included in the relevant regional aggregates.

k Data from years 1992-2002 referred to the Federal Republic of Yugoslavia. Data from before 1992 referred to the Socialist Federal Republic of Yugoslavia.

m Palestinian Territory.

x Indicates data that refer to years or periods other than those specified in the column heading, differ from the standard definition or refer to only part of a country.

TABLE 4: Economic and Development Indicators

	GNI per capita US$ 2004	GNI per capita Purchasing power parity (PPP) per capita ($) 2004	GDP per capita % of 2003-2004	Human Development Index (HDI) rank 2004	Distribution of income or consumption by quintiles[k] 1983-2004[t] Lowest 20%	Second quintile	Third quintile	Fourth quintile	Highest 20%	Ratio of highest 20% to lowest 20%[e]	Total central government expenditure (% of GDP) 2004	Public education expenditure (% of GDP) 2002-2004[t,y]	Military expenditure (% of GDP) 2004	Per capita energy consumption (kg. of oil equivalent) 2003	Average annual deforestation[m] (% of total forest) 1990-2005
Developing Countries	..	..	..	..	..	..	..	..	..	..	..	..	..	..	..
Africa (sub-Saharan)	601	1,842	2.6	..	..	..	..	..	..	..	..	..	..	681	0.6
Angola	930	1,930[c]	7.9	161	..	..	..	..	..	..	..	..	4.2	606	0.2
Benin	450	1,090	-0.5	163	7.4	11.3	15.4	21.5	44.5	6.01	..	3.3[s]	..	292	2.0
Botswana	4,360	9,580	5.0	131	2.2	4.9	8.2	14.4	70.3	31.95	..	..	3.8	..	0.9
Burkina Faso	350	1,170[c]	0.6	174	6.9	10.9	14.5	20.5	47.2	6.84	..	..	1.3	..	0.3
Burundi	90	660[c]	1.9	169	5.1	10.3	15.1	21.5	48.0	9.41	..	5.2	6.3	..	3.2
Cameroon	810	2,120	2.4	144	5.6	9.3	13.7	20.4	50.9	9.09	..	3.8	1.4	429	0.9
Cape Verde	..	..	..	106	..	..	..	..	..	..	..	7.3	0.7	..	..
Central African Republic	310	1,100[c]	0.0	172	2.0	4.9	9.6	18.5	65.0	32.50	..	..	1.2	..	0.1
Chad	250	1,340	25.5	171	..	..	..	..	..	..	..	..	1.0	..	0.6
Comoros	..	..	..	132	..	..	..	..	..	..	..	3.9	..	..	..
Congo, Dem. Rep.	110	680[c]	3.2	167	..	..	..	..	..	..	7.8[aa]	..	3.0	293	0.3
Congo, Rep.	760	740	0.6	140	..	..	..	..	..	..	19.9[aa]	3.2[s]	..	273	0.1
Côte d'Ivoire	760	1,470	0.1	164	5.2	9.1	13.7	21.3	50.7	9.75	17.5	..	..	374	-0.1
Djibouti	..	..	..	148	..	..	..	..	..	..	..	6.1	..	..	..
Equatorial Guinea	..	..	..	120	..	..	..	..	..	..	..	0.6[s]	..	..	..
Eritrea	190	960[c]	-2.5	157	..	..	..	..	..	..	..	3.8	..	..	0.3
Ethiopia	110	750[c]	10.9	170	9.1	13.2	16.8	21.5	39.4	4.33	26.7[aa]	4.6[s]	..	299	0.9
Gabon	4,080	5,700	-0.2	124	..	..	..	..	..	..	..	..	1.7	1,256	0.1
Gambia	280	1,890[c]	5.4	155	4.8	8.7	12.8	20.3	53.4	11.13	..	1.9[s]	0.4	..	-0.4
Ghana	380	2,220[c]	3.6	136	5.6	10.1	14.9	22.9	46.6	8.32	20.9	..	0.8	400	1.7
Guinea	410	2,160	0.4	160	6.4	10.4	14.8	21.2	47.2	7.38	..	..	..	..	0.6
Guinea-Bissau	160	690[c]	1.2	173	5.2	8.8	13.1	19.4	53.4	10.27	..	..	..	..	0.4
Kenya	480	1,130	2.0	152	6.0	9.8	14.3	20.8	49.1	8.18	20.6[aa]	7.0	1.6	494	0.3
Lesotho	730	3,250[c]	2.5	149	1.5	4.3	8.9	18.8	66.5	44.33	38.0[aa]	9.0[s]	2.3	..	-4.0
Liberia	120	..	1.8	..	..	..	..	..	..	..	..	..	..	..	1.5
Madagascar	290	840	2.4	143	4.9	8.5	12.7	20.4	53.5	10.92	63.0	3.3	..	..	0.4
Malawi	160	630	4.4	166	4.9	8.5	12.3	18.3	56.1	11.45	..	6.0	..	..	0.9
Mali	330	950	-0.8	175	4.6	8.0	11.9	19.3	56.2	12.22	..	..	1.9	..	0.7
Mauritania	530	2,050[c]	3.7	153	6.2	10.6	15.2	22.3	45.7	7.37	..	3.4	1.4	..	2.4
Mauritius	4,640	11,950	3.2	63	..	..	..	..	..	..	21.8[aa]	4.7	0.2	..	0.3
Mozambique	270	1,170[c]	5.1	168	6.5	10.8	15.1	21.1	46.5	7.15	..	..	1.3	430	0.3
Namibia	2,380	7,520[c]	4.7	125	1.4[bb]	3.0[bb]	5.4[bb]	11.5[bb]	78.7[bb]	56.21	31.1[aa]	7.2	3.1	635	0.8
Niger	210	780[c]	-2.4	177	2.6	7.1	13.9	23.1	53.3	20.50	..	2.3	1.1	..	2.3
Nigeria	430	970[c]	3.7	159	5.0	9.6	14.5	21.7	49.2	9.84	..	..	1.0	777	2.4
Rwanda	210	1,240	2.5	158	9.7	13.2	16.5	21.6	39.1	4.03	..	..	2.2	..	-3.4
Senegal	630	1,660[c]	3.7	156	6.4	10.3	14.5	20.6	48.2	7.53	15.6[aa]	4.0	1.4	287	0.5
Sierra Leone	210	550	3.0	176	1.1	2.0	9.8	23.7	63.4	57.64	..	..	1.2	..	0.6
Somalia	..[d]	..	..	..	..	..	..	..	..	..	..	..	..	..	0.9
South Africa	3,630	10,960[c]	4.4	121	3.5	6.3	10.0	18.0	62.2	17.77	29.4[aa]	5.4	1.4	2,587	0.0
Sudan	530	1,810[c]	4.0	141	..	..	..	..	..	..	..	..	0.0	477	0.8
Swaziland	1,660	5,650	0.8	146	2.7[bb]	5.8[bb]	10.0[bb]	17.1[bb]	64.4[bb]	23.85	23.2[aa]	6.2	..	..	-1.0
Tanzania	320[n]	670	4.3	162	7.3	12.0	16.1	22.3	42.4	5.81	..	..	1.1	465	1.0
Togo	310	1,510[c]	0.4	147	..	..	..	..	..	..	..	2.6	1.6	445	2.9
Uganda	250	1,450[c]	2.1	145	5.9	10.0	14.0	20.3	49.7	8.42	22.8[aa]	5.2[s]	2.3	..	1.8
Zambia	400	890	2.9	165	6.1	10.2	14.2	20.7	48.8	5.03	..	2.8[s]	..	592	0.9
Zimbabwe	620	2,040	-4.7	151	4.6	8.1	12.2	19.3	55.7	12.11	..	..	..	752	1.4
South Asia	594	2,854	5.0	..	..	..	..	..	..	..	15.1	..	..	474	-0.2
Afghanistan	..[d]	..	..	..	..	..	..	..	..	..	13.2	..	..	..	2.3
Bangladesh	440	1,970	4.3	137	9.0	12.5	15.9	21.2	41.3	4.59	8.8[aa]	2.2	1.2	159	0.1
Bhutan	..	..	..	135	..	..	..	..	..	..	..	..	..	..	..
India	620	3,120[c]	5.4	126	8.9	12.3	16.0	21.2	43.3	4.87	15.9[aa]	3.3	3.0	520	-0.4
Maldives	..	..	..	98	..	..	..	..	..	..	..	8.1[s]	..	..	..
Nepal	250	1,480	1.4	138	6.0	9.0	12.4	18.0	54.6	9.10	..	3.4	1.7	336	1.6
Pakistan	600	2,170	3.9	134	9.3	13.0	16.3	21.1	40.3	4.33	14.7[aa]	2.0	3.4	467	1.7
Sri Lanka	1,010	4,210	4.5	93	8.3	12.5	16.0	21.0	42.2	5.08	22.9[aa]	..	2.8	421	1.2

	GNI per capita		GDP per capita	Human Development Index	Distribution of income or consumption by quintiles[k] 1983-2004[t]					Ratio of highest 20% to lowest 20%[e]	Total central government expenditure (% of GDP)	Public education expenditure (% of GDP)	Military expenditure (% of GDP)	Per capita energy consumption (kg. of oil equivalent)	Average annual deforestation[m] (% of total forest)
	US$ 2004	Purchasing power parity (PPP) per capita ($) 2004	% of 2003-2004	(HDI) rank 2004	Lowest 20%	Second quintile	Third quintile	Fourth quintile	Highest 20%		2004	2002-2004[t,v]	2004	2003	1990-2005
East Asia and the Pacific	**1,416[q]**	**5,332[q]**	**8.1[q]**	..	..	..	..	..	..	..	**12.0**	..	..	**1,007[q]**	**-0.2**
Brunei	..	..	..	34	..	..	..	..	..	..	..	..	..	..	..
Cambodia	350	2,310[c]	5.6	129	6.9	10.7	14.7	20.1	47.6	6.90	9.1	2.0	2.2	..	1.3
China	1,500	5,890[u]	9.4	81	4.7	9.0	14.2	22.1	50.0	10.64	10.4	..	2.4	1,094	-1.7
Hong Kong[a]	26,660	31,560	6.9	22	5.3[bb]	9.4[bb]	13.9[bb]	20.7[bb]	50.7[bb]	9.57	..	4.7	..	2,428	..
Fiji	..	..	..	90	..	..	..	..	..	..	..	..	6.4	1.2	..
Indonesia	1,140	3,480	3.7	108	8.4	11.9	15.4	21.0	43.3	5.15	16.8[aa]	0.9	1.1	753	1.6
Korea, DPR (North)	..[d]	..	..	..	..	..	..	..	..	..	..	..	..	896	1.6
Korea, Rep. (South)	14,000	20,530	4.1	26	7.9[bb]	13.6[bb]	18.0[bb]	23.1[bb]	37.5[bb]	4.75	18.6[aa]	4.6	2.4	4,291	0.1
Lao, PDR	390	1,880	3.9	133	8.1	11.9	15.6	21.1	43.3	5.35	..	2.3	..	..	0.5
Malaysia	4,520	9,720	5.2	61	4.4[bb]	8.1[bb]	12.9[bb]	20.3[bb]	54.3[bb]	12.34	20.1[aa]	8.0	2.3	2,318	0.4
Mongolia	600	2,040	9.2	116	5.6	10.0	13.8	19.4	51.2	9.14	30.8	5.6	2.0	..	0.7
Myanmar (Burma)	..[d]	..	..	130	..	..	..	..	..	..	..	..	..	276	1.2
Papua New Guinea	560	2,280[c]	0.4	139	4.5	7.9	11.9	19.2	56.5	12.56	23.4[aa]	..	0.6	..	0.4
Philippines	1,170	4,950	4.2	84	5.4	8.8	13.1	20.5	52.3	9.69	..	3.2	0.9	525	2.2
Singapore	24,760	27,370	7.0	25	5.0[bb]	9.4[bb]	14.6[bb]	22.0[bb]	49.0[bb]	9.80	15.5[aa]	..	4.7	5,359	0.0
Solomon Islands	..	..	..	128	..	..	..	..	..	..	..	..	..	..	..
Thailand	2,490	7,930	5.3	74	6.3	9.9	14.0	20.8	49.0	7.78	17.1	4.2	1.2	1,406	0.6
Vietnam	540	2,700	6.6	109	7.5	11.2	14.8	21.1	45.4	6.05	..	..	..	544	-2.5
Latin America and the Caribbean	**3,576**	**7,661**	**4.4**	..	..	..	..	..	..	..	..	..	..	**1,148**	**0.4**
Argentina	3,580	12,530	7.9	36	3.2[bb,cc]	7.0[bb,cc]	12.1[bb,cc]	20.7[bb,cc]	56.8[bb,cc]	17.75	18.3	3.5	1.1	1,575	0.4
Belize	..	..	..	95	..	..	..	..	..	..	..	5.1	..	..	..
Bolivia	960	2,600	1.6	115	1.5	5.9	10.9	18.7	63.0	42.00	27.2	6.4[s]	2.0	504	0.4
Brazil	3,000	7,940	3.5	69	2.6[bb]	6.2[bb]	10.7[bb]	18.4[bb]	62.1[bb]	23.88	..	4.1	1.5	1,065	0.5
Chile	5,220	10,610	4.9	38	3.3[bb]	6.6[bb]	10.5[bb]	17.4[bb]	62.2[bb]	18.85	18.4	3.7	3.9	1,647	-0.4
Colombia	2,020	6,940[c]	2.5	70	2.5[bb]	6.2[bb]	10.6[bb]	18.0[bb]	62.7[bb]	25.08	22.9	4.9	3.8	642	0.1
Costa Rica	4,470	9,220[c]	2.3	48	3.9[bb]	8.1[bb]	12.8[bb]	20.4[bb]	54.8[bb]	14.05	22.7[aa]	4.9	0.0	880	0.5
Cuba	..[h]	..	0.8	50	..	..	..	..	..	..	..	..	..	1,000	-2.1
Dominican Republic	2,100	6,860[c]	0.5	94	3.9[bb]	7.8[bb]	12.1[bb]	19.4[bb]	56.8[bb]	14.56	13.2[aa]	1.1	0.5	923	0.0
Ecuador	2,210	3,770	5.4	83	3.3	7.5	11.7	19.4	58.0	17.58	..	..	2.4	708	1.4
El Salvador	2,320	4,890[c]	-0.2	101	2.7[bb]	7.5[bb]	12.8[bb]	21.2[bb]	55.9[bb]	20.70	17.0	2.8[s]	0.7	675	1.4
Guatemala	2,190	4,260[c]	0.2	118	2.9[bb]	7.0[bb]	11.6[bb]	19.0[bb]	59.5[bb]	20.52	11.1[aa]	..	0.4	608	1.1
Guyana	..	..	..	103	..	..	..	..	..	..	..	5.5	..	..	..
Haiti	400	..	-1.0	154	2.4	6.2	10.4	17.7	63.4	26.42	..	..	..	270	0.6
Honduras	1,040	2,760[c]	2.3	117	3.4[bb]	7.1[bb]	11.6[bb]	19.6[bb]	58.3[bb]	17.15	..	..	0.7	522	2.5
Jamaica	3,300[i]	3,950	0.4	104	6.7	10.7	15.0	21.7	46.0	6.87	41.1[aa]	4.9	0.7	1,543	0.1
Mexico	6,790	9,640	2.9	53	4.3	8.3	12.6	19.7	55.1	12.81	..	5.8	0.4	1,564	0.5
Nicaragua	830[p]	3,480	3.0	112	5.6	9.8	14.2	21.1	49.3	8.80	19.7[aa]	3.1[s]	0.7	588	1.4
Panama	4,210	6,730[c]	4.4	59	2.5[bb]	6.4[bb]	11.2[bb]	19.6[bb]	60.3[bb]	24.12	23.2[aa]	3.9[s]	0.0	836	0.1
Paraguay	1,140	4,820[c]	1.6	91	2.2[bb]	6.3[bb]	11.3[bb]	18.8[bb]	61.3[bb]	27.86	12.9[aa]	4.3	0.7	679	0.9
Peru	2,360	5,400	3.3	82	3.2[bb]	7.1[bb]	11.8[bb]	19.3[bb]	58.7[bb]	18.34	16.9[aa]	3.0	1.2	442	0.1
Suriname	..	..	..	89	..	..	..	..	..	..	..	..	..	..	..
Trinidad and Tobago	8,730	11,430	5.9	57	5.5[bb]	10.3[bb]	15.5[bb]	22.7[bb]	45.9[bb]	8.35	..	4.3	..	8,553	0.3
Uruguay	3,900	9,030	11.1	43	5.0[bb,cc]	9.1[bb,cc]	14.0[bb,cc]	21.5[bb,cc]	50.5[bb,cc]	10.10	27.5[aa]	2.2	1.2	738	-4.4
Venezuela	4,030	5,830	15.8	72	4.7[bb]	9.4[bb]	14.5[bb]	22.1[bb]	49.3[bb]	10.49	25.2[aa]	..	1.2	2,112	0.6
Middle East and North Africa	**1,972[r]**	**5,734[r]**	**3.8[r]**	..	..	..	..	..	..	..	..	..	..	**1,144[r]**	**-0.5**
Algeria	2,270	6,320[c]	3.6	102	7.0	11.6	16.1	22.7	42.6	6.09	24.6[aa]	..	3.4	1,036	-1.8
Bahrain	..	..	..	39	..	..	..	..	..	..	..	..	4.4	..	..
Cyprus	..	..	..	29	..	..	..	..	..	..	..	7.4	1.5	..	..
Egypt	1,250	4,200	2.2	111	8.6	12.1	15.4	20.4	43.6	5.07	..	..	2.8	735	-3.5
Iran	2,320	7,530	4.6	96	5.1	9.4	14.1	21.5	49.9	9.78	20.2[aa]	4.8	4.5	2,055	0.0
Iraq	..[h]	..	..	..	..	..	..	..	..	..	..	..	..	..	-0.2
Jordan	2,190	4,770[c]	5.1	86	6.7	10.8	14.9	21.3	46.3	6.91	31.9[aa]	..	8.2	1,027	0.0
Kuwait	22,470	21,610[c]	4.5	33	..	..	..	..	..	..	43.3[aa]	8.2	7.9	9,566	-6.7
Lebanon	6,010	5,550	5.2	78	..	..	..	..	..	..	30.8	2.6	3.8	1,700	-0.8

TABLE 4: Economic and Development Indicators

	GNI per capita US$ 2004	GNI per capita Purchasing power parity (PPP) per capita ($) 2004	GDP per capita % of 2003-2004	Human Development Index (HDI) rank 2004	Distribution of income or consumption by quintiles[k] 1983-2004[l] Lowest 20%	Second quintile	Third quintile	Fourth quintile	Highest 20%	Ratio of highest 20% to lowest 20%[e]	Total central government expenditure (% of GDP) 2004	Public education expenditure (% of GDP) 2002-2004[l,y]	Military expenditure (% of GDP) 2004	Per capita energy consumption (kg. of oil equivalent) 2003	Average annual deforestation[m] (% of total forest) 1990-2005
Libya	4,400	..	2.5	64	..	..	..	..	..	..	..	..	2.0	3,191	0.0
Morocco	1,570	4,250	0.7	123	6.5	10.6	14.8	21.3	46.6	7.17	..	6.3	4.5	378	-0.1
Oman	9,070	14,680	2.2	56	..	..	..	..	..	..	26.9aa	4.6s	12.0	4,975	0.0
Qatar	..	..	..	46	..	..	..	..	..	..	..	..	..	..	..
Saudi Arabia	10,140	13,810c	2.5	76	..	..	..	..	..	..	..	..	8.3	5,607	0.0
Syria	1,230	3,500	-0.4	107	..	..	..	..	..	..	..	..	6.6	986	-1.6
Tunisia	2,650	7,430	4.9	87	6.0	10.3	14.8	21.7	47.3	7.88	28.4aa	8.1	1.5	837	-4.3
Turkey	3,750	7,720	7.4	92	5.3	9.7	14.2	21.0	49.7	9.38	..	3.7	3.1	1,117	-0.3
United Arab Emirates	23,770	24,090	1.5	49	..	..	..	..	..	..	..	1.6s	2.4	9,707	-1.8
West Bank and Gaza[w]	1,120	..	-5.6	100	..	..	..	..	..	..	..	..	..	..	..
Yemen	550	810	-0.5	150	7.4	12.2	16.7	22.5	41.2	5.57	..	..	6.3	289	0.0
Countries in Transition[b]	..	..	..	..	..	..	..	..	..	..	..	..	..	..	..
Albania	2,120	5,070	5.3	73	9.1	13.5	17.3	22.8	37.4	4.11	..	2.8s	1.2	674	0.0
Armenia	1,060	4,160	7.4	80	8.5	12.3	15.7	20.6	42.8	5.04	18.6aa	3.2	2.6	660	1.2
Azerbaijan	940	3,810	9.2	99	12.2	15.8	18.7	22.2	31.1	2.55	..	3.3s	1.8	1,493	0.0
Belarus	2,140	6,970	11.6	67	8.5	13.2	17.3	22.7	38.3	4.51	28.5aa	5.8	1.4	2,613	-0.5
Bosnia and Herzegovina	2,040	7,230	6.4	62	9.5	14.2	17.9	22.6	35.8	3.77	38.6	..	2.5	1,137	0.1
Bulgaria	2,750	7,940	6.4	54	8.7	13.7	17.2	22.1	38.3	4.40	35.3aa	4.2	2.4	2,494	-0.6
Croatia	6,820	11,920	3.8	44	8.3	12.8	16.8	22.6	39.6	4.77	42.0aa	4.5	1.7	1,976	-0.1
Czech Republic	9,130	18,420	4.3	30	10.3bb	14.5bb	17.7bb	21.7bb	35.9bb	3.49	36.1	4.6	1.8	4,324	-0.1
Estonia	7,080	13,630	8.2	40	6.7	11.8	16.3	22.4	42.8	6.39	26.7aa	5.7	1.8	3,631	-0.4
Georgia	1,060	2,900c	7.3	97	5.6	10.5	15.3	22.3	46.4	8.29	14.4aa	2.9	1.4	597	0.0
Hungary	8,370	15,800	4.9	35	9.5	13.9	17.6	22.4	36.5	3.84	41.6	6.0	1.5	2,600	-0.7
Kazakhstan	2,250	6,930	8.8	79	7.4	11.9	16.4	22.8	41.5	5.61	14.9aa	2.4	1.0	3,342	0.2
Kyrgyzstan	400	1,860	5.9	110	8.9	12.8	16.4	22.5	39.4	4.43	15.8aa	4.4s	2.9	528	-0.3
Latvia	5,580	11,820	8.9	45	6.6	11.2	15.5	22.0	44.7	6.77	28.1aa	5.4	1.7	1,881	-0.4
Lithuania	5,740	12,690	7.2	41	6.8	11.6	16.0	22.3	43.2	6.35	28.8	5.2	1.7	2,585	-0.5
Macedonia, Republic of	2,420	6,560	2.7	66	6.1	10.8	15.5	22.2	45.5	7.46	..	3.4	2.6	..	0.0
Moldova	720g	1,950	7.6	114	7.8	12.2	16.5	22.1	41.4	5.31	27.1aa	4.9s	0.4	772	-0.2
Poland	6,100	12,730	5.5	37	7.5	11.9	16.1	22.2	42.2	5.63	39.3aa	5.8	2.0	2,452	-0.2
Romania	2,960	8,330	8.6	60	8.1	12.9	17.1	22.7	39.2	4.84	25.9aa	3.6	2.1	1,794	0.0
Russian Federation	3,400	9,680	7.7	65	6.1	10.5	14.9	21.8	46.6	7.64	21.9	3.7	3.9	4,424	0.0
Serbia and Montenegro[v]	2,680o	..	8.3	..	..	..	..	..	..	..	39.9aa	..	..	1,991	-0.4
Slovakia	6,480	14,480	5.4	42	8.8bb	14.9bb	18.7bb	22.8bb	34.8bb	3.95	36.8	4.4	1.7	3,443	0.0
Slovenia	14,770	20,830	4.5	27	9.1bb	14.2bb	18.1bb	22.9bb	35.7bb	3.92	41.2aa	6.0	1.6	3,518	-0.4
Tajikistan	280	1,160	9.4	122	7.9	12.3	16.5	22.4	40.8	5.16	13.8aa	2.8	2.2	501	0.0
Turkmenistan	..	..	..	105	6.1	10.2	14.7	21.5	47.5	7.79	..	..	..	3,662	0.0
Ukraine	1,270	6,330	13.0	77	9.2	13.6	17.3	22.4	37.5	4.08	33.0aa	4.6	2.6	2,772	-0.2
Uzbekistan	450	1,860	6.1	113	9.2	14.1	17.9	22.6	36.3	3.95	..	..	..	2,023	-0.6
Industrial Countries	..	..	..	..	..	..	..	..	..	..	..	..	..	..	..
Australia	27,070	29,340	1.8	3	5.9bb	12.0bb	17.2bb	23.6bb	41.3bb	7.00	25.5	4.8	1.9	5,668	0.2
Austria	32,280	31,800	1.5	14	8.6bb	13.3bb	17.4bb	22.9bb	37.8bb	4.40	40.1	5.5	0.8	4,086	-0.2
Belgium	31,280	31,530	2.5	13	8.5bb	13.0bb	16.3bb	20.8bb	41.4bb	4.87	43.9	6.2	1.3	5,701	0.1f
Canada	28,310	30,760	1.8	6	7.2bb	12.7bb	17.2bb	23.0bb	39.9bb	5.54	18.3aa	5.2	1.1	8,240	0.0
Denmark	40,750	31,770	2.1	15	8.3bb	14.7bb	18.2bb	22.9bb	35.8bb	4.31	35.2	8.4	1.5	3,853	-0.8
Finland	32,880	29,800	3.4	11	9.6bb	14.1bb	17.5bb	22.1bb	36.7bb	3.82	36.9	6.5	1.2	7,204	-0.1
France	30,370z	29,460	1.7	16	7.2bb	12.6bb	17.2bb	22.8bb	40.2bb	5.58	47.1	6.0	2.6	4,519	-0.5
Germany	30,690	28,170	1.6	21	8.5bb	13.7bb	17.8bb	23.1bb	36.9bb	4.34	31.3	4.8	1.4	4,205	-0.2
Greece	16,730	22,230	3.9	24	6.7bb	11.9bb	16.8bb	23.0bb	41.5bb	6.19	..	4.3	4.2	2,709	-0.9
Ireland	34,310	32,930	3.0	4	7.4bb	12.3bb	16.3bb	21.9bb	42.0bb	5.68	..	4.3	0.7	3,777	-3.5
Israel	17,360	23,770	2.8	23	5.7bb	10.5bb	15.9bb	23.0bb	44.9bb	7.88	48.8	7.3	8.7	3,086	-0.7
Italy	26,280	28,020	1.4	17	6.5bb	12.0bb	16.8bb	22.8bb	42.0bb	6.46	40.0	4.9	2.0	3,140	-1.3
Japan	37,050	29,810	2.5	7	10.6bb	14.2bb	17.6bb	22.0bb	35.7bb	3.37	..	3.7	1.0	4,053	0.0
Luxembourg	..	..	..	12	..	..	..	..	..	..	..	..	0.9	..	..
Netherlands	32,130	31,360	1.1	10	7.6bb	13.2bb	17.2bb	23.3bb	38.7bb	5.09	42.6	5.3	1.7	4,982	-0.4
New Zealand	19,990	22,260	3.1	20	6.4bb	11.4bb	15.8bb	22.6bb	43.8bb	6.84	31.5	6.9	1.0	4,333	-0.5
Norway	51,810	38,680	2.6	1	9.6bb	14.0bb	17.2bb	22.0bb	37.2bb	3.88	37.2	7.7	2.0	5,100	-0.2

| | GNI per capita | | GDP per capita | Human Development Index | Distribution of income or consumption by quintiles[k] 1983-2004[t] | | | | | Ratio of highest 20% to lowest 20%[e] | Total central government expenditure (% of GDP) | Public education expenditure (% of GDP) | Military expenditure (% of GDP) | Per capita energy consumption (kg. of oil equivalent) | Average annual deforestation[m] (% of total forest) |
	US$ 2004	Purchasing power parity (PPP) per capita ($) 2004	% of 2003-2004	(HDI) rank 2004	Lowest 20%	Second quintile	Third quintile	Fourth quintile	Highest 20%		2004	2002-2004[t,y]	2004	2003	1990-2005
Portugal	14,220	19,240	0.4	28	5.8[bb]	11.0[bb]	15.5[bb]	21.9[bb]	45.9[bb]	7.91	41.9	5.9	2.3	2,469	-1.5
Spain	21,530	24,750	1.4	19	7.0[bb]	12.1[bb]	16.4[bb]	22.5[bb]	42.0[bb]	6.00	29.7	4.5	1.1	3,240	-2.2
Sweden	35,840	29,880	3.2	5	9.1[bb]	14.0[bb]	17.6[bb]	22.7[bb]	36.6[bb]	4.02	37.5	7.0	1.6	5,754	0.0
Switzerland	49,600	35,660	1.4	9	7.6[bb]	12.2[bb]	16.3[bb]	22.6[bb]	41.3[bb]	5.43	19.1[aa]	5.4	1.0	3,689	-0.4
United Kingdom	33,630	31,430	2.6	18	6.1[bb]	11.4[bb]	16.0[bb]	22.5[bb]	44.0[bb]	7.21	39.9	5.5	2.8	3,893	-0.6
United States	41,440	39,820	3.2	8	5.4[bb]	10.7[bb]	15.7[bb]	22.4[bb]	45.8[bb]	8.48	20.9	5.9	4.0	7,843	-0.1
World	**6,329**	**8,844**	**2.9**	..	..	..	..	..	..	..	**27.3**	..	..	**1,734**	**0.1**

The number '0' (zero) means zero or less than half the unit of measure.

..   Data not available.

a   Special Administrative Region, data exclude China.

b   Central and Eastern European countries and the newly independent states of former Soviet Union.

c   Estimate based on regression; others are extrapolated from the latest International Comparison Program benchmark estimates.

d   Estimated to be low-income ($735 or less).

e   Bread For the World Institute estimate.

f   Includes Luxembourg.

g   Excludes data for Transnistria.

h   Estimated to be lower middle income ($766-$3,035).

i   Included in the aggregates for lower-middle-income economies based on earlier data.

k   Refers to expenditure shares by percentiles of population, ranked by per capita expenditure, except as noted.

m   Positive data indicate loss of forest; negative data indicate gain in forest.

n   Data refer to mainland Tanzania only.

o   Excludes data for Kosovo.

p   Included in the aggregates for low-income economies based on earlier data

q   Data exclude Hong Kong.

r   Data include West Bank and Gaza. Data exclude Kuwait, Qatar, Turkey and United Arab Emirates.

s   Date refer to UNESCO Institute for Statistics estimate when national estimate is not available.

t   Data refer to most recent year available during the period specified in the column heading.

u   Based on a 1986 bilateral comparison of China and the United States employing a different methodology than that used for other countries

v   Data from years 1992-2002 refer to the Federal Republic of Yugoslavia. Data from before 2002 refer to the Socialist Federal Republic of Yugoslavia.

w   Palestinian Territory.

y   Other private flows combine non-debt-creating portfolio equity investment flows, portfolio debt flows and bank and trade-related lending.

z   Data include French Guiana, Guadeloupe, Martinique and Reunion.

aa   Data were reported on a cash basis and have been adjusted to the accrual framework.

bb   Refers to income shares by percentiles of population, ranked by per capita income.

cc   Urban data.

TABLE 5: Economic Globalization

	Trade 2004						Investment 2004				Debt 2004	
	Exports of goods and services (% of GDP)		Manufactured exports (% of merchandise exports)	Food Trade		Imports of goods and services (% of GDP)	Gross capital formation (% of GDP)	Foreign direct investment ($ millions)	Aid (% of gross capital formation)	Foreign direct investment (% of GDP, net inflows)	Total external debt (US $ millions)	Debt service (% of exports of goods, services and income)
	1990	2004		Food exports (% of merchandise exports)	Food imports (% of merchandise imports)							
Developing Countries	..	..	..	..	..	..	..	..	..	..	..	..
Africa (sub-Saharan)	**27**	**32**	**31**	**16**	**12**	**33**	**19**	**11,276**	**26.1**	**2.2**	**235,056**	**7.9**
Angola	39	71	..	..	..	55	12	1,444	49.1	7.4	9,521	14.8
Benin	14	15	9	41	24	26	20	60	45.6	1.5	1,916	..
Botswana	55	40	..	..	..	32	31	47	1.4	0.5	524	..
Burkina Faso	11	9	8	16	12	23	19	35	66.2	0.7	1,967	..
Burundi	8	9	5	92	9	25	11	3	501.4	0.5	1,385	..
Cameroon	20	26	5	19	18	26	17	0	31.8	0.0	9,496	..
Cape Verde	..	..	..	..	..	..	..	..	..	..	..	..
Central African Republic	15	12	37	2	23	16	18	-13	45.6	-1.0	1,078	..
Chad	14	52	..	..	..	36	25	478	30.6	11.3	1,701	..
Comoros	..	..	..	..	..	..	..	..	..	..	..	..
Congo, Dem. Rep.	30	19	..	..	..	22	13	0	213.9	0.0	11,841	..
Congo, Rep.	54	85	..	..	..	57	24	0	11.0	0.0	5,829	..
Côte d'Ivoire	32	48	20	56	22	38	11	175	9.2	1.1	11,739	6.9
Djibouti	..	..	..	..	..	..	..	..	..	..	..	..
Equatorial Guinea	..	..	..	..	..	..	..	..	..	..	..	..
Eritrea	11	13	..	..	..	86	22	30	129.0	3.2	681	..
Ethiopia	8	19	11	62	21	40	21	545	107.7	6.8	6,574	5.3
Gabon	46	61	7	1	24	40	25	323	2.1	4.5	4,150	..
Gambia	60	42	27	63	38	52	24	60	63.3	14.5	674	..
Ghana	17	35	14	72	21	54	28	139	54.9	1.6	7,035	6.6
Guinea	31	21	25	2	23	23	11	100	68.6	2.6	3,538	19.9
Guinea-Bissau	10	35	..	..	..	49	12	5	219.4	1.8	765	..
Kenya	26	26	21	40	10	32	18	46	21.6	0.3	6,826	8.6
Lesotho	17	48	..	..	..	105	42	123	18.8	9.4	764	4.5
Liberia	..	..	..	..	..	48	12	20	346.8	4.1	2,706	..
Madagascar	17	32	22	61	14	48	28	45	103.2	1.0	3,462	..
Malawi	24	27	16	78	13	49	11	16	229.4	0.9	3,418	..
Mali	17	28	..	..	..	36	20	180	59.2	3.7	3,316	..
Mauritania	46	29	..	..	..	70	22	300	54.5	19.6	2,297	..
Mauritius	64	56	71	27	18	56	24	14	2.6	0.2	2,294	7.4
Mozambique	8	30	3	19	11	38	20	245	100.6	4.0	4,651	4.5
Namibia	52	46	41	48	15	45	26	..	12.3	..	..	..
Niger	15	16	8	30	34	26	16	0	109.3	0.0	1,950	..
Nigeria	43	55	2	0	15	37	22	1,875	3.6	2.6	35,890	8.2
Rwanda	6	10	10	52	12	27	21	8	121.8	0.4	1,656	11.2
Senegal	25	28	39	35	28	41	23	70	57.9	0.9	3,938	..
Sierra Leone	22	23	7	92	23	39	16	26	211.3	2.4	1,723	10.9
Somalia	10	..	..	..	..	..	..	9	..	..	2,849	..
South Africa	24	27	58	9	5	27	18	585	1.6	0.3	28,500	6.4
Sudan	..	18	2	10	16	21	20	1,511	20.9	7.2	19,332	6.0
Swaziland	75	84	76	15	18	92	18	68	26.6	2.9	470	1.7
Tanzania	13	19e	20	53	15	29e	19e	249	83.8	2.3	7,799	5.3
Togo	34	34	47	24	18	47	18	60	16.5	2.9	1,812	..
Uganda	7	14	15	64	17	28	23	222	75.5	3.3	4,822	6.9
Zambia	36	20	10	16	7	27	26	334	77.1	6.2	7,279	..
Zimbabwe	23	36	28	31	19	44	13	60	31.0	1.3	4,797	..
South Asia	**9**	**19**	**76**	**11**	**8**	**22**	**23**	**7,151**	**3.3**	**0.8**	**193,933**	**12.4**
Afghanistan	..	..	..	..	..	..	..	..	..	..	..	..
Bangladesh	6	16	90	8	19	21	24	449	10.3	0.8	20,344	5.2
Bhutan	..	..	..	..	..	..	..	..	..	..	..	..
India	7	19	73	10	4	23	24	5,335	0.4	0.8	122,723	..
Maldives	..	..	..	..	..	..	..	..	..	..	..	..

	Exports of goods and services (% of GDP)		Manufactured exports (% of merchandise exports)	Food Trade Food exports (% of merchandise exports)	Food imports (% of merchandise imports)	Imports of goods and services (% of GDP)	Gross capital formation (% of GDP)	Foreign direct investment ($ millions)	Aid (% of gross capital formation)	Foreign direct investment (% of GDP, net inflows)	Total external debt (US $ millions)	Debt service (% of exports of goods, services and income)
	1990	2004										
Nepal	11	18	74	21	17	31	26	0	24.2	0.0	3,354	5.5
Pakistan	16	16	85	10	11	15	17	1,118	8.5	1.2	35,687	21.2
Sri Lanka	29	36	74	21	12	46	25	233	10.4	1.2	10,887	8.5
East Asia and the Pacific	**24**[g]	**43**[g]	**80**[g]	**6**[g]	**5**[g]	**40**[g]	**34**[g]	**64,563**[g]	**0.7**[g]	**2.5**[g]	**588,888**[g]	**6.8**[g]
Brunei	..	..	..	..	..	..	..	..	..	..	..	..
Cambodia	6	65	97	1	8	76	26	131	38.0	2.7	3,377	0.8
China	19	34	91[l]	4	4	31[c]	39[c]	54,936	0.2	2.8	248,934	3.5
Hong Kong[a]	132	193	96[m]	1[m]	3	184	22	34,034	0.0	20.9	..	..
Fiji	..	..	..	..	..	..	..	..	..	..	..	..
Indonesia	25	31	56	14	10	27	23	1,023	0.1	0.4	140,649	22.1
Korea, DPR (North)	..	..	..	..	..	..	..	..	..	..	..	..
Korea, Rep. (South)	28	44	92	1	5	40	30	8,189	0.0	1.2	..	..
Lao, PDR	12	29	..	..	..	42	..	17	..	0.7	2,056	..
Malaysia	75	121	76	8	6	100	23	4,624	1.1	3.9	52,145	..
Mongolia	24	75	38	3	14	87	37	93	44.3	5.8	1,517	2.9
Myanmar (Burma)	3	..	..	..	..	..	..	214	..	..	7,239	3.8
Papua New Guinea	41	71	6	21	16	60	..	25	..	0.7	2,149	..
Philippines	28	52	55	6	6	51	17	469	3.1	0.6	60,550	20.9
Singapore	..	..	84[m]	2[m]	3	..	18	16,032	0.0	15.0	..	..
Solomon Islands	..	..	..	..	..	..	..	..	..	..	..	..
Thailand	34	71	75	14	5	66	27	1,412	0.0	0.9	51,307	10.6
Vietnam	36	66	53	23	6	74	36	1,610	11.4	3.6	17,825	..
Latin America and the Caribbean	**17**	**26**	**56**	**16**	**7**	**23**	**21**	**60,843**	**1.6**	**3.0**	**778,970**	**26.4**
Argentina	10	25	29	48	2	18	19	4,084	0.3	2.7	169,247	28.5
Belize	..	..	..	..	..	..	..	..	..	..	..	..
Bolivia	23	31	14	27	12	26	12	116	70.7	1.3	6,096	18.6
Brazil	8	18	54	28	5	13	21	18,166	0.2	3.0	222,026	46.8
Chile	35	36	13	21	7	30	23	7,603	0.2	8.1	44,058	24.2
Colombia	21	21	38	17	11	22	19	3,052	2.8	3.1	37,732	33.0
Costa Rica	35	47	63	33	9	49	22	620	0.3	3.4	5,700	7.3
Cuba	..	..	..	..	..	..	..	..	..	..	..	..
Dominican Republic	34	50	..	..	..	49	21	645	2.3	3.5	6,965	6.4
Ecuador	33	27	9	31	9	29	28	1,160	1.9	3.8	16,868	36.0
El Salvador	19	27	60	32	18	44	16	466	8.6	2.9	7,250	8.8
Guatemala	21	18	42	45	12	32	18	155	4.5	0.6	5,532	7.4
Guyana	..	..	..	..	..	..	..	..	..	..	..	..
Haiti	18	12	..	..	..	39	27	7	..	0.2	1,225	..
Honduras	36	37	27	63	16	54	29	293	..	4.0	6,332	7.8
Jamaica	48	41	65	23	15	58	31	602	2.7	6.8	6,399	14.8
Mexico	19	30	80	5	6	32	21	17,377	0.1	2.6	138,689	22.9
Nicaragua	25	26	11	85	17	54	28	250	95.3	5.5	5,145	5.8
Panama	87	63	10	84	14	65	21	1,012	1.3	7.4	9,469	14.3
Paraguay	33	36	13	75	9	37	22	92	0.0	1.3	3,433	13.5
Peru	16	21	20	24	13	18	19	1,816	3.8	2.6	31,296	17.1
Suriname	..	..	..	..	..	..	..	..	..	..	..	..
Trinidad and Tobago	45	60	35	4	9	48	20	1,001	0.0	8.0	2,926	..
Uruguay	24	30	32	55	9	28	13	311	1.3	2.4	12,376	34.9
Venezuela	40	36	12	1	15	20	22	1,518	0.2	1.4	35,570	16.0
Middle East and North Africa	**26**[h]	**34**[h]	**20**[h]	**6**[h]	**17**[h]	**34**[h]	**26**[h]	**5,340**[h]	**6.4**[h]	**1.1**[h]	**163,935**[h]	**10.6**[h]
Algeria	23	40	2	0	22	26	33	882	1.1	1.0	21,987	..
Bahrain	..	..	..	..	..	..	..	..	..	..	..	..

TABLE 5: Economic Globalization

	Exports of goods and services (% of GDP) 1990	Exports of goods and services (% of GDP) 2004	Manufactured exports (% of merchandise exports)	Food exports (% of merchandise exports)	Food imports (% of merchandise imports)	Imports of goods and services (% of GDP)	Gross capital formation (% of GDP)	Foreign direct investment ($ millions)	Aid (% of gross capital formation)	Foreign direct investment (% of GDP, net inflows)	Total external debt (US $ millions)	Debt service (% of exports of goods, services and income)
Cyprus	..	..	..	..	..	..	..	..	..	..	..	..
Egypt	20	29	31	10	22	29	17	1,253	11.1	1.6	30,291	7.6
Iran	22	32	9	4	11	30	37	500	0.3	0.3	13,622	..
Iraq	..	..	..	..	..	..	..	..	..	..	..	..
Jordan	62	48	72	14	17	80	24	620	21.1	5.4	8,175	8.2
Kuwait	45	60	..	..	..	33	14	-20	0.0	0.0	..	..
Lebanon	18	21	68	19	18	41	21	288	5.7	1.3	22,177	..
Libya	40	47	..	..	17	36	14	..	..	..	..	..
Morocco	27	33	69	19	11	39	25	769	5.6	1.5	17,672	14.0
Oman	47	57	12	4	14	43	18	-17	1.3	-0.1	3,872	6.9
Qatar	..	..	..	..	..	..	..	..	..	..	..	..
Saudi Arabia	41	53	12	1	16	25	19	..	0.1	..	..	..
Syria	28	35	11	15	17	34	21	275	2.2	1.1	21,521	3.5
Tunisia	44	45	78	11	9	48	25	593	4.7	2.1	18,700	13.7
Turkey	13	29	85	9	3	35	26	2,733	0.3	0.9	161,595	35.9
United Arab Emirates	66	82	..	..	..	65	22	..	0.0	..	..	..
West Bank and Gaza[o]	10	..	..	..	..	49	3	..	..	..	..	..
Yemen	14	25	3	4	28	34	17	144	11.5	1.1	5,488	3.5
Countries in Transition[b]	..	..	..	..	..	..	..	..	..	..	..	..
Albania	15	21	82	6	19	43	24	426	20.2	5.6	1,549	..
Armenia	35	39	62	12	22	53	20	219	40.5	7.1	1,224	8.1
Azerbaijan	44	50	10	4	12	74	55	3,556	3.8	41.7	1,986	5.3
Belarus	46	69	60	8	10	74	28	169	0.7	0.7	3,717	2.1
Bosnia and Herzegovina	..	26	..	..	..	55	21	613	37.8	7.2	3,202	3.7
Bulgaria	33	58	62	10	5	69	24	2,005	11.0	8.3	15,661	17.1
Croatia	78	48	72	9	8	56	30	1,243	1.2	3.6	31,548	27.2
Czech Republic	45	72	90	3	5	72	28	4,454	0.9	4.2	45,561	10.5
Estonia	60	78	77	7	9	86	31	1,049	3.9	9.3	10,008	15.7
Georgia	40	31	37	32	21	48	29	499	20.7	9.6	2,082	11.2
Hungary	31	64	88	7	4	68	24	4,608	1.3	4.6	63,159	25.2
Kazakhstan	74	55	16	4	7	46	24	4,104	2.7	10.1	32,310	38.0
Kyrgyzstan	29	43	43	18	13	53	14	77	84.9	3.5	2,100	14.2
Latvia	48	44	61	9	11	60	33	699	3.7	5.1	12,661	21.2
Lithuania	52	54	58	11	8	61	24	773	4.8	3.5	9,475	14.3
Macedonia, Republic of	26	40	77	15	14	61	22	157	21.5	2.9	2,044	10.5
Moldova	48	51	36	53	12	82	25	81	18.0	3.1	1,868	12.1[f]
Poland	29	39	81	8	6	41	20	12,613	3.1	5.2	99,190	34.6
Romania	17	37	82	3	6	47	25	5,440	5.0	7.4	30,034	17.2
Russian Federation	18	35	21	1	17	22	21	12,479	1.1	2.1	197,335	9.8
Serbia and Montenegro[k]	..	24	57	23	11	52	17	966	29.0	4.0	15,882	..
Slovakia	27	77	86	4	5	80	26	1,122	2.2	2.7	22,068	..
Slovenia	91	60	90	3	6	61	27	827	0.7	2.6	..	..
Tajikistan	28	46	..	..	..	65	9	272	124.7	13.1	896	6.8
Turkmenistan	..	66	..	..	..	57	26	..	2.4	..	..	..
Ukraine	28	61	67	13	6	54	19	1,715	2.9	2.6	21,652	10.7
Uzbekistan	29	40	..	..	..	33	20	140	10.2	1.2	5,007	..
Industrial Countries	..	..	..	..	..	..	..	..	..	..	..	..
Australia	17	18	25	19	5	21	25	42,469	n/a	6.7	..	..
Austria	38	51	84	6	6	46	22	4,022	n/a	1.4	..	..
Belgium	71	84	81	9	8	81	20	118,758[j]	n/a	30.9[j]	..	..
Canada	26	38	60	7	6	34	20	6,284	n/a	0.6	..	..
Denmark	36	44	66	19	12	38	20	-8,804	n/a	-3.6	..	..
Finland	23	37	83	2	6	32	19	3,075	n/a	1.7	..	..
France	21	26	83	11	8	26	20	24,521	n/a	1.2	..	..

	Trade 2004						Investment 2004				Debt 2004	
	Exports of goods and services (% of GDP)		Manufactured exports (% of merchandise exports)	Food Trade		Imports of goods and services (% of GDP)	Gross capital formation (% of GDP)	Foreign direct investment ($ millions)	Aid (% of gross capital formation)	Foreign direct investment (% of GDP, net inflows)	Total external debt (US $ millions)	Debt service (% of exports of goods, services and income)
				Food exports (% of merchandise exports)	Food imports (% of merchandise imports)							
	1990	2004										
Germany	25	38	84	4	7	33	17	-34,903	n/a	-1.3	..	..
Greece	18	21	59	20	11	30	26	1,355	n/a	0.7	..	..
Ireland	57	80	86	8	8	65	25	11,040	n/a	6.1	..	..
Israel	35	44	94	3	6	49	17	1,664	2.4	1.4	..	..
Italy	20	27	88	7	9	26	20	16,772	n/a	1.0	..	..
Japan	10	12	93	0	12	10	24	7,805	n/a	0.2	..	..
Luxembourg	..	..	..	..	..	..	..	..	n/a	..	..	..
Netherlands	55	65	70	15	10	60	21	377	n/a	0.1	..	..
New Zealand	27	29	31	49	8	29	23	2,271	n/a	2.3	..	..
Norway	40	44	19	6	7	30	19	502	n/a	0.2	..	..
Portugal	33	31	85	8	12	38	24	825	n/a	0.5	..	..
Spain	16	26	77	14	10	29	28	16,594	n/a	1.6	..	..
Sweden	30	46	81	3	8	38	16	-588	n/a	-0.2	..	..
Switzerland	36	44	93	3	6	37	20	-797	n/a	-0.2	..	..
United Kingdom	24	25	76	6	9	28	17	72,561	n/a	3.4	..	..
United States	10	10	82	7	4	14	18	106,831	n/a	0.9	..	..
World	**19**	**24**	**77**	**7**	**7**	**24**	**21**	**624,797**	**..**	**1.6**	**..**	**..**

The number '0' (zero) means zero or less than half the unit of measure.

n/a Not applicable.

.. Data not available.

a Special Administrative Region, data exclude China.

b Central and Eastern European countries and the newly independent states of the former Soviet Union.

c China has revised its national accounts data from 1993 onwards, but revised expenditure data are not available. The data shown here are based on earlier series.

e Mainland Tanzania only.

f Data are from debt sustainability analyses undertaken as part of the Heavily Indebted Poor Countries Initiative.

g Data exclude Hong Kong and Singapore.

h Data exclude Kuwait, Turkey and United Arab Emirates.

j Data include Luxembourg.

k Data from years 1992-2002 referred to the Federal Republic of Yugoslavia. Data from before 1992 referred to the Socialist Federal Republic of Yugoslavia.

l Data for Taiwan, China.

m Data Include re-exports.

o Palestinian Territory.

TABLE 6: United States—National Hunger and Poverty Trends

	1970	1980	1990	1995	2000	2001	2002	2003	2004	2005
Total population (millions)	**205.1**	**227.8**	**249.4**	**262.9**	**281.4**	**284.8**[d]	**288.0**[d]	**290.8**[d]	**293.6**[d]	**296.4**[d]
Food insecurity prevalence estimates[j]										
All U.S. households – food insecure (%)	..	..	..	11.9	10.5	10.7	11.1	11.2	11.9	11.0
Without hunger	..	..	..	7.8	7.3	7.4	7.6	7.7	8.0	7.1
With hunger	..	..	..	4.2	3.1	3.3	3.5	3.5	3.9	3.9
Adult members (total) – food insecure (%)	..	..	..	11.0	10.1	10.2	10.5	10.8	11.3	10.4
Without hunger	..	..	..	7.4	7.3	7.3	7.5	7.7	7.9	7.0
With hunger	..	..	..	3.6	2.8	3.0	3.0	3.1	3.4	3.5
Child members (total) – food insecure (%)	..	..	..	19.5	18.0	17.6	18.1	18.2	19.0	16.9
Without hunger	..	..	..	13.4	13.9	16.9	17.3	17.6	18.2	16.1
With hunger	..	..	..	6.1	4.1	0.6	0.8	0.6	0.7	0.8
Percent of federal budget spent on food assistance[a]	**0.5**	**2.4**	**1.9**	**2.48**	**1.83**[e,f]	**1.83**[e,f]	**1.9**[e,f,i]	**1.97**[e,f,i]	**2.02**[e,f,i]	**2.04**[e,f,i]
Total infant mortality rate (per 1,000 live births)	**20.0**	**12.6**	**9.1**	**7.6**	**6.9**	**6.9**	**7.0**	**6.9**	**..**	**..**
White	17.8	11.0	7.7	6.3	5.7	..	5.8	5.7	..	..
White, non-Hispanic	..	..	..	..	5.7[c]	..	..	..	..	..
African American	32.6	21.4	17.0	15.1	14.1	..	14.4	14.0	..	..
Hispanic	..	..	7.8	..	5.6[c]	..	..	..	..	..
American Indian	..	..	..	..	7.4[c]	..	..	..	..	..
Asian or Pacific Islander	..	..	..	..	4.1[c]	..	..	..	..	..
Total poverty rate (%)	**12.6**	**13.0**	**13.5**	**13.8**	**11.3**	**11.7**	**12.1**	**12.5**	**12.7**	**12.6**
Northeast	..	..	10.2	12.5	10.3	10.7	10.9	11.3	11.6	11.3
Midwest	..	..	11.9	11.0	9.5	9.4	10.3	10.7	11.6	11.4
South	..	..	15.9	15.7	12.5	13.5	13.8	14.1	14.1	14.0
West	..	..	11.6	14.9	11.9	12.1	12.4	12.6	12.6	12.6
White	9.9	10.2	10.7	11.2	9.4	9.9	10.2	10.6	10.8	10.6
non-Hispanic	..	..	..	..	7.5	7.8	8.0	8.2	8.6	8.3
African American	33.5	32.5	31.9	29.3	22.1	22.7	24.1	24.3	24.7	24.9
Hispanic	..	25.7	28.1	30.3	21.2	21.4	21.8	22.5	21.9	21.8
American Indian/Alaskan Native	..	..	..	..	25.9[b]	..	..	20.0[h]	..	..
Asian and Pacific Islander	..	..	..	..	10.8	10.2	10.2	11.8	9.8	11.1
Elderly (65 years and older)	24.6	15.7	12.2	10.5	10.2	10.1	10.4	10.2	9.8	10.1
Female-headed households	38.1	36.7	33.4	32.4	24.7	26.4	26.5	28.0	28.4	28.7
Total child poverty rate (%) (18 years and under)	**15.1**	**18.3**	**20.6**	**20.8**	**16.2**	**16.3**	**16.7**	**17.6**	**17.8**	**17.6**
White	..	13.9	15.9	16.2	13.0	13.4	13.6	14.3	14.8	14.4
non-Hispanic	..	..	..	..	9.4	9.5	9.4	9.8	10.5	10.0
African American	..	42.3	44.8	41.9	30.9	30.2	32.3	34.1	33.6	34.5
Hispanic	..	33.2	38.4	40.0	28.0	28.0	28.6	29.7	28.9	28.3
Asian and Pacific Islander	..	..	17.6	19.5	14.5	11.5	11.7[g]	12.5	10.0	11.1
Unemployment rate (%)	**4.9**	**7.1**	**5.6**	**5.6**	**4.0**	**4.8**	**5.8**	**6.0**	**5.5**	**5.1**
White	4.5	6.3	4.8	4.9	3.5	4.2	5.1	5.2	4.8	4.4
African American	..	14.3	11.4	10.4	7.6	8.7	10.2	10.8	10.4	10.0
Hispanic	..	10.1	8.2	9.3	5.7	6.6	7.5	7.7	7.0	6.0

TABLE 6: United States—National Hunger and Poverty Trends

	1970	1980	1990	1995	2000	2001	2002	2003	2004	2005
Household income distribution (per quintile in %)										
All races										
Lowest 20 percent	4.1	4.2	3.9	3.7	3.6	3.5	3.5	3.4	3.4	3.4
Second quintile	10.8	10.2	9.6	9.1	8.9	8.7	8.8	8.7	8.7	8.6
Third quintile	17.4	16.8	15.9	15.2	14.8	14.6	14.8	14.8	14.7	14.6
Fourth quintile	24.5	24.8	24.0	23.3	23.0	23.0	23.3	23.4	23.2	23.0
Highest 20 percent	43.3	44.1	46.6	48.7	49.6	50.1	49.7	49.8	50.1	50.4
Ratio of highest 20 percent to lowest 20 percent[e]	10.6	10.5	11.9	13.2	13.8	14.3	14.2	14.6	14.7	14.8
White										
Lowest 20 percent	4.2	4.4	4.2	4.0	3.7	3.7	3.7	3.6	3.6	3.6
Second quintile	11.1	10.5	10.0	9.3	9.0	8.9	9.0	8.9	8.8	8.9
Third quintile	17.5	17.0	16.0	15.3	14.9	14.7	15.0	14.8	14.8	14.7
Fourth quintile	24.3	24.6	23.9	23.3	22.9	22.9	23.2	23.2	23.1	22.9
Highest 20 percent	42.9	43.5	46.0	48.1	49.4	49.8	49.2	49.4	49.6	49.9
Ratio of highest 20 percent to lowest 20 percent[e]	10.2	9.9	11.0	12.0	13.4	13.5	13.2	21.4	13.8	13.9
African American										
Lowest 20 percent	3.7	3.7	3.1	3.2	3.2	3.0	2.9	2.9	2.8	2.8
Second quintile	9.3	8.7	7.9	8.2	8.6	8.6	8.2	8.2	8.3	8.0
Third quintile	16.3	15.3	15.0	14.8	15.2	15.0	14.5	14.7	14.6	14.5
Fourth quintile	25.2	25.2	25.1	24.2	23.8	24.2	23.3	24.0	23.8	23.7
Highest 20 percent	45.5	47.1	49.0	49.6	49.3	49.2	51.1	50.2	50.5	50.9
Ratio of highest 20 percent to lowest 20 percent[e]	12.3	12.7	15.8	15.5	15.4	16.4	17.6	17.3	18.0	18.2
Hispanic										
Lowest 20 percent	..	4.3	4.0	3.8	4.3	4.0	3.9	3.9	3.8	3.9
Second quintile	..	10.1	9.5	8.9	9.8	9.4	9.4	9.4	9.3	9.5
Third quintile	..	16.4	15.9	14.8	15.7	15.2	14.8	15.0	14.9	15.2
Fourth quintile	..	24.8	24.3	23.3	23.8	23.2	22.9	23.1	22.9	23.3
Highest 20 percent	..	44.5	46.3	49.3	46.4	48.3	49.0	48.6	49.1	48.1
Ratio of highest 20 percent to lowest 20 percent[e]	..	10.3	11.6	13.0	10.8	12.1	12.6	12.5	12.9	12.3

..   Data not available.
a   Data refer to fiscal year.
b   3-year average: 1998, 1999 and 2000.
c   Preliminary.
d   U.S. Census estimate.
e   Bread for the World Institute estimate.
f   "Food Assistance" includes the following programs: Food Stamp Program, child nutrition programs, supplemental food (including WIC) programs, and elderly nutrition programs.
g   Data for 2002 is "Asian alone," or "people who reported Asian and did not report any other race category." (U.S. Census Bureau, *Poverty in the United States: 2002*, 32).
h   3-year average: 2001, 2002 and 2003.
i   Estimate was made by adding the budgets of USDA Food and Nutrition programs and the budget of Senior Nutrition Programs under Health and Human Services (HHS). The total budget for food assistance programs was then divided by the federal budget. All figures are taken from the U.S. Budget.
j   The U.S. Department of Agriculture has reclassified food insecurity and food insecurity with hunger as "low food security" and "very low food security." The methodology for measuring food insecurity and food insecurity with hunger has not changed. Cross comparisons can still be made between years.

TABLE 7: United States—State Hunger and Poverty Statistics

	Total population (millions) July 2005	Food insecure (% of households) 2003-2005[c,d]	Food insecure with hunger (% of households) 2003-2005[c,d]	Infant mortality rate (per 1,000 live births) 2003 All races	White	African American	% Population in poverty 2003-2005	Unemployment rate (%) 2005
Alabama	4.56	12.3	3.4	8.72	6.53	14.05	16.2	4.0
Alaska	0.66	12.2	4.9[b]	7.04	5.70	..	9.6	6.8
Arizona	5.94	12.2	3.8	6.52	6.18	14.72	14.4	4.7
Arkansas	2.78	14.7[b]	5.6[b]	8.65	7.56	13.54	15.6	4.9
California	36.13	11.7	3.6	5.21	4.86	12.61	13.2	5.4
Colorado	4.67	12.0	3.9	6.06	5.51	20.43	10.4	5.0
Connecticut	3.51	8.2[b]	2.6[b]	5.36	4.66	11.18	9.2	4.9
Delaware	0.84	6.6[b]	1.9[b]	9.44	6.67	18.23	8.5	4.2
District of Columbia	0.55	11.4	3.8	10.50	..	12.38	18.3	6.5
Florida	17.79	9.4[b]	3.5	7.46	5.76	13.65	11.8	3.8
Georgia	9.07	12.4	5.1[b]	8.46	6.14	13.76	13.1	5.3
Hawaii	1.28	7.8[b]	2.8[b]	7.51	6.49	..	8.8	2.8
Idaho	1.43	14.1[b]	3.7	6.33	6.48	..	10.0	3.8
Illinois	12.76	9.1[b]	3.2[b]	7.74	6.18	16.19	12.1	5.7
Indiana	6.27	11.1	4.1[b]	7.65	6.72	15.79	11.4	5.4
Iowa	2.97	10.9	3.5	5.63	5.18	19.43	10.4	4.6
Kansas	2.74	12.3	4.6[b]	6.64	6.20	14.48	11.6	5.1
Kentucky	4.17	12.8[b]	4.2	6.90	6.50	11.75	15.6	6.1
Louisiana	4.52	12.8	3.6	9.32	6.38	13.69	17.3	7.1
Maine	1.32	12.3	4.6[b]	4.91	4.86	..	11.9	4.8
Maryland	5.60	9.4[b]	3.6	8.23	5.41	14.15	9.4	4.1
Massachusetts	6.40	7.8[b]	3.0[b]	4.84	4.42	9.42	9.9	4.8
Michigan	10.12	11.5	4.1	8.54	6.71	17.37	12.2	6.7
Minnesota	5.13	7.7[b]	3.0[b]	4.63	4.34	7.65	7.5	4.0
Mississippi	2.92	16.5[b]	4.4	10.74	6.92	15.25	18.3	7.9
Missouri	5.80	11.7	4.0	7.92	6.77	15.05	11.5	5.4
Montana	0.94	11.2	4.6	6.83	6.50	..	14.4	4.0
Nebraska	1.76	10.3[b]	4.0	5.44	4.75	15.67	9.6	3.8
Nevada	2.41	8.4[b]	3.0[b]	5.71	5.31	12.07	10.8	4.1
New Hampshire	1.31	6.5[b]	2.2[b]	3.96	4.03	..	5.6	3.6
New Jersey	8.72	8.1[b]	2.6[b]	5.65	4.52	11.78	7.8	4.4
New Mexico	1.93	16.8[b]	5.7[b]	5.75	5.45	..	17.5	5.3
New York	19.25	10.4[b]	3.1[b]	6.04	5.00	11.39	14.6	5.0
North Carolina	8.68	13.2[b]	4.5[b]	8.21	6.06	15.72	14.4	5.2
North Dakota	0.64	6.4[b]	2.2[b]	7.28	6.97	..	10.2	3.4
Ohio	11.46	12.6[b]	3.8	7.74	6.50	15.35	11.6	5.9
Oklahoma	3.55	14.6[b]	4.8[b]	7.79	7.31	14.92	13.1	4.4
Oregon	3.64	11.9	3.9	5.57	5.48	..	12.1	6.1
Pennsylvania	12.43	9.8[b]	2.9[b]	7.33	6.15	14.92	11.0	5.0
Rhode Island	1.08	12.4	4.1	6.66	6.41	..	11.7	5.0
South Carolina	4.26	15.5[b]	6.3[b]	8.32	5.85	13.53	14.2	6.8
South Dakota	0.78	9.5[b]	3.2[b]	6.71	4.94	..	12.7	3.9
Tennessee	5.96	13.0	4.2	9.25	6.99	18.03	15.0	5.6
Texas	22.86	16.0[b]	5.1[b]	6.58	5.74	13.78	16.5	5.3
Utah	2.47	14.5[b]	5.1	4.99	4.88	..	9.4	4.3
Vermont	0.62	9.5[b]	3.9	5.01	4.99	..	8.0	3.5
Virginia	7.57	8.4[b]	2.7[b]	7.69	6.15	13.58	9.5	3.5
Washington	6.29	11.2	3.9	5.60	5.53	9.71	11.4	5.5
West Virginia	1.82	8.9[b]	3.0	7.26	6.89	..	15.6	5.0
Wisconsin	5.54	9.5[b]	2.7[b]	6.51	5.44	15.71	10.8	4.7
Wyoming	0.51	11.1	4.1	5.82	4.93	..	10.1	3.6
Puerto Rico	..	..	..	9.70	10.51	..	..	..
United States	**296.41**	**11.4**	**3.8**	**6.85**[a]	**5.72**[a]	**14.01**[a]	**12.6**	**5.1**

.. Data not available.   a Excludes data for Puetro Rico, Virgin Islands, Guam, American Samoa, and Northern Marianas.   b Difference from U.S. total was statistically significant with 90 percent confidence (t > 1.645).   c Prevalence rates for 1996-98 reported in Prevalence of Food Insecurity and Hunger, by State, 1996-1998 (Nord et al., 1999) are not directly comparable with the rates reported here because of differences in screening procedures in the CPS Food Security Supplements from 1995-98.
d The U.S. Department of Agriculture has reclassified food insecurity and food insecurity with hunger as "low food security" and "very low food security." The methodology for measuring food insecurity and food insecurity with hunger has not changed. Cross comparisons can still be made between years.

TABLE 8: United States—Nutrition and Assistance Programs

	Food Stamp Participation: Monthly Average by State								
	1997[c]	1998[c]	1999[c]	2000[c]	2001[c]	2002[c]	2003[c]	2004[c]	2005[c]
Alabama	469,268	426,819	405,273	396,057	411,292	443,547	472,066	497,591	558,596
Alaska	45,234	42,451	41,262	37,524	37,897	46,165	50,687	49,323	55,567
Arizona	363,779	295,703	257,362	259,006	291,372	378,722	466,153	529,556	550,291
Arkansas	265,854	255,710	252,957	246,572	256,441	283,909	310,359	346,441	373,764
California	2,814,761	2,259,069	2,027,089	1,831,697	1,668,351	1,710,306	1,708,354	1,859,486	1,990,919
Colorado	216,748	191,015	173,497	155,948	153,952	178,490	208,053	241,780	245,926
Connecticut	209,529	195,866	178,168	165,059	157,031	168,591	180,512	195,980	204,146
Delaware	53,655	45,581	38,571	32,218	31,886	39,628	46,027	55,642	61,586
District of Columbia	90,391	85,396	84,082	80,803	73,494	74,271	81,777	88,655	88,799
Florida	1,191,664	990,571	933,435	882,341	887,256	985,130	1,041,315	1,202,227	1,381,804
Georgia	698,323	631,720	616,600	559,468	573,537	645,633	750,208	867,148	921,427
Hawaii	126,901	122,027	125,155	118,041	108,313	106,370	100,382	98,589	93,548
Idaho	70,413	62,393	57,201	58,191	59,667	69,998	81,524	91,395	93,441
Illinois	1,019,600	922,927	820,034	779,420	825,295	886,344	953,929	1,069,596	1,158,271
Indiana	347,772	313,116	298,213	300,314	346,551	410,884	470,182	526,324	556,285
Iowa	161,184	141,067	128,790	123,322	126,494	140,729	153,816	179,179	206,696
Kansas	148,734	119,218	114,875	116,596	124,285	170,403	160,705	169,528	177,782
Kentucky	444,422	412,028	396,440	403,479	412,680	450,102	502,677	544,744	570,277
Louisiana	575,411	536,834	516,285	599,851	518,384	588,458	655,300	705,700	807,896
Maine	123,767	115,099	108,749	101,598	104,383	111,147	132,582	141,929	152,910
Maryland	354,436	322,653	264,393	219,180	208,426	228,329	252,294	273,872	288,943
Massachusetts	339,505	292,997	261,021	231,829	219,223	242,542	292,200	334,939	368,122
Michigan	838,917	771,580	682,680	602,857	641,269	750,037	837,629	943,713	1,047,594
Minnesota	260,476	219,744	208,062	196,050	197,727	216,960	234,631	247,465	259,937
Mississippi	399,062	329,058	288,057	275,856	297,805	324,882	355,783	376,864	391,485
Missouri	477,703	410,966	408,331	419,959	454,427	515,006	591,532	699,616	766,425
Montana	66,605	62,328	60,898	59,466	61,957	63,347	71,320	77,478	80,870
Nebraska	97,176	94,944	92,404	82,414	80,652	88,459	99,243	113,900	117,415
Nevada	82,419	71,531	61,673	60,905	69,396	97,035	111,352	120,275	121,707
New Hampshire	46,000	39,578	37,438	36,266	35,554	41,053	44,783	48,449	52,310
New Jersey	491,337	424,738	384,888	344,677	317,579	319,799	339,047	368,695	392,416
New Mexico	204,644	174,699	178,439	169,354	163,245	170,457	194,795	222,716	240,637
New York	1,913,548	1,627,170	1,540,784	1,438,568	1,353,542	1,346,644	1,435,986	1,598,143	1,754,861
North Carolina	586,415	527,790	505,410	488,247	493,672	574,369	649,426	747,274	799,747
North Dakota	37,688	33,801	33,442	31,895	37,755	36,781	39,663	41,421	42,204
Ohio	873,562	733,565	639,786	609,717	640,503	734,679	855,401	945,435	1,007,172
Oklahoma	321,894	287,577	271,351	523,287	271,001	316,684	380,299	411,840	424,402
Oregon	258,615	238,446	223,978	234,387	283,705	359,138	398,377	419,736	429,358
Pennsylvania	1,008,864	906,735	834,898	777,112	748,074	766,615	822,696	960,941	1,042,809
Rhode Island	84,627	72,301	76,394	74,256	71,272	71,933	74,068	77,528	76,085
South Carolina	349,137	333,017	308,570	295,335	315,718	379,310	450,556	497,218	521,125
South Dakota	46,901	45,173	44,065	42,962	44,594	47,663	51,176	53,459	56,095
Tennessee	585,889	538,467	510,828	496,031	521,510	598,012	728,305	806,490	849,703
Texas	2,033,750	1,636,175	1,400,526	1,332,785	1,360,642	1,554,428	1,872,473	2,258,951	2,441,975
Utah	98,338	91,764	88,163	81,945	79,716	89,899	105,630	123,411	133,263
Vermont	53,005	45,702	44,287	40,831	38,874	39,914	41,333	42,862	45,218
Virginia	476,088	396,581	361,581	336,080	332,312	352,172	393,911	485,877	488,481
Washington	444,800	364,418	306,654	295,061	308,589	350,373	403,992	453,497	508,472
West Virginia	287,035	269,140	247,249	226,897	221,361	235,736	246,890	255,936	262,442
Wisconsin	232,103	192,887	182,206	193,021	215,786	262,310	296,719	324,047	345,748
Wyoming	28,584	25,452	23,477	22,459	22,539	23,530	25,306	25,649	25,482
Guam	17,783	25,249	19,758	22,234	22,723	24,457	23,934	25,725	27,277
Puerto Rico	n/a	n/a	n/a	n/a	..	..	..	..	..
United States	22,854,273	19,788,115	18,182,595	17,155,093	17,312,974	19,093,798	21,260,293	23,857,607	25,674,369

TABLE 8: United States—Nutrition and Assistance Programs

	WIC[a] Annual Participation by State								
	1997[c]	1998	1999	2000	2001	2002	2003	2004	2005
Alabama	118,899	117,319	115,172	103,930	111,049	118,616	120,377	120,310	118,751
Alaska	23,537	23,829	26,131	24,395	23,628	25,094	25,512	26,616	26,840
Arizona	145,849	142,000	142,488	145,544	147,285	151,186	156,353	176,223	177,538
Arkansas	87,310	82,939	82,882	82,131	79,826	84,153	85,607	89,113	88,463
California	1,224,224	1,216,253	1,229,495	1,219,430	1,243,509	1,266,542	1,274,489	1,292,737	1,309,413
Colorado	75,068	74,679	74,801	71,967	72,124	77,501	81,196	83,409	84,013
Connecticut	59,368	60,267	58,299	50,867	49,252	51,329	51,721	52,130	52,059
Delaware	15,581	15,635	15,274	15,844	16,568	17,241	17,839	18,353	19,361
District of Columbia	16,747	16,593	16,406	15,060	15,204	15,117	15,572	16,019	15,923
Florida	354,971	345,150	337,559	296,298	316,758	340,954	354,568	373,214	371,365
Georgia	230,153	232,258	224,069	216,319	226,365	237,124	246,296	259,992	267,452
Hawaii	30,807	34,098	34,137	32,080	32,467	32,986	32,788	33,221	32,586
Idaho	31,475	31,678	31,543	31,286	32,641	33,448	34,754	36,279	37,850
Illinois	236,068	237,262	241,016	243,655	251,329	260,080	266,975	275,833	275,094
Indiana	132,700	131,099	128,269	120,648	117,880	124,462	124,683	131,485	134,706
Iowa	66,293	65,885	63,996	60,793	60,664	63,010	64,585	66,188	67,823
Kansas	54,754	52,896	52,345	52,773	53,260	57,898	61,229	63,987	68,218
Kentucky	122,948	122,910	122,056	112,182	111,004	113,112	113,109	117,201	121,644
Louisiana	139,223	136,866	135,430	130,042	125,916	129,200	133,403	141,661	143,362
Maine	26,663	25,786	24,646	22,073	20,962	21,470	21,743	22,916	23,454
Maryland	91,412	92,744	93,338	94,194	93,829	96,153	101,283	107,542	108,540
Massachusetts	118,818	117,681	115,042	113,842	112,623	113,176	113,957	115,657	114,161
Michigan	218,371	217,924	215,138	213,049	214,951	215,989	216,684	222,077	226,601
Minnesota	94,807	95,101	90,101	90,093	96,192	102,008	110,117	116,677	123,275
Mississippi	100,124	99,097	96,863	95,836	98,874	102,272	103,244	102,738	101,694
Missouri	131,638	128,176	126,640	123,738	125,144	128,029	129,961	132,763	132,227
Montana	21,679	21,428	21,346	21,288	21,413	21,402	21,320	21,302	21,102
Nebraska	33,041	31,770	33,047	32,793	34,427	37,074	38,286	39,668	40,818
Nevada	37,324	37,972	37,415	38,781	40,646	41,297	44,551	46,355	48,803
New Hampshire	19,179	18,678	18,100	17,049	16,507	16,894	16,701	16,722	16,677
New Jersey	141,514	140,732	129,603	127,013	128,577	133,946	136,272	143,341	146,888
New Mexico	54,040	56,183	56,494	57,802	59,464	59,914	62,253	63,530	64,216
New York	478,980	482,882	476,563	466,818	460,252	454,577	458,177	473,058	482,807
North Carolina	194,566	1,979,544	196,389	190,258	200,678	208,377	211,574	218,930	225,252
North Dakota	16,868	15,810	14,930	14,303	14,053	13,823	13,969	14,117	14,248
Ohio	254,668	250,815	245,994	242,921	247,092	253,923	256,095	267,300	272,632
Oklahoma	108,348	109,581	108,485	108,375	105,907	109,391	111,688	116,145	119,779
Oregon	89,299	31,341	92,831	86,061	93,246	97,058	96,457	100,135	102,793
Pennsylvania	257,018	246,337	235,526	230,914	226,434	222,879	229,628	240,836	240,754
Rhode Island	22,596	22,768	22,454	21,783	21,925	22,451	22,739	22,780	22,914
South Carolina	118,966	118,556	110,850	108,204	111,408	109,575	104,967	106,784	108,341
South Dakota	21,945	20,507	20,445	20,409	20,505	20,278	20,631	21,608	21,580
Tennessee	150,289	148,692	148,824	148,662	149,490	153,212	152,828	155,394	155,330
Texas	683,583	691,292	707,872	737,206	750,122	786,530	824,449	867,586	892,195
Utah	57,511	57,391	59,592	57,549	58,928	61,445	64,070	66,848	68,147
Vermont	16,133	16,308	16,051	16,401	15,966	15,903	16,201	16,290	16,306
Virginia	129,520	132,317	131,304	128,163	130,094	129,103	5,491	131,832	138,221
Washington	145,147	144,052	141,089	145,850	150,138	152,055	152,520	159,233	160,703
West Virginia	55,065	53,962	52,335	50,996	50,064	50,265	49,837	50,436	49,961
Wisconsin	108,886	108,352	104,041	100,574	100,128	102,776	105,702	110,186	112,942
Wyoming	12,447	11,789	11,583	10,907	11,103	11,353	12,037	12,381	12,699
Guam	..	..	..	..	6,210	6,208	5,382	5,994	6,514
Puerto Rico	211,454	206,968	205,228	214,651	219,620	209442	207,838	209,610	205,831
United States	**7,406,866**	**7,367,397**	**7,311,206**	**7,192,604**	**7,305,577**	**7,490,841**	**7,631,8008**	**7,904,435**	**8,022,615**

TABLE 8: United States—Nutrition and Assistance Programs

	TANF[b] Individual Recipients: Monthly Average by State								
	1997[c]	1998[c]	1999[c]	2000[c]	2001[c]	2002[c]	2003[c]	2004[c]	2005[c]
Alabama	77,096	54,164	49,470	55,858	49,100	42,706	44,704	45,377	48,223
Alaska	34,434	29,599	25,221	22,425	16,997	17,623	15,190	13,768	12,048
Arizona	140,161	100,216	88,665	84,458	82,595	94,279	112,952	114,970	99,294
Arkansas	49,156	32,633	29,023	28,704	27,751	27,731	25,425	22,360	18,759
California	2,318,036	1,997,709	1,661,769	1,283,356	1,228,605	1,160,882	1,111,558	1,103,152	1,087,877
Colorado	71,088	53,089	35,207	27,880	27,132	31,491	35,391	38,162	38,313
Connecticut	151,801	115,941	77,947	63,903	59,566	53,102	44,964	42,782	40,109
Delaware	21,139	10,547	16,613	15,338	12,355	12,357	12,697	12,723	12,530
District of Columbia	64,663	55,949	50,035	45,748	43,425	42,159	42,342	43,610	41,980
Florida	403,838	252,257	184,486	143,078	124,586	123,247	120,013	116,208	107,210
Georgia	254,243	182,274	147,581	137,782	120,501	128,177	133,772	124,239	90,123
Hawaii	60,593	46,724	44,069	42,306	40,645	30,466	25,715	22,908	20,307
Idaho	12,277	4,059	2,545	2,333	2,246	2,374	3,124	3,405	3,311
Illinois	563,129	474,976	335,395	246,469	182,673	133,708	98,049	89,018	96,336
Indiana	119,429	109,114	107,688	101,380	115,519	138,885	140,302	131,125	124,777
Iowa	75,864	66,212	57,539	52,363	51,392	53,434	52,170	44,753	42,884
Kansas	49,463	34,718	33,912	35,300	32,967	35,808	39,745	43,640	46,026
Kentucky	150,900	119,161	95,488	86,501	81,750	77,658	76,963	78,174	75,005
Louisiana	166,395	134,370	101,257	82,934	65,504	60,704	57,775	45,506	34,491
Maine	46,944	39,537	33,757	27,506	26,134	26,039	27,091	26,651	25,509
Maryland	153,367	115,728	81,736	71,326	68,221	65,565	61,789	59,362	54,412
Massachusetts	199,403	167,315	121,784	98,144	95,057	108,068	109,093	107,630	103,906
Michigan	428,622	332,240	243,818	199,185	195,369	201,695	200,557	212,182	214,547
Minnesota	151,907	139,993	120,788	123,838	112,688	94,584	94,605	88,302	72,968
Mississippi	92,211	52,667	36,191	34,013	35,710	40,434	45,743	42,459	34,695
Missouri	186,396	147,035	128,703	124,535	121,364	118,753	101,893	99,613	96,611
Montana	24,326	17,727	13,618	14,230	15,401	16,440	17,294	14,284	12,224
Nebraska	37,439	35,657	31,838	27,183	23,802	25,500	26,876	26,749	26,430
Nevada	28,787	25,472	18,203	16,438	19,461	27,640	25,256	20,956	15,601
New Hampshire	19,248	16,045	15,203	13,739	13,501	14,499	14,152	14,032	14,150
New Jersey	242,285	189,418	155,753	125,050	113,481	102,657	102,564	107,703	109,202
New Mexico	71,573	75,237	79,183	68,986	56,105	47,338	44,081	45,926	45,314
New York	1,017,878	908,776	793,366	694,950	613,353	412,530	338,668	336,236	323,134
North Carolina	230,819	172,813	124,004	97,053	91,526	91,084	84,214	77,119	67,644
North Dakota	10,633	8,682	8,123	8,646	8,881	8,344	8,677	7,871	7,373
Ohio	466,524	340,179	262,806	236,976	199,352	190,998	187,557	186,272	179,422
Oklahoma	80,294	69,316	49,715	32,281	33,895	36,923	36,830	34,229	27,876
Oregon	57,672	46,395	46,761	41,072	41,976	40,916	42,722	42,362	44,707
Pennsylvania	437,898	357,684	278,036	231,983	215,175	210,595	210,405	231,260	253,352
Rhode Island	55,286	53,369	49,020	44,246	41,628	38,957	35,514	31,929	27,101
South Carolina	81,944	60,110	41,029	40,179	40,266	50,866	50,561	38,567	36,069
South Dakota	12,550	9,609	7,680	6,656	6,365	6,603	6,285	6,001	6,065
Tennessee	166,582	149,440	153,286	147,902	155,094	164,823	180,940	190,132	186,025
Texas	530,281	370,857	310,698	346,753	349,279	331,363	334,406	249,634	201,365
Utah	32,067	28,934	28,151	23,188	21,815	19,892	21,812	23,012	22,758
Vermont	21,086	19,644	17,585	15,626	15,060	13,407	12,701	12,257	11,466
Virginia	122,766	100,358	85,933	69,315	65,051	67,262	58,198	26,883	28,241
Washington	246,202	202,573	166,100	148,444	141,397	137,755	135,893	136,747	136,882
West Virginia	82,899	44,179	30,150	33,470	39,037	41,643	40,699	35,559	27,218
Wisconsin	98,732	41,651	41,984	38,186	40,030	45,231	49,019	54,314	46,609
Wyoming	5,679	2,586	1,576	1,118	987	823	733	633	548
Guam	..	..	..	..	9,729	10,783	10,783	10,783	10,783
Puerto Rico	140,344	121,402	102,806	87,354	75,114	67,413	53,506	48,904	41,543
United States	**10,376,224**	**8,347,041**	**6,836,093**	**5,821,857**	**5,469,184**	**5,146,132**	**4,965,419**	**4,784,042**	**4,555,755**

n/a   Not Applicable.
a   Special Supplemental Nutrition Program for Women, Infants and Children.
b   Temporary Assistance for Needy Families.
c   Data refer to fiscal year.

Sources for Tables

TABLE 1: Global Hunger—Life and Death Indicators

Total population, projected population, projected growth rate, life expectancy: The Population Reference Bureau, *2006 World Population Data Sheet*, data posted at http://www.prb.org.

Population under age 15: Statistics and Population Division of the U.N. Secretariat, "Indicators of Youth and Elderly Populations," data posted at http://unstats.un.org/unsd/demographic/products/socind/youth.htm.

Total fertility rate, urban population, infant mortality, low-birth weight infants, children immunized, under-5 mortality rate, maternal mortality rate: U.N. Children's Fund, *The State of the World's Children, 2006 (SWC)* (New York: UNICEF, 2005).

Refugees: U.S. Committee for Refugees and Immigrants, *World Refugees Survey 2006* (Washington, DC: Immigration and Refugee Services of America, 2005) data posted at http://www.refugees.org.

TABLE 2: Global Food, Nutrition and Education

Per capita dietary energy supply, FAO, *The State of Food Insecurity in the World, 2006* (Rome: FAO, 2006).

Food production per capita: Food and Agriculture Organization of the United Nations (FAO) Database, http://faostat.fao.org.

Vitamin A supplementation coverage, gender-related primary school enrollment: *SWC, 2006*.

Total adult literacy rate, gender-based adult literacy rate, total net primary school enrollment, combined educational enrollment: U.N. Development Program, *Human Development Report, 2006 (HDR)* (New York: Hoechstetter Printing Co., 2006).

TABLE 3: Hunger, Malnutrition and Poverty

Undernourished population: FAO, *SOFI, 2006*.

Underweight, wasting, stunting, safe water: *SWC, 2006*.

Population in poverty: The World Bank, *World Development Indicators, 2006 (WDI)* (Washington, DC: The World Bank, 2006).

TABLE 4: Economic and Development Indicators

GNP data, PPP data, GDP data, distribution of income or consumption, central government expenditures, per capita energy consumption, annual deforestation: *WDI, 2006*.

Human Development Indicators rank, public education expenditures, military expenditures: *HDR, 2006*.

TABLE 5: Economic Globalization

Exports, imports, net private capital flows, gross capital formation, investment, aid, debt: *WDI, 2006*.

TABLE 6: United States—National Hunger and Poverty Trends

Total population: U.S. Bureau of the Census, data posted at http://quickfacts.census.gov/qfd/states/00000.html.

Food insecurity prevalence: U.S. Department of Agriculture (USDA), *Household Food Security in the United States, 2005*. (USDA, Economic Research Service, 2006).

Percentage of federal budget spent on food assistance: BFWI estimate based on data from the *US Federal Budget for Fiscal Year 2007*, available at http://www.gpoaccess.gov/usbudget/fy07/pdf/appendix/agr.pdf.

Infant mortality: Centers for Disease Control and Prevention, National Center for Health Statistics, *National Vital Statistics Reports, Vol. 54, No. 13*, data posted at http://www.cdc.gov/nchs/products/pubs/pubd/nvsr/nvsr.htm.

National poverty rate, poverty rates by race, region and age, and income: U.S. Census Bureau, *Income, Poverty and Health Insurance Coverage in the United States: 2005*. August 2006. Report posted at http://www.census.gov/prod/2006pubs/p60-231.pdf.

Total child poverty rate by race: U.S. Census Bureau, Historical Poverty Tables, data posted at http://www.census.gov/hhes/www/poverty/histpov/hstpov3.html.

Unemployment by race: U.S. Department of Labor, Bureau of Labor Statistics, data posted at http://www.bls.gov.

Income: U.S. Census Bureau, Historical Income Tables by Race-Household, data posted at http://www.census.gov/hhes/www/income/histinc/h02ar.html.

TABLE 7: United States—State Hunger and Poverty Trends

Total population: U.S. Census Bureau, data posted at http://www.census.gov/popest/datasets.html

Food insecurity prevalence: USDA, *Household Food Security in the United States, 2005*.

Infant mortality: Centers for Disease Control and Prevention, National Center for Health Statistics, *National Vital Statistics Reports, Vol. 54, No. 13*.

Percent of population in poverty: U.S. Census Bureau, *Current Population Survey*, data available at http://www.census.gov/hhes/www/cpstc/cps_table_creator.html.

Unemployment by state: U.S. Department of Labor, Bureau of Labor Statistics, data posted at http://www.bls.gov/lau/lastrk05.htm.

TABLE 8: United States—Nutrition and Assistance Programs

Food stamp participation: USDA, Food and Nutrition Service Program Data, data posted at http://www.fns.usda.gov/pd/fsfypart.htm.

Special Supplemental Nutrition Program for Women, Infants, and Children (WIC) participation: USDA, Food and Nutrition Service Program Data, http://www.fns.usda.gov/pd/wifypart.htm.

Temporary Assistance for Needy Families (TANF): U.S. Department of Health and Human Services, Administration for Children and Families, data posted at http://www.acf.hhs.gov/programs/ofa/caseload/caseloadindex.htm.

Sponsors

Benefactor
(Gifts of $10,000 or more)

The Community of Christ World Hunger Committee seeks to engage the church and others in a response to the needs of hungry people throughout the world. Its primary purpose is to support programs of food production, storage and distribution; fund projects to provide potable water; supply farm animals; instruct in food preparation and nutrition; and educate in marketing strategies for produce. It also seeks to advocate for the hungry and educate about the causes and alleviation of hunger in the world.

The majority of proposals reviewed by the committee originate with Outreach International and World Accord, agencies recognized by the church as engaged in participatory human development that is global in scope. Direct grants to Community of Christ jurisdictions for community hunger projects, as well as disaster relief, also are considered.

> 1001 W. Walnut
> Independence, MO 64050-3562
> Phone: (816) 833-1000, ext. 3073
> Fax: (816) 521-3096
> Web site: www.CofChrist.org/hunger

Covenant World Relief is the relief and development arm of The Evangelical Covenant Church. Covenant World Relief was formed in response to the Covenant's historic commitment to being actively involved in Christ's mission to respond to the spiritual and physical needs of others.

> 5101 N. Francisco Avenue
> Chicago, IL 60625-3611
> Phone: (773) 784-3000
> Fax: (773) 784-4366

E-mail: jimsundholm@covchurch.org
Web site: www.covchurch.org

Episcopal Relief and Development is the international relief and development agency of the Episcopal Church of the United States. An independent 501(c) 3 organization, ERD saves lives and builds hope in communities around the world. For over 65 years, ERD has worked in more than 100 countries. ERD provides emergency assistance in times of crisis and rebuilds after disasters. ERD enables people to climb out of poverty by offering long-term solutions in areas of food security and health care, including HIV/AIDS and malaria.

> 815 Second Avenue
> New York, NY 10017 USA
> Phone: (800) 334-7626 ext. 5129
> Fax: (212) 687-5302
> E-mail: er-d@er-d.org
> Web site: www.er-d.org

Evangelical Lutheran Church in America World Hunger Program is a 30-year-old ministry that confronts hunger and poverty through long-term sustainable development, emergency relief, education, organizing, advocacy and lifestyle stewardship. Approximately 72 percent of the program works internationally and 28 percent works within the United States. Lutheran World Relief (Baltimore) and Lutheran World Federation (Geneva) are key implementing partners in international relief and development throughout the world.

> 8765 W. Higgins Road
> Chicago, IL 60631-4190
> Phone: (800) 638-3522, ext. 2717
> Fax: (773) 380-2707
> Web site: www.elca.org/hunger

Heifer International is a nonprofit charity working to end world hunger and poverty by giving cows, goats and other livestock, along with training, in animal husbandry, strategic planning and environmentally sound community development to impoverished families around the globe. Recipients give offspring of their livestock to others, multiplying the benefits of each donated animal. "Passing on the gift" is fundamental to Heifer's approach as part of its holistic development solution. As people share their animals' offspring with others along with their knowledge and resources, an ever-expanding network of hope, dignity and self-reliance is created that is expanding around the globe.

Since it began in 1944, Heifer has impacted more than 38 million people in more than 125 countries and 38 U.S. states. Each year Heifer's message of hope reaches still others through the media and through its own publications, such as it quarterly World Ark magazine. Heifer's three learning centers in Arkansas, California and Massachusetts offer hands-on educational experiences with seminars, service learning projects and hunger immersion experiences. Heifer is the 2004 recipient of the $1 million Conrad N. Hilton Humanitarian Award.

> 1 World Avenue
> Little Rock, AR 72202
> Phone: (501) 907-2600
> Fax: (501) 907-2602
> Web site: www.heifer.org

Oxfam America is dedicated to creating lasting solutions to global poverty and hunger by working in partnership with grassroots organizations promoting sustainable development in Africa, Asia, the Caribbean and the Americas, including the United States. Oxfam's grant awards and advocacy work aim to challenge the structural barriers that foster conflict and human suffering and limit people from gaining the skills, resources and power to become self-sufficient. Oxfam America envisions a world in which all people one day shall know freedom—freedom to achieve their fullest potential and to live secure from the dangers of hunger, deprivation and oppression—through the creation of a global movement of economic and social justice.

226 Causeway Street, Floor 5
Boston, MA 02114-2206
Phone: (800) 77-OXFAM
Fax: (617) 728-2594
E-mail: info@oxfamamerica.org
Web site: www.oxfamamerica.org

For 35 years, the **Presbyterian Hunger Program** has provided a channel for congregations to respond to hunger in the United States and around the world. With a commitment to the ecumenical sharing of human and financial resources, the program provides support for direct food relief efforts, sustainable development and public policy advocacy. A network of 100 Hunger Action Enablers leads the Presbyterian Church (USA) in the study of hunger issues, engagement with communities of need, advocacy for just public policies, and the movement toward simpler corporate and personal lifestyles.

100 Witherspoon Street
Louisville, KY 40202-1396
Phone: (502) 569-5832
Fax: (502) 569-8963
Web site: www.pcusa.org/hunger

Since 1984, **Share Our Strength** has led the fight against hunger and poverty by inspiring individuals and businesses to share their strengths. Today, their priority is to end childhood hunger in America. By raising funds to support the most effective community-based programs that feed hungry children, partnering with organizations pursuing long-term solutions, and helping families help themselves through nutrition education programs, Share Our Strength will ensure that the nearly 14 million children facing hunger have access to the nutritious food they need to learn, grow and thrive. For more information, please visit www.strength.org.

1730 M Street, NW
Suite 700
Washington, DC 20036
Phone: (202) 393-2925
Fax: (202) 347-5868
E-mail: info@strength.org
Web site: www.strength.org

United Methodist Committee on Relief (UMCOR) is the global humanitarian aid organization of the United Methodist Church. UMCOR works in more than 70 countries worldwide, including the United States. Our mission is to alleviate human suffering—whether caused by war, conflict or natural disaster—with open minds and hearts to all people. We partner with people to rebuild their livelihoods, health, and homes. In times of acute crisis we mobilize aid to stricken areas—emergency supplies, fresh water, and temporary shelter—and then stay, as long as it takes, to implement long-term recovery and rehabilitation. UMCOR is a member of several global alliances that share the same mission to restore well-being to women, children and men. Together with these and many local partners, UMCOR embodies the life-saving humanitarian presence of the people of the United Methodist Church.

475 Riverside Drive, Room 330
New York, NY 10115
Phone: (212) 870-3816
Phone: (800)-554-8583
Fax: (212) 870-3624
E-mail: umcor@gbgm-umc.org
Web site: www.umcor.org

Sponsors
(Gifts of $5,000 or more)

The **Adventist Development and Relief Agency** (ADRA) International is an independent humanitarian agency established in 1984 for the specific purpose of providing individual and community development and disaster relief. Committed to improving quality of human life, ADRA serves people in need without regard to their ethnic, political or religious association.

ADRA's development and relief work is divided among five core activities: food security, economic development, primary health, disaster preparedness and response, and basic education. In addition to feeding the hungry, ADRA works to prevent hunger through long-term development programs. Struggling families and individuals learn how to support and feed themselves by using agricultural methods that do not hurt the environment. ADRA also helps improve access to food and ensures equitable distribution of food among community members.

12501 Old Columbia Pike
Silver Spring, MD 20904 USA
Phone: (800) 424-2372
Web site: www.adra.org

Baptist World Aid (BWAid), the relief and development arm of the Baptist World Alliance (BWA), empowers grassroots solutions to local needs—clean drinking water, sustainable food supply, village health workers, improved farming, environmental care, small loans and business skills training, and HIV/Aids initiatives.

The Baptist World Alliance (BWA) is a fellowship of 211 Baptist unions and conventions comprising a membership of more than 47 million baptized believers. This represents a community of approximately 110 million Baptists ministering in more than 200 countries. The BWA unites Baptists worldwide, leads in world evangelism, responds to people in need and defends human rights.

405 North Washington Street
Falls Church, VA 22046
Phone: (703) 790-8980
Fax: (703) 790-5719
E-mail: bwaid@bwanet.org
Web site: www.bwanet.org

Canadian Foodgrains Bank is a partnership of Canadian church-based agencies working to end hunger in developing countries by increasing and deepening the involvement of Canadians in efforts to end hunger; supporting partnerships and activities to reduce hunger on both an immediate and sustainable basis; and influencing changes in public policies necessary to end hunger. In addition to cash donations, substantial amounts of food grain are donated directly from Canadian farmers and from more than 200 community groups that collectively grow crops for donation to the Canadian Foodgrains Bank. Each year, approximately $7 million in grain and cash donations are collected in addition to the $16 million matching support from the Canadian International Development Agency. Hunger related programming supported by the Foodgrains Bank through its 13 member agencies include food aid, food security, nutrition programming, and food justice.

Box 767, 400-280 Smith Street
Winnipeg, Manitoba
Canada R3C 2L4
Phone: (204) 944-1993
Fax: (204) 943-2597
E-mail: cfgb@foodgrainsbank.ca
Web site: www.foodgrainsbank.ca

Catholic Relief Services (CRS) is the overseas relief and development agency of the U.S. Catholic community. Founded in 1943, CRS provides more than $300 million in development and relief assistance in more than 80 nations worldwide. Working in partnership with the Catholic church and other local institutions in each country, CRS works to alleviate poverty, hunger and suffering, and supports peace-building and reconciliation initiatives. Assistance is given solely on the basis of need. Even while responding to emergencies, CRS supports more than 2,000 development projects designed to build local self-sufficiency. CRS works in conjunction with Caritas Internationalis and CIDSE, worldwide associations of Catholic relief and development agencies. Together, these groups build the capacity of local nonprofit organizations to provide long-term solutions. In the United States, CRS seeks to educate and build awareness on issues of world poverty and hunger and serves as an advocate for public policy changes in the interest of poor people overseas.

209 W. Fayette Street
Baltimore, MD 21201-3443 USA
Phone: (410) 625-2220
Fax: (410) 685-1635
E-mail: webmaster@catholicrelief.org
Web site: www.catholicrelief.org

Christian Children's Fund (CCF) is a global force for children, helping the world's poorest and most vulnerable children survive and thrive to reach their full potential. One of the world's oldest and most respected international child development organizations, CCF works in 33 countries and assists approximately 10.5 million children and family members worldwide, without regard to religion, race or gender.

CCF is a member of ChildFund International, a network of 12 affiliated worldwide organizations, working for the well-being of children in 55 countries. CCF supports locally led initiatives that strengthen families and communities, helping them overcome poverty and protect the rights of their children. CCF programs seek to be holistic and comprehensive, incorporating health, education, nutrition and livelihood interventions to protect, nurture and develop children in a sustainable way. CCF works in any environment where poverty, conflict and disaster threaten the well-being of children.

2821 Emerywood Parkway
Richmond, VA 23294 USA
Phone: (800) 776-6767
Web site:
www.christianchildrensfund.org

The **Cooperative Baptist Fellowship** is a fellowship of Baptist Christians and churches who share a passion for the Great Commission of Jesus Christ and a commitment to Baptist principles of faith and practice. The Fellowship's purpose is to serve Christians and churches as they discover and fulfill their God-given mission. One of the Fellowship's strategic initiatives is engaging in holistic missions and ministries among the most neglected in a world without borders. With more than 1,900 contributing churches and more than 3,000 individual contributors, the Fellowship supports a global missions field force of 163 personnel.

PO Box 450329
Atlanta, GA 31145
Phone: (770) 220-1600
Website: www.thefellowship.info

Church World Service is the global relief, development and refugee-assistance ministry of Protestant, Orthodox and Anglican denominations. Founded in 1946, CWS works in partnership with local organizations worldwide to support sustainable self-help development, meet emergency needs, and address the root causes of poverty and powerlessness.

475 Riverside Drive, Suite 700
New York, NY 10115-0050 USA
Phone: (800) 297-1516
Fax: (212) 870-3523
Web site: www.churchworldservice.org

Foods Resource Bank is a Christian response to world hunger. Its goal is for hungry people to know the dignity and pride of feeding themselves by making it possible for them, through sustainable agricultural programs, to produce food for their families with extra to share, barter or sell. Foods Resource Bank endeavors to twin rural and urban communities in "growing projects" in the United States, allowing participants to give a gift only they can give. These volunteers grow crops, sell them in the United States and the resulting money is used by implementing members (many of the mainline denominations) to establish food security programs abroad. Foods Resource Bank creates solidarity between America's bounty and the needs of the world's hungry.

2141 Parkview
Kalamazoo, MI 49008
Phone: (269) 349-3467
Web site: www.FoodsResourceBank.org

International Orthodox Christian Charities (IOCC), a humanitarian relief and development agency of Orthodox Christians, was established in 1992. Since its inception, IOCC has administered more than $226 million in aid and development programs in more than 30 countries. All assistance is provided solely on the basis of need, giving help to some of the most vulnerable people, including orphans, refugees and displaced persons, the elderly, school children, families and people with disabilities.

The mission of IOCC is to respond to the call of our Lord Jesus Christ to minister to those who are suffering and in need throughout the world, sharing with them God's gifts of food, shelter, economic self-sufficiency and hope.

110 West Road, Suite 360
Baltimore, Maryland 21204
Phone: (410) 243-9820
Fax: (410) 243-9824
E-mail: relief@iocc.org
Web site: www.iocc.org

Lutheran Church-Missouri Synod (LCMS) World Relief and Human Care is the alliance of disaster relief, self-help and human care ministries of LCMS. The mission of the Church through LCMS World Relief and Human Care is to reach out in mercy and compassion to those in need, in the clear name of Christ and his gospel, and according to the Lutheran confessions.

Phone: (314) 996-1380
Toll Free: (800)-248-1930 ext. 1380
Fax: (314) 996-1128

Lutheran World Relief (LWR) is a ministry of the Evangelical Lutheran Church in America (ELCA), The Lutheran Church–Missouri Synod (LCMS), individuals and parish groups in international relief, development, advocacy and social responsibility.

LWR acts on behalf of U.S. Lutherans in response to natural disasters, humanitarian crises and chronic poverty in some 35 countries in Africa, Asia, Latin America and the Middle East. In partnership with local organizations, LWR supports community projects to improve food production, health care, environment and employment, with special emphasis on training and gender equity. LWR monitors legislation on foreign aid and development, and advocates for public policies that address the root causes of hunger and poverty. LWR values the God-given gifts that each person can bring to the task of promoting peace, justice and human dignity. LWR began its work in 1945.

700 Light Street
Baltimore, MD 21230-3850
Phone: (410) 230-2700
or (800) LWR-LWR-2
Fax: (410) 230-2882

LWR Washington D.C. Office
110 Maryland Ave. NE
Washington, DC 20002
Phone: (202) 547-6243
Fax: (202) 547-6246
E-mail: lwr@lwr.org

The mission of **Physicians Against World Hunger** is to alleviate chronic hunger by supporting programs that implement microlending and education to break the hunger cycle. As part of this educational service, Physicians Against World Hunger also makes available a speaker to societies and organizations that wish to know more about world hunger.

2 Stowe Road, Suite 13
Peekskill, NY 10566 USA
Phone: (914) 737-8570
Fax: (914) 737-6016
Web site: www.pawh.org

The **U.N. World Food Program (WFP)** is the food-aid arm of the United Nations and the primary U.N. agency fighting to eradicate world hunger. Each year, WFP feeds close to 100 million people to meet their nutritional needs—two-thirds of them children—in more than 80 of the world's poorest countries. As the world's largest humanitarian organization, WFP has developed sophisticated techniques to assess the need for food aid not only in emergencies but in situations of chronic hunger, channeling its assistance to the poorest and most vulnerable groups—typically women, children and the elderly. Fifty-seven percent of WFP's expenditure is directed to Least-Developed Countries—as compared to 42 percent of bilateral ODA, more than half is directed to Africa. Programs include "food for education," which enables poor children, especially girls, to attend school; and "food for work," which seeks to build assets and promote self-reliance within poor communities. WFP envisions a world in which every woman, man and child has access, at all times, to the food needed for a healthy and productive life.

WFP Headquarters
Via C.G. Viola 58
Parco dei Medici
00148 – Rome – Italy
Phone: +39-06-65131
Fax: +39-06-6513-2840
E-mail: wfpinfo@wfp.org

Since 1944, **World Relief** has been helping churches to assist suffering people worldwide in the name of Jesus. As the humanitarian arm of the National Association of Evangelicals, World Relief equips churches to minister to hurting people's physical, emotional and spiritual needs. Working with local churches, World Relief serves in some of the poorest countries in the world. Its innovative ministries focus on microenterprise development, maternal and child health, HIV/AIDS, agricultural assistance, refugee care and emergency relief.

7 East Baltimore Street
Baltimore, MD 21202 USA
Phone: (443) 451-1900 or
(800) 535-LIFE
E-mail: worldrelief@wr.org
Web site: www.worldrelief.org

World Vision is a Christian relief and development organization dedicated to helping children and their communities worldwide reach their full potential by tackling the causes of poverty. Motivated by our faith in Jesus, we serve the poor, regardless of a person's religion, race, ethnicity, or gender, as a demonstration of God's unconditional love for all people. World Vision provides emergency assistance to children and families affected by natural disasters and civil conflict, works with communities to develop long-term solutions to alleviate poverty, and advocates for justice on behalf of the poor. World Vision serves more than 100 million people in nearly 100 countries around the world.

34834 Weyerhaeuser Way South
Federal Way, WA 98001 USA
Phone: (888) 511-6593
Web site: www.worldvision.org

Friends
(Gifts under $5,000)

Academy for Educational Development
www.aed.org

Congressional Hunger Center
www.hungercenter.org

Freedom from Hunger
www.freefromhunger.org

Islamic Society of North America
www.isna.net

Mennonite Central Committee
www.mcc.org

Moravian Church in North America
www.moravia.org

Nazarene Compassionate Ministries
www.nazcompassion.com

Reformed Church in America
www.rca.org

UCC Wider Church Ministries
www.ucc.org

U.S. Fund for UNICEF
www.unicefusa.org

World Hope International
www.worldhope.org

Study Guide 2007

The following outline covers five one-hour sessions on *Hunger 2007: Healthy Food, Farms and Families*. Groups should not feel restricted to covering just these topics. However, even if groups choose to discuss other issues in the report, this guide will still serve as a useful starting point.

Session One: Farming in the United States (1 hour)

"He has told you, O mortal, what is good; and what does the Lord require of you but to do justice, and to love kindness, and to walk humbly with your God?"

Micah 6:8,
New Revised Standard Version (NRSV)

For reflection: Read Micah 6:1-8. What is the controversy God has with the community? How does the community respond to God? Verse 8 sums up Israel's prophetic tradition. Discuss the three requirements the prophet puts before the community. What do you think Micah would say to us today about the current U.S. farm policy?

1. According to Tim Nissen, the farmer described on page 19, the current farm system discourages farmers from diversifying their business and thinking more creatively about their planting decisions. Given what you've learned from reading this report, what do you think are the reasons U.S. farmers would be struggling?

2. Chapter One discusses four myths about farm subsides (pages 20-23). Why are these myths so powerful and continue to seem plausible to so many Americans?

Session Two: Life in Rural America (1 hour)

"Faithfulness will spring up from the ground, and righteousness will look down from the sky. The LORD will give what is good, and our land will yield its increase. Righteousness will go before him, and will make a path for his steps."

Psalm 85:11-13, NRSV

For reflection: Read all of Psalm 85. This psalm is a lament and plea to God for restoration. What is the psalmist lamenting? What would be the lament of people living in rural communities today? The last four verses paint a vision of peace and justice. Note that the vision includes the land as well as the people. How would you translate this vision for rural communities today?

1. What are the advantages and disadvantages to living in rural America, and in what ways can government programs strengthen rural America?

2. Box stores like Wal-Mart offer rural communities low-cost items, employment opportunities, and tax revenue. However, they also make it difficult for small, local business to compete and are known for paying low wages and providing minimal employee benefits. Are there ways to create an environment that welcomes outside development to rural areas but also encourages local small business development?

Session Three: Trade and Agriculture (1 hour)

"I do not mean that there should be relief for others and pressure on you, but it is a question of a fair balance between your present abundance and their need, so that their abundance may be for your need, in order that there may be a fair balance."

II Corinthians 8:13-14, NRSV

For reflection: Read II Corinthians 8:1-15. Why does Paul compliment the Macedonian churches? Why is Paul appealing to the church in Corinth? Paul seems to be equating generosity and grace; do you agree? Do you think Paul's appeal is relevant to the issue of agricultural trade today? If yes, then in what ways? If no, then why not? What would be a "fair balance" among nations today in terms of trade?

1. There are nearly 3 billion people in the world living on less than $2 per day. Raising their incomes to $5 or $9 per day could give a substantial boost to U.S. farmers by expanding the available markets for agricultural exports. But raising incomes from $2 per day to $5 or $9 per day does not happen overnight. Nor is it likely to happen without reform of U.S. agricultural trade policies. What are the reforms that U.S. agriculture needs to adopt to achieve the gains described in the paragraph above?

2. A new multilateral trade deal could make a big difference for the future of agriculture in developing countries, but as this chapter explains, simply improving developing countries' access to international markets is not everything. What issues outside of the trade policies of developed countries need to be addressed to improve the ability of developing countries to compete in the global market?

Session Four: Obesity and Malnutrition (1 hour)

"Taking the five loaves and the two fish, [Jesus] looked up to heaven, and blessed and broke the loaves, and gave them to his disciples to set before the people; and he divided the two fish among them all. And all ate and were filled; and they took up twelve baskets full of broken pieces and of the fish. Those who had eaten the loaves numbered five thousand men."

Mark 6:41-44, NRSV

For reflection: This story occurs in all four Gospels and twice in Matthew and Mark. Why is it such an important story? What's the miraculous part of the story? Would ending hunger in the United States take a miracle? If not, then what would it take?

1. The fact is that in high-poverty areas where obesity levels are highest, hunger is also lurking. It may sound like a paradox, but hunger, poverty and obesity can and do co-exist. Severe hunger in the United States…has been cut sharply since the 1960s, but the more common form of hunger today, "food insecurity," affects a startling number of people." What does Chapter 4 tell us about the relationship between hunger, poverty and obesity?

2. Come up with 5 creative ideas that school administrators could use to combine nutrition education with the school lunch program? For starters, perhaps you should

consider Figure 4.5 on page 83, showing the difference between annual spending on food and beverage advertising and spending on nutrition education.

Session Five: Looking Forward (1 hour)

"When a great crowd gathered and people from town after town came to him, he said in a parable: 'A sower went out to sow his seed; and as he sowed, some fell on the path and was trampled on, and the birds of the air ate it up. Some fell on the rock; and as it grew up, it withered for lack of moisture. Some fell among thorns, and the thorns grew with it and choked it. Some fell into good soil, and when it grew, it produced a hundredfold.' As he said this, he called out, 'Let anyone with ears to hear listen!'"

Luke 8:4-8, NRSV

For reflection: Most scholars think that parables have just one point. What is the point of this parable? How does this parable inform the work of social justice?

1. "… policymakers must develop solutions that help struggling U.S. farmers, strengthen rural communities, provide an adequate, nutritious diet for hungry people in this country, and support the efforts of small farmers in developing countries to get their products to market and feed their families." This report has tried to present a vision that can accomplish all the above objectives. How would you inform someone indifferent to the farm bill that these objectives converge there, and what recommendations do you think are the strongest to achieve progress in reducing hunger through the farm bill?

2. What are some ways your church or campus could promote policies that are recommended in this report?

Index